János Wildmann (Ed.)

Religions and Churches in a Common Europe

Wildmann, János (Ed.)

Religions and Churches in a Common Europe

ISBN/EAN: 978-3-86741-768-6
First published in 2012 by Europaeischer Hochschulverlag GmbH & Co KG, Bremen, Germany.

© Europaeischer Hochschulverlag GmbH & Co KG, Fahrenheitstr. 1, D-28359 Bremen (www.eh-verlag.de). All rights reserved.

No part of this publication may be reproduced or transmitted, in any form or by any means, electronic, mechanical, photocopying, recording or otherwise, or stored in any retrieval system of any nature, without the written permission of the copyright holder and the publisher, application for which shall be made to the publisher.

János Wildmann (Ed.)

Religions and Churches in a Common Europe

Contents

Introduction — 1
  János Wildmann

Europe and the religions — 2

The Price of Secularisation — 3
  Reinhold Knoll

Secularisation, Individualization or Market Approach? Results from the "Church and Religion in an Enlarged Europe" Project — 9
  Gert Pickel

Vital coexistence: Religion and Secularism in further European integration. Tomas Masaryk Revisited — 49
  Lucia Faltin

Religious Euro-skepticism in Hungary — 57
  János Wildmann

The churches in Europe — 71

The Church as a "Creative Minority". On being church in today's Europe — 72
  Arne Rasmusson

Churches in Europe in Light of the Thoughts of Simone Weil — 89
  Endre Nagy

Church and State Relations in Portugal — 99
  Alejandro Torres Gutiérrez

Historical Background of the Relationship between the State and Churches in Hungary — 112
  Adam Rixer

Church and Society — 121

Religious messages and the world of the media: Trends and experiences in Europe in the field of religious communication and information systems — 122
  Marco Ricceri

Scenes of church communication – results of an empiric investigation — 159
  Márta Korpics

The Economic Teaching of World Religions. Cosmological and Material Beliefs — 168
  Katalin Botos

Religious Identities and Environmental Attitudes in Hungary   177
  Benedek Jávor

Religious Research Perspectives   198

Religious Research in Europe   199
  Viggo Mortensen

The Necessity of the Study and Research of Jewish-Christian Relations as a Coherent Field of Academic Inquiry   210
  Judit Hermann

What is Emerging in Western Europe / USA? The Emerging Church in the Post-Christendom Culture – Strengths, Weaknesses, Opportunities and Threats   216
  Norbert Izsák

Authors   231

Introduction

János Wildmann

With the support of the Hungarian Scientific Research Fund (Hungarian abbreviation: OTKA) the sociology of religion research project "Religions and Churches in a Common Europe" was conducted in Hungary in 2006–2009. The aim of the Working Group, based at the University of Pécs, was to ascertain, after Hungary's accession to the European Union (2004), the basic attitudes especially of religious people to Europe and the European Union, as well as what religion and the church mean to them under the historic new circumstances. The detailed report on this representative survey has already appeared in Hungarian.[1]

Although this research project was restricted to Hungary, it was an explicit goal of the research group to link up its work with similar European projects. This took place primarily through cooperation with the Network for the Study of Religious Innovation and Pluralism in Contemporary Europe (RIPE). Other European scholars also showed an interest in cooperation, but they pursued their own research interests and goals, and had their own methods. However, there was a conference at which all participants were able to present their results. It took place in Pécs in 2009.

The present volume gathers together most of the presentations given at the Pécs conference. The reader will appreciate that in this book only the basic framework – Religions and Churches in a Common Europe – is given (only one study extends its considerations beyond Europe, taking in also the USA), but the studies are complex. It is not a thematic, but rather a diverse volume. Readers are offered an opportunity to look briefly at the results of various research efforts. For a deeper insight, the respective research reports must be examined.

I would like to take this opportunity to thank all the authors for their active participation in the project and for their contribution. Particular thanks are due to the Hungarian Scientific Research Fund, which also funded the publication of this volume, as well as to the RIPE Network, especially its former chairman, Professor Viggo Mortensen, and its new head, Professor Marco Ricceri, who did so much to promote international cooperation, championed the conference in Pécs and supported the publication of this book.

---

[1] Márta Korpics and János Wildmann: Vallások és egyházak az egyesült Európában. Magyarország (Religions and Churches in a Common Europe. Hungary), Budapest: Typotex, 2010.

Europe and the religions

The Price of Secularisation

Reinhold Knoll

Taking a look at sociological theories in general, we notice that from the very beginning, the interest in the relationship between state and society was a constantly declining one. The reason for this can be found in the notion that the post-French-revolution state, as an enduring form of government, seemed not to deserve a closer analysis compared to the more interesting subject of society itself. Theories of society on the other hand seemed to have been deduced from the diversity of social systems which after all had led society out of servitude and therefore had proven their unique political creativity. Thus the development towards democracy could be seen as a reliable mechanism. The economic development was seen as proof of this assumption. The state was reduced to claiming only a residual function, by which the continued execution of the social contract seemed guaranteed within a solid framework. The state was no longer host to society, as it was common in the 18th century. The dominant conviction in the theories of the time was that the state, not only had to guarantee the free development of the societal powers in the form of liberalism, but also that the state itself would be the achievement of society's will. The state had to be a representation of the civic self-determination and emancipation. Thus the label „laissez faire state „was an appropriate one. The guiding functions of the state were seen as disruptive to society's independent existence, therefore administrative functions and their executing authorities were preferred over political responsibilities – the state became a quasi-service industry for society.

The eagerness of civic revolutions to domesticate the formerly absolute state into an instrument of their making was however only one side of the coin. The other side shows us the simultaneous development of a strengthening of the authoritarian state which facilitated totalitarian movements to a high degree, beginning with Napoleon and ending in the 20th century. This put into effect the exact opposite of what was intended in the theories of civic societies. One could almost speak of unintended synergistic effects because out of these common liberal values of civic origin emerged capitalism and it was able to adapt to totalitarian authorities quite well depending on the respective political traditions of the countries.

This modern form of the totalitarian state came into being almost as a natural process although it would have astounded everyone should they have foreseen this consequence in their theories of society – of course with the exception of Marxist theory, which had however always maintained the hypothesis that the traditional state would eventually have to succumb to the reign of a classless proletariat. To view the history of the past 200 years from this perspective is not new, yet it has not been described consistently enough. Only rarely have sociological insights been regarded as the hypotheses of empiric historic interpretation even though the motifs of a history of society had been taken into account in the discipline of economic and social history. This account however was seen as an apolitical course of events – historical and societal phenomena regarded as separated from the facts of political history. At the same time political historiography remained locked in the hard shadows of two world wars and after these catastrophic events was put into the service of depicting the peaceful post war social order, even though this order had come about only as the result of the stalemate between the super powers during the Cold War period. Consequently sociology and social history continued for a prolonged period to be a field of arbitrary description and theory beyond and detached from statehood. The political options of "nations" were considerably limited. Socio-politically however, states saw their duty in providing an interest-led interpretation of a universal "social contract", with the aim of either reforming constitutions or creating a variant of economic democracy or free markets.

It is a long-established and justifiable historical tradition that political constellations which seek to combine state and society are explained in a dualistic form. In late antiquity Saint Augustine contrasted theocracy and civitas terrena. Later similar comparisons tended to remove an ideal model either into the domain of utopia or resigned by accepting earth as the best of all possible worlds. The various interpretations, beginning with theology and philosophy, seemed to have been trapped in this interplay only to be newly phrased in social sciences. The Enlightenment however did consider a departure from this dualism, even though this world view continued to remain in the focus of the politico-philosophical discourse. Secularisation was this attempt to get rid of the clasp of a political theology which saw man ensnared in world history and salvific history. A term from canon law, used in the peace accords of 1648 to signify devolution of former clerical possessions into worldly hands, thus became an expression in political philosophy and the brand of a modern emancipatory intellectual movement. At the moment the process of secularisation not only seems to have been completed but has also brought about lasting changes, which may not at all be the desired avenue towards liberation and self-determination. "We tend to overlook the essential meaning of this beginning process of alienation from the world because we are so used to equating secularisation with the receding influence of the religious domain. But secularisation as a tangible historical event is nothing more than the separation of church and state, of religion and politics and thus signifies, from a religious point of view, nothing more than the return to "giving to Caesar what is Caesar's..." This has nothing to do with a loss of spirituality and transcendence or a newly awakened interest in worldly matters... World history has proved that a loss of faith has not made us reflect on the world or the here and now but rather reduced us to ourselves."[2]

Upon the beginning of the Enlightenment a-religious society seemed to have evolved from Christendom, transforming "heaven", still a favourite object of citation in the apotheosis of the Baroque, into history, future, progress. Nature and body cease to be "objects of condemnation and (become) subjects of transformation".[3] The transformation of Christianity towards a more modern, "western" version also changed the missionary task into an all-over colonisation and "conversion" of nature into resource, which was executed with the same zeal as the crusade against the Moslems. Colonisation of what is yet to come is the intention of science and with pious fury it seeks to conquer the cosmos.[4]

Now the preceding events of secularisation in mediaeval times, which had been the result of a political "dualism" between emperor and pope, resulted in the paradoxical situation that the church's claim on what is holy – exemplified by the sacramental consecration of Gregor VII – was now nullified; a fact which established an unintended "immanent sovereignty". Furthermore the conflict led to the formation of a church whose self-conception expressed itself in quasi-governmental institutions. At the same time principalities adopted sacral traits which, by the time of the renaissance, had culminated in the identification with the world of the deities of the antiquity. [5]

Now it is extremely difficult to follow the further development of secularisation since one has legitimate reason to claim that, especially from the 19th century onward, this dualistic metaphor and its "interpretation of the world", though it had managed to evolve from political theory, had completely lost its significance. Modernity simply adopted a completely different model of interpretation. It claimed to possess a new independence disconnected from previous history. The categories "world history",

---

[2] Hannah Arendt, Vita activa, München 1981, p. 248 f.
[3] cf. Giacomo Marramao, Die Säkularisierung der westlichen Welt, Frankfurt 1969, p. 11.
[4] Octavio Paz, Verbindungen – Trennungen, Frankfurt 1969, p. 138 f.
[5] cf. Marc Bloch, Les rois thaumaturges. Etudes sur la caractére surnaturel attribué à la puissance royale particulièrement en France et en Angleterre, Paris 1961, p. 90 ff.

"universal history" or the diversity of "cultural histories" formulated by Friedrich Schlegel flattened out the Christian dualism and its potential for conflict. Historical events do not orient themselves towards the "last days". Therefore the eschatological framework ceases to apply and in the historicist historiography in the manner of the Leopold von Ranke, transcendence is no longer included among the issues the scholar must deal with. Ranke regarded "Papal history" merely as a special form of national positivity.

The term "Säkularisierung" – secularisation – fades out of fashion and through a process of rephrasing by Hegel it is replaced by "Verweltlichung" – "worldification"[6] which loses the religious connotation. The effect of this rephrasing is fully expressed in Hegel's works. "Verweltlichung" is given ample treatment in "The Phenomenology of Spirit". In the midst of all these examples of "Verweltlichung" the human "self" comes undone and simultaneously a surprising number of new "Spirits" begin to determine history, for example "Zeitgeist2, "Weltgeist" or "Volksgeist". While the "genuine consciousness" vis à vis civil society, in the style of Diderot's novel, "Rameau's Nephew", can only be commented on with irony, the arrival of these new "spiritual phenomena", which add colour to the collective consciousness of a society, is disconcerting.

This "Verweltlichung" is in fact the fruition of the overcoming of Christendom but it requires its historical manifestation, without which this transition is not possible. This was alluded to by Hegel and he simultaneously escalated it into anti-Judaism of an incredible scale, as noted by Emmanuel Levinas, by calling called the continued existence of Jewish communities a scandal, a resistance against the course of world history. At the same time all indicators point towards the conclusion that it is only within the framework of a Christian "Occident" that the secular processes of civilisation can guarantee the continuation of history. Karl Marx aligns himself with this attitude in his early work, where he stipulates a religious spirit as a condition for democracy – and insists that the spirit can emerge in a political context in this way only

"That which is a creation of fantasy, a dream, a postulate of Christianity, i.e., the sovereignty of man – but man as an alien being different from the real man – becomes, in democracy, tangible reality, present existence, and secular principle."[7] Thus it follows that not even democracy can forego political theology.

---

[6] Translator's note: literal translation
[7] Cf. keywords in: Geschichtliche Grundbegriffe. Historisches Lexikon zur politisch-sozialen Sprache in Deutschland. Hg. Otto Brunner, Reinhart Koselleck, Stuttgart 1957. eg.: „Geschichte", „Fortschritt", „Revolution".

The implications of this philosophical/practical outlook led the 19th century theologian Richard Rother to the conviction that both institutions, state and church, had become caught in a "counter-ambitious relationship": "In the same proportion by which the state de-secularizes, church secularizes, and, being only an increasingly insufficient, makeshift accommodation for the Christian spirit, takes a step back, until the time that His true abode has been completed."[8] He arrived at this belief by having observed the overcoming of Catholicism by Protestantism. It is obvious that the state, the aim of this theological interpretation, is to him the embodiment of morality. It includes the religious element, so that the idea of God's realm is realized not in the institution of the church but in the state!

One has to make the astonishing realisation that what have been considered secular motivations of the modern political period are beginning to turn around on their axis. A new construct of state – but also its de-secularized form – is being evoked and simultaneously addressed as a kind of renewed church in which the confining isolation of Christians is lifted. It would be of great interest to note at what point in these deliberations the state – existing in its 19th century reality – began showing signs of this intended political "ecclesification"[9].

History so far has been written according to whatever concepts are prevalent the prevalent concepts, always in antithesis to these observations. "Säkularisierung", which formed the basis of the absolutistic state, was possible due to powerful forms of substitution. Reformation – as we all know – split the former unity of Christianity. The legitimation of political power and authority could no longer be deduced from the political metaphysics of the monarchs which is why, pursuant to the typology of power of Max Weber; a transition from legitimate power to lawful power became necessary. Thus the commitment to universality of the sciences replaced the philosophical theology. Political theology was replaced by administration theory and jurisprudence. A framework which continued to be valid as a common "Weltanschauung", due to the universally accepted aesthetic of the baroque, became established in the common language of architecture, painting and music[10]. Thus a phenomenon, which Hegel had so clearly identified as the "Kunstreligion" – sacralised art – comes into play in opposition to political demands. In this context art may be viewed as the first

---

[8] Karl Marx, Zur Judenfrage; MEW I, S. 590. (1844)
[9] Translator's note: my coinage
[10] cf. Alois Dempf, Unsichtbare Bilderwelt; Eine Geistesgeschichte der Kunst, Einsiedeln 1959.

element of de-secularisation in a universal project to visualize and hypostatize representation, state power and claims to domination.

The metaphysics of the old imperial crown was no longer needed to authenticate political power. Nevertheless, metaphysics had been a highly problematic construct. Since Otto I, rulers had seen themselves in succession to the biblical kings as depicted on eight enamel plates and they took care to conceal the division between political and spiritual authority brought about by Christ. Maximilian I and later Maximilian II found themselves in this dilemma and consequently entertained the thought of uniting empire and papacy in their person.

If we now WITHOUT THE HISTORICAL PERSPECTIVE interpret the development of modern societies according to this European political paradigm as a process of secularisation, we firstly learn nothing about the context of the rationale for the state and secondly our knowledge of these developments remains uncertain, especially because of the variations in the meaning and significance of "secularisation". The framework of the state may be realised as Bismarck's authoritarian state just as well as the constitutional monarchy in its British or Austro-Hungarian manifestation, or the French republic or for that matter the reconstructed Italian monarchy under Victor Emanuel.

Secularisation, Individualization or Market Approach? Results from the "Church and Religion in an Enlarged Europe" Project

Gert Pickel

1. Introduction – Church and Religion in Europe

For decades, the secularization theory was the dominating paradigm in the sociology of religion (Berger 1967; Wilson 1982; Bruce 2002). Starting out from the French Enlightenment critiques of religion, the hypothesis developed that the process of modernization, including rationalization, functional differentiation, democratization, urbanization, burocratization and the absence of existential social threats did not really fit with religion and leads to a continuous loss of the relevance of religion in (modern) society. Especially in Europe empirical evidence of secularization processes was found repeatedly. This regional pattern did not come as a surprise as the most rapid processes of modernization took place in Europe and the largest number of advanced societies worldwide could be found in Europe.

However, these conclusions were increasingly questioned in the last decade. On the one hand, it was stated that a revival of religiosity or spirituality which did not take place within but rather outside the traditional Christian churches could be observed everywhere (Graf 2004; Zulehner 2002). New religious movements or individualized forms of religiosity which no longer needed the ecclesiastic institutionalization of the 'old' popular churches were particularly popular. Furthermore, considering church attendance rates was assumed to hinder insights into the increase or stability of *privatized or individualized religiosity* (Luckmann 1967, 1991; Davie 2001). The individual religiosity become more and more diffused (Cipriani 2006) or syncretistic, all in all a "patchwork religiosity". These positions are mentioned in the sociology of religion as individualization thesis of religion.

On the other hand, the inevitability of a secularization process was criticized with reference to the outer-European regions in general and with regard to the United States of America in particular. Is the situation in Europe a special one, resulting from specific historical paths and didn't the prevailing conditions of religion influence its vitality (Casanova 1994; Finke/Stark 2006; Iannaccone 1991; Stark/Bainbridge 1987; Stark/Finke 2000)? The process of "desecuralization" (Berger 1999) in Latin America and the ongoing high religious vitality in the United States seems to be significant indicators for the stronger evidence of an approach, called the *market model of religion*. Therefore, it is no surprise, that Steven Warner (1993) named the market model the "new paradigm" of the sociology of religion, replacing the secularization theory.

These different points of view resulted in a broad academic debate, which of the mentioned theoretical positions is more related to the reality of religion and its development in modernity. However, after years of discussions we may conclude: even if we disagree with the premises and assumptions of the secularization theory, we cannot deny its continuing relevance for the debate in the sociology of religion, because none of the proponents of the both alternative approaches can do without referring to the secularization theory (most of the time they do so by distancing themselves from it). This raises the question whether this ‚old paradigm' of explanation of the development in Europe may actually still be valid or whether it is – as its critics claim – an out-dated model, worth only to forget it as fast as possible. An answer to this question is only possible, if we analyse the societal reality in Europe. For that, it is necessary to take meaningful empirical evidence into account. This entails three premises: First, we need to clarify what we *mean by secularization* in modern societies. Second, for the analyses, it would be helpful to bear opposing opinions or *alternative models of explanations* in mind as points of reference. Third, we *need data* which provide measures of secularization and include indicators of alternative explanations. All in all we need concrete empirical analysis.

Therefore, the study ‚Church and Religion in an enlarged Europe 2006 (C&R)' was carried out, to give information to answer the question mentioned before. In the study – mainly based on survey research – indicators not only for secularization, but for all of the three potential models of explanation were taken into account. The idea was to confront the potential of the three approaches with each other, to come to a conclusion, which approach fits best to the reality. Western and Eastern European countries were included in the analysis. The study comprised nine countries, namely Germany (West and East), Portugal, Ireland, Finland, Estonia, Poland, Hungary, Croatia and Russia. A *"Most-different-system-design"* (Przeworski/Teune 1970) was applied in selecting the countries under research and to allow comparative merit. For the benefit of focusing on a culturally homogeneous research area as well as for pragmatic reasons (limited resources); we did not take non-European countries into account. The systematic selection serves to avoid fallacies with regard to generalizable developments, which occasionally occur in regional or single case studies (Lauth/Pickel/Pickel 2008: 58-79). Therefore, the approach of the analysis focuses on the macro-level and tries to answer the distribution of religiosity by their societal, political and historical conditions.

The four key questions of the empirical analyses are: (1) Are there differences in the levels and in the developments of religious vitality (integration in church/subjective religiosity) in European comparison? (2) Are the ideas of the secularization theory outdated or is it possible to use these ideas for the analysis of European religiosity.

(3) Which of the actual theoretical models in the sociology of religion (Secularization, Individualization, and Market Model) is consistent with the European reality? (4) What are the main sources for the different levels of religiosity in Europe?

2. The theoretical prerequisites – three general models in contrast

Like mentioned in the introduction, the secularization theory[11] has been the reference point for decades, dealing with questions of religion and religiosity, or – like the market model names it – religious vitality. The secularization theory refers to the persistent *loss of the social relevance* of church and religion in modern societies (Berger 1967; Bruce 2002; Dobbelaere 2002; Wilson 1982) and maintain the assumption that modernity or rather modernization and religion do not get along well. This *tense relationship* is a result of the processes of *rationalization* and *functional differentiation* but also democratization and urbanization inherent in modernization. While the former undermines the credibility of religious explanations (Berger 1967) due to proliferating rational and scientific explanations, the latter results in an increasing loss of the function of religion. At the same time, religion is increasingly ousted from public life (privatization), is becoming less relevant in the everyday life of the people and the norms set by the religions decreasingly succeed in committing the members of society to them. In addition, the number of people who turn away from the churches as social form of religion is growing as they no longer need it to alleviate existential problems and social hardship. Compared to the past, deprivation no longer presents such a threat to the citizens due to the increasing socioeconomic welfare of modern service societies – and thus the desire for security provided by religion wanes (Norris/Inglehart 2004). With a certain time lag, the above-mentioned "loss of the communal basis of religion" (Bruce 2002: 19-21) may in the end actually lead to a decrease in faith and subjective religiosity in modernizing societies.[12] However, secularization theory does not consider the latter point

---

[11] In the following, we will use the term secularization theory even though a variety of different approaches are subsumed under this expression.
[12] It needs to be pointed out, though, that hardly any of the prominent secularization theorists (Wilson 1982; Bruce 2002) assume that religiosity will vanish entirely.

to be the main issue to be explained. It is rather a forward projection consistent with its assumptions. The concept of the secularization theory is deduced from the situation in Europe, which serves to provide the main examples as evidence of the theory.

Currently, the *religious market model* is probably the most relevant alternative explanatory approach. It regards the situation in the USA as a prime example of the social development of religion and religiosity and points to a European peculiar path and the status of "Europe as an exceptional case". According to its proponents (Iannaccone 1991; Stark/Finke 2000; Stark/Iannaccone 1994; Froese/Pfaff 2001, 2009), Europe as a special case merely distracts the attention from the generally valid relationship between religious supply and religious demand. In the market model, religious vitality – the main issue of the market model as well as secularization theory – is mainly determined by taking the services offered by the churches and the *degree of regulation* of this market by the state into account (Iannaconne 1991, 1992; Finke/Stark 2006; Fox 2008).[13] The monopoly churches can no longer satisfy the continually widening interests of the individualized believers – and in the market model, every citizen is in some way an individualized believer. On the one hand, the religious choices they provide are too unspecific due to their popular church character; on the other hand, their dedication to the believers is decreasing, as they are not pressured by any exposure to competition (Stark/Bainbridge 1987). If the religious market continues to be limited to these established suppliers (churches), this will surely result in a decrease in the religious vitality of the citizens. This is particularly true in the case of the quasi monopoly churches, which are predominantly located in Europe. *Competitors* and competition[14] on this religious market will revive religious vitality as the religious providers will then be forced to develop suitable choices and to attend to the believers after all. The assumptions in which the market model crucially differs from

---

Rather, they believe that a small amount of subjective religiosity will remain due to the inevitability of questions of meaning. However, this group will diminish in the course of advancing modernization and will be split up among several types of religious organizations (see Bruce 2002: 41-43). We also need to be aware of the fact that the core of the claim of the secularization theory refers to the *loss of social relevance* and not to the board assumption of the global disappearance of religion (Beckford 2003: 51).

[13] In return, proponents of the secularization theory accused supporters of the market model of choosing an ‚exceptional case' and argued that their research results depended on this selectively drawn sample.

[14] In certain cases, conflicts among religions or between religions and the state may serve as a substitute for competition (for example in the case of Northern Ireland or Poland) (Froese/Pfaff 2009).

secularization theory is that religious pluralism has a positive effect on religious vitality[15], the fact that modernization does not necessarily lead to a loss of relevance of religion in society and that every individual is in search of a religious model in order to find an answer to the „ultimate" questions of meaning.[16]

A third standpoint whose proponents also argue against secularization theory, differentiates between the developments on the personal level of faith and one's commitment to the church. This approach, which is discussed in particular in the European realm under the term *"thesis of religious individualization"* (Luckmann 1967; Davie 1994, 2007; Beck 2008), now has a number of supporters. As in the case of the market model, individual religiosity is conceived as an anthropological constant which is inherent in the nature of man (Luckmann 1967; 1991: 77-86). The social form of religion may lose importance; however, individual religiosity merely modifies its form (Luckmann 1991: 96-103), which does not necessarily have to manifest itself publicly. This results in the development of a *'invisible religion'*, which suggests a loss of faith, even though this does not occur. The new types of religiosity may take on entirely different forms than what we are accustomed to with respect to the hitherto common commitment to traditional churches. Secularization theory in turn is criticized for focusing too narrowly on questions related to the sociology of the church as well as a substantial concept of religion which is no longer in line with functionally differentiated modern societies. According to the critics, the tendentiously Christian substantial concept of religion particularly limits the scope to conventional religious phenomena and loses sight of the new forms. Thus, the false assumption of secularization does not come as a surprise. Without further ado, the proponents of the individualization thesis also concur with an inauspicious interpretation of the development of the integration of the church. But at the same time, they disapprove of assigning this loss of relevance to the subjective level of religiosity (also Cipriani 2006: 126-127). In addition, they emphasize the development of new social movements, which in part take on the social functions of traditional religions.

---

[15] This constrasts Peter L. Berger's assumption (1967: 127-154) that religious pluralization undermines the plausibility structures of the (in his case Christian) belief system and thus reduces religious vitality in the long run.

[16] Consequently, it is a rational choice approach which focuses exclusively on the supply side since – per definition – there is constant demand for religious explanations. It is thus referred to as the „supply-side approach" (Stark/Iannaccone 1994). Stolz (2008: 7) as well as Froese/Pfaff (2005: 401-402) point out that regulations such as social control and political repression, can also affect the demand. This possible effect is not included as such in the basic model of the market approach and was added to a more broad rational choice perspective of religion only recently.

Apart from their different ways of explaining the developments, the proponents of the market model and the supporters of the religious individualization thesis mainly agree in one respect – they *rebut the secularization theory* as an unsuitable explanatory pattern of the development of religion in current societies. They particularly feel uneasy about the inevitability of the decline of religion inherent in the secularization theory. Thus it is not entirely surprising that meanwhile they rather speak of a 'return of religions' (Riesebrodt 2001; Casanova 1994) or the "return of the religious or the gods" (Zulehner 2002; Graf 2004) rather than concerning themselves any longer with the assumptions of the secularization theory. Still, the results of the empirical analysis of religion indicate secularization effects (Bruce 2002; Jagodzinski/Dobbelaere 1995; Norris/Inglehart 2004; Pollack/Pickel 2003, 2007, 2008; Voas 2008). However, the structure of the evidence is not entirely linear but is often interrupted by other explanatory factors or reflects path dependent developments. This in turn does not necessarily indicate that the secularization theory does not hold true but rather that the processes which it refers to are more complex. It may be necessary to differentiate the secularization theory with regard to its effects, as it consists of a whole range of assumptions and hypotheses on the one hand and closely refers to modernization theory on the other hand. Such a procedure includes observing secularization on different levels. Especially the work of Karel Dobbelaere (1981, 2002) seems to be from great interest here.[17]

Dobbelaere (1981, 2002) differentiates between „societal secularization", "organizational secularization", and "individual secularization". *Individual secularization* refers to the process of citizens' growing dissociation from religion. This encompasses a slackening of the involvement in religious events as well as a decrease in or transformation of subjective religiosity[18]

---

[17] Another possibility are the thoughts of Jose Casanova (1994: 19-39). He discerns the process of differentiation at the societal level, which manifests itself particularly in the relation between the church and the state, from the secularization assumption of a decrease in faith or a process of privatization of religion. He concludes that only the former process of differentiation of social spheres occurs in a continous manner, while the latter two processes are contingent on the historical constellations in certain regions and countries. With regard to the conditions, Casanova frequently falls back on conceptions of the market model, in particular on the relation between the church and the state.

[18] Dobbelaere (2002: 137) points to two possible trends: on the one hand, a general decrease in religious convictions and religious faith may occur, on the other hand, there is the option to recombine religious convictions – i.e. a transformation of individual religiosity. However, Dobbelaere also underlines that both processes, the

(Dobbelaere 2002: 38-39, 137-140). *Organizational secularization* addresses the issue of a decline of religious societies in the course of rationalization. At the same time, it refers to the inner secularization of religion, in the sense of a change in the social form and the self- image of the churches. It thus focuses mainly on the organization of the church and its development. *Societal secularization* is to be conceived of as a consequence of the functional differentiation of modern societies (Dobbelaere 2002: 45-46). Different subsystems fulfill functions in society, which were originally carried out by religion. In this respect, the role of social integration through norms and religious commandments has to be particularly emphasized. In modern societies, both constantly become less important for the citizens. Even when considering them separately, all three processes of secularization are associated and interact.

Chart 1: The dimensions of secularization

Societal Secularization
... is the consequence of functional differentiation within the society and results in a loss of functions of religion for society. Especially the social significance of norm-settings and education decline.
Organizational Secularization
... refers to the ddecline of religious organizations and the internal rationalization of churches as reaction to (modernization and value change) developments in the modern societies.
Individual Secularization
... describes the pprocess of increasing distance of the individuals towards religion, including the decline in integration in church and subjective religiosity.

Source: Own composition; following Dobelaere 2002.

A lot of current thoughts in the sociology of religion run along the same vein (Bruce 2002: 4; Martin 1978; Pickel 2009a; Stolz 2009). Consequently, the project ‚Church and Religion in an enlarged Europe' presented here is based on the differentiation as suggested by Dobbelaere. Accordingly, the research question of the article at hand reads as follows: *Is the secularization theory able to provide explanatory patterns for the development of religious vitality or do its assumptions fail to stand up to an empirical test?*. The extent of *religious vitality* is our main object of research. It comprises both the integration in church as well as religious beliefs. It is necessary to extend the term (which

---

former in the short run, the latter in the long run, contribute or lead to a loss of relevance of religion.

usually refers to religious practices in the US)[19] to the level of religious beliefs as it enables us to compare the theses of secularization and individualization. At the current stage of the project, the organizational level of secularization has not yet been fully elaborated. Therefore, I will thus focus my analyses on the levels of individual and societal secularization.[20] As the contentious issues between the three theoretical approaches presented here refer to these two levels (explanation of religious vitality, development of subjective religiosity), the suggested focus appears to be a viable solution for the empirical analysis.

3. Case Selection and Measurement

Most of the empirical results presented in this article are based on the study 'Church and Religion in an enlarged Europe 2006', which is the product of the Project 'Church and Religion in an enlarged Europe', financed by the Volkswagen Foundation since 2004. The joint directors of the project are Detlef Pollack (University of Münster) and Gert Pickel (University of Leipzig). Olaf Müller is the project coordinator. The international project partners are: Helena Vilaca (Portugal), Marat Shterin (Russia), Miklos Tomka and Gergely Rosta (Hungary), Kati Niemelä and Kimmo Kääriäinen (Finland); Sinisa Zrinscak and Krunoslav Nikodem (Croatia); Karen Andersen and Tom Inglis (Ireland); Tadeusz Doktor † and Dorota Hall (Poland) and Eva-Liisa Jannus (Estonia). The reference survey was carried out in the Fall of 2006.

The *criteria for selecting the countries* included in the survey are based on the findings in previous studies and conceptual considerations, using a *"Most-different-system-design"* (Przeworski/Teune 1970). The first criterion is the *cultural-religious heritage* of the country, which arises from its religious-cultural tradition. This in turn is derived from the denominational orientation of the citizens and its historical roots. The idea behind this selection criterion is the assumption that the membership of the citizens in different denominations can cause differences regarding the religious vitality. A number of analyses (Haller 1988; Pickel 1998; Martin 1978) point to a higher ability of Catholicism to develop a commitment to the church among its members in comparison with Protestantism or the Orthodox Church for

---

[19] The local discussion does not specifically differentiate between the integration in church and faith. Both are considered to be related both in the market model as well as in the secularization theory. However, concerning the empirical analysis, actions are of greater interest to Northern American scientists' research. This is in line with the reasoning of the rational choice approach upon which it is based.

[20] Due to the fact that the secularization theory and the thesis of the individualization of religion can only be differentiated at the individual level, focusing on the level of individual secularization is advantageous.

example. The second criterion is the *political situation in the past 50 years*. We assume that the actually existing socialism and its hostile orientation to religion has left its mark in the minds of the citizens. The third criterion is the degree of *socio-economic modernization* which is considered to be an indicator to designate secularization processes.

Chart 2: The sample collection of the project

	Cultural heritage (religious denomination)	Political heritage (Socialist experience)	Level of socioeconomic modernization
Portugal	Catholic		23
Ireland	Catholic		12
West Germany	Mixed denominations		18
Finland	Protestant		14
Poland	Catholic	Socialist experience	35
Croatia	Catholic	Socialist experience	47
Hungary	Mixed denominations	Socialist experience	38
Russia	Orthodox	Socialist experience	63
Estonia	Protestant	Socialist experience	41
East Germany	Protestant	Socialist experience	(18)

Source: Own composition.

The countries were selected due to the fact that each of them exemplifies a trend. However, it soon became apparent that we could not rigidly apply the "Most-different-system-design" due to the fact that the selection criteria overlapped. First, several of the ideal type combinations of the three selection variables do not occur in reality, second, the different general conditions (the degree of modernization and socialist past) overlap and their effects are not independent of each other. Nevertheless, selecting the cases in this manner was helpful in carrying out a systematic comparative analysis. In addition to the countries which were selected as described above, Ireland (perpetual religiously charged conflict with Northern Ireland) and Poland (high historical confluence of the nation and its religion) were included as special cases. They complement the wide spread image of the European development.

In order to test the certainty of the three theoretical models in the sociology of religion, it is necessary to include different *indicators* with an informative value with regard to religious vitality. In particular with regard to the debate on the discrepancy between the individualization thesis and the secularization theory it is important to differentiate between those indicators that facilitate conclusions with regard to the integration in the church as well as indicators that are intended to measure the individual, subjective faith or the religiosity of the individual.[21] If the assumptions of the secularization theory hold true, then we should be able to observe a decrease in the bonding to the church as well as subjective religiosity. In a comparative perspective, both should be higher in countries with a lower degree of modernization than in countries with a high degree of modernization. In addition, we should be able to observe a negative relation between prosperity and religiosity on the individual level, as proponents of one branch of the secularization theory assume that an increase in material security causes a decrease in *deprivation* (Norris/Inglehart 2004; Stolz 2007). The latter cause's high religiosity, as people do not seek solace in religion as much in fortunate social situations as when they experience existential threats to life. The relation between education (as a proxy of rationalization) and religiosity is quite similar. People with a higher degree of formal education should exhibit a lower degree of religiosity than people with a lower formal degree of education.

We seek to determine the *societal secularization* through citizens' attitude toward the differentiation of the different subareas of life. The segregation of religion and politics is of particular importance in this respect. From the point of view of the secularization theory, it is also of interest in how far the citizens approve of the supposed tension between ‚rational modernity' (exemplified by the sciences) and religion. If they widely support such a discrepancy, which increases further with the level of modernization, then we may assume that an extensive societal secularization is taking place, which emerges from a process of social differentiation.

In order to consider the assumptions of the market model, we also seek to determine whether citizens want a religiously plural landscape in general. If this is not the case, then we may hardly expect that a growing number of religious choices will increase religious vitality. It would speak for the secularization theory if countries with a higher degree of pluralisation had a rather low religious vitality or if their citizens became religiously inactive due to an increasing number of religious choices. Due to our focus on a limited number of countries, we can only test this claim to a certain degree, as it is located on the macro-level of observation (Fox 2008; Pollack/Pickel 2009).

---

[21] According to Charles Y. Glock's considerations (1954), these indicators belong to the sphere of religious rituals or rather religious practice or to the area of religious beliefs (see also Huber 2003).

4. Societal and Individual Secularization in Europe?

The *societal secularization* – the dimension I will start with – focuses on the loss of relevance of religious norms and the process of *functional differentiation*. Three indicator groups are chosen – religion and politics, science and education. The *segregation of religion and politics* or between the church and the state is deeply rooted in the minds of the people of all the European states under research. According to the citizens, religion has only little place in politics. The response styles in the countries hardly vary. It appears to be a basic constant in modern (European) societies. Consequently, it does not come as a surprise that the explicit inclusion of a reference to God in the preamble of the European Constitution was rejected by most of the citizens in our nine countries under research. The opinions on this issue strongly diverge between the Catholic and non-Catholic countries: In Croatia and Poland, there is a slim majority and in Portugal and Ireland a large minority which would approve of an explicit reference to God in the European Constitution while there are only small minorities in favour of this issue in the other countries. However, this also implies that even in countries with a predominantly positive disposition toward a reference in the constitution, usually half of the citizens (and thus a large number of the faithful and church members) oppose this political decision.

Chart 3: Indicators of societal secularization

	WG	Port	Irl	Fin	EG	Pol	Hun	Cro	Est	Rus
Religion and Politics										
"Religious Leaders should not try to influence government decisions"	70	75	67	62	70	73	68	73	80	75
"The constitution of the European Union should make explicit reference to God"	27	48	46	22	20	51	39	58	18	37
Religion and Science										
"Scientific Research should not be restricted by religious norms and values"	72	68	62	82	74	58	77	69	88	87
Religion and School										
"Education at school should be free from religion"	42	31	30	34	60	27	29	36	64	42
"Religious symbols, such as crosses, should be forbidden in state schools"	31	27	20	11	55	16	13	30	28	33

Source: Own Calculations on C&R; percent of positive answers (a lot + quite a lot).

The citizens also have a clear position on the *influence of religion on science*. According to them, religious norms and values should not interfere with scientific research. Again, there are differences between Catholic and non-Catholic countries, however, there is no country with a majority which rejects the given statements. People least agree with them in the two special cases of religious vitality – Ireland and Poland. Science and religion are perceived as separate spheres. Both indicators lead to the conclusion, that societal secularization is common to all European societies. But while the differentiation between the functional spheres of religion, politics and science is apparently firmly rooted in the belief systems of the European citizens, the *attitudes toward the influence of religion on the educational system* are far from clear-cut. Not only are Estonia and East Germany the only countries where the majority of citizens favours a school education without religious elements, a strict segregation between the church and the state in the sense of keeping state schools clear of religious symbols, is approved of only to a very limited extent. Apparently, there is a common Christian *cultural heritage* and its transmission is generally regarded as beneficial, even though not all of the respondents are very closely committed to the church and religion. This is possibly one of the last bastions of religion apart from its own limited functional sphere. As in the case of the other indicators, the countries are distributed as usual when it comes to the assessment of the desired relationship between religion and school. In Catholic countries, there is a far more open-minded attitude toward the presence of religion in schools than in Protestant countries.

We can conclude that societal secularization in the European realm has progressed to a large extent. This does not imply that there is no longer any potential for conflict. Rather, it depends on the specific areas in society. In cases where the influence of religion has endured, some of the groups who are integrated in church fight fierce rear-guard battles. In the long run, we will most likely witness a progression in the differentiation of society and, subsequently, an increasing loss of the social relevance of religion as illustrated by the existing broad acceptance of a segregation of religion and politics or religion and science. This appears to be such a wide-ranging process that we can hardly make out any differences between the countries in this respect as to their degree of modernization. On the one hand, socio-economic differences may simply be too small to produce any perceivable variation; on the other hand, the respective differences are largely covered up by the dominant structures of influence of the cultural traditions. Thus, at the societal level, Catholic countries usually resist the secularization processes longer than Orthodox or Protestant countries. The question that follows is in how far this applies to individual secularization.

Individual Secularization

This reference to the communal basis of religion points to one of the main starting points of every secularization debate: the declaration that church attendance rates and membership in religious organizations are decreasing (Bruce 2002a: 3; Dobbelaere 2002: 137-140). A closer look reveals that in this instance, religion is in fact not disappearing. Apart from the two ‚problem cases' of Estonia and East Germany, a broad *culture of church affiliation* remains prevalent in the European realm. In Hungary and Russia as well as in Estonia and Croatia, we even find that membership rates have increased since 2000. In Russia, these changes have turned out to be particularly drastic. The abolition of the political repressions has led many people to return to the church in Eastern European countries – at least during the first years after the radical changes (also Tomka et al. 1999). In Finland, Ireland and Portugal, the membership rates have remained rather stable during the past 15 years according to survey data. Only in Germany do we find a continuous decrease in church membership rates in our group of countries. With different data, we can make out a similar trend in Great Britain and the Netherlands as well – both states have a mixed denominational culture (Pickel 2009a: 14). The developments in East Germany should be emphasized: it is the only ‚Eastern European country' which does not have a positive balance between those leaving and those joining the church. Here, the de-ecclasiasticalization appears to have passed a certain threshold, which prevents a revitalization of the participation in church.

Chart 4: Integration in Church and religious practice

	WG	Port	Irl	Fin	EG	Pol	Hun	Cro	Est	Rus
Membership										
2006	81	92	96	88	29	96	78	95	45	74
1999/2000	83	92	96	88	29	96	67	89	25	51
1990/1991	89	89	96	88	35	96	65	-	35	43
Attendance at church										
2006	10	17	34	4	3	33	8	16	3,5	4
1999/2000	11	21	35	4	3,5	33	8	20	3,5	3
1990/1991	12	23	43	4	3,5	38	14	-	3,5	3
Frequency of prayer										
At least once a week	39	55	79	30	17	69	48	52	15	32
Never	26	16	10	22	65	3	20	11	57	33

Source: Own Calculations on C&R; calculations for 1999/2000 means of the results of EVS 1999/PCE 2000; calculations for 1990/1991 means of the results of WVS 1990/ISSP 1990/1991 percent of positive answers (a lot + quite a lot); percent of positive answers (a lot + quite a lot); pilgrimage = "Have you ever taken part in pilgrimage".

Because membership rates are a relatively imprecise indicator for measuring religious vitality, as they hardly provide any information on the active involvement in church life, considering the *church attendance rates* appears to be a much more informative indicator, as it presupposed a minimum of active participation of the respective persons. Here, the empirical point of reference of the secularization theory becomes more evident, as the number of churchgoers in all Western European countries has continuously decreased independent of the level of this activity in the respective country.[22] Using the average annual rate of churchgoers[23] as a benchmark, we find that Finland (which has the same values as Sweden or Norway, see chart 5) is the only country where the number of churchgoers have not decreased. This may be less due to Finland's exceptional position than due to the already low attendance rate of four church services per year on average. It remains to be seen whether a lower threshold of integration in the church

---

[22] Ireland – the country which had the highest church attendance rates for decades – is characterized by the most prominent decrease. Without a doubt, this is also owing to the particularly high initial level, which allows for more variations than in less religiously vital countries.

[23] The aggregate indicator of average church attendance is more informative than the share of regular churchgoers as it also takes developments within the large group of peripheral church members into account.

has been reached, as the average rates in Russia and East Germany are not considerably lower. Thus, a large number of church members hardly pursue any religious activities and they remain (often passive) church members out of tradition, due to their socialization or social desirability.

As depicted in Chart 4 and 5, the churches' hopes for a broad wave of return to religion with regard to religious activity were fulfilled only in part in the post-socialist states of Central and Eastern Europe – especially in the orthodox Russian region or nations, in which religion and the national identity go hand in hand. Even though we can assert an increase in membership rates in all Eastern European countries except for East Germany, if anything, the religious activities – church service attendance – decreased after an initial increase after the radical changes or stabilized at a relatively low level.[24] *Based on these results, we cannot speak of a broad revitalization of bonding to the church in Eastern Europe.*[25] This may possibly be due to an adjustment process during which the Eastern European countries adapt to ‚normality'. Consequently, the growth rates increase the level in the Eastern European countries to a degree which they would have reached due to their degree of modernization if it had not been for their socialist past. According to the assumptions of the secularization theory, they would join the common European process at this point.

Chart 5: Integration in Church in European comparison

	1981	1990 - 1991	1994 - 1998	2000 - 2002	2003 - 2006		1990 (1981)	1991	1994 - 1998	2000 - 2002	2003 - 2006
Italy	23	23	21	24	20	Poland	38	37	32	33	33
Portugal	-	23	22	21	17	Lithuania	-	14	12	12	10
Spain	24	18	17	15	11	Slovakia	20	22	-	20	20
Cyprus	-	-	11	-	11	Slovenia	15	14	14	12	12
Ireland	45	43	38	35	34	Hungary	14	8	11	8	8
France	7	7	8	6	6	Croatia	-	-	15	20	16
Luxemburg	23	19	15	14	10	Czech Republic	4,5	9	6	5	4,5
Belgium	18	16	14	11	6,5	Germany (O)	-	3	3	3,5	3,5

---

[24] Due to missing valid survey data, we cannot sketch the return movement to the churches.
[25] This contrasts with Zulehner's (2002) and Tomka's et al. (1999) statements. However, they link the developments of the differences to the different age cohorts and refer to different countries of observation.

Country						Country					
Austria	-	18	16	15	11	Latvia	4	6	6	6	5
Netherlands	16	13	10	9	8	Estonia	-	4	3,5	3,5	3,5
Switzerland	-	16	10	9	8,5	Romania	13	17	-	17	17
Germany (W)	13	12	11	11	10	Bulgaria	4	6	6	7	6
Great Britain	10	10	10	9	8,5	Macedonia	-	11	8	14	-
Northern Irl.	30	30	27	27	-	Serbia-Monten.	-	-	6	8	9,5
Sweden	5	4,5	4,5	4	3,5	Russia	2	4	3	3	4
Denmark	4	4	4,5	4	3,5	Belorussia	3	4	5	5	-
Norway	5	5	4,5	4	4	Ukraine	-	8	7	7	7,5
Finland	5	4	4	4	4	Georgia	-	10	9	8	-
Island	3,5	3,5	-	4	4	Moldavia	-	10	8	11	10
Greece	17	16	15,5	11,5	17	Albania	-	9	-	13	-
Turkey	-	20	23	21,5	19,5	Bosnia-Herzeg.	-	-	19	18	-

Source: Own Calculations different data-sets.

The *distribution of church attendance*, as well as the frequency of individual prayer across the countries show a similar pattern to that of the membership rates. Poland and Ireland have the largest number of church service attenders, followed by Croatia, Portugal and Hungary, where at least about half of those questioned pray at least once a week. Again, the difference between Catholic and Protestant countries becomes apparent. In historically Catholic countries, the commitment of the faithful to their church in the sense of personal activities is generally higher than in Protestant, denominationally mixed or even Orthodox countries. If we define religious vitality as religious activity, Protestant countries in Europe report a rather low level of religious vitality. In order to verify the individualization thesis,[26] it is necessary to consider *personal religiosity*, as it alone informs us about the validity or invalidity of a comprehensive loss of social relevance of religion according to Luckmann (1991). Maybe the commitment of the people to the church is decreasing – however, in the course of a change in the form of religion, they make out other possibilities to satisfy their anthropologically

---

[26] Individualization has to be understood as a general social phenomenon which pertains to entire societies and not individuals. It must not be confused with „egoism" (Beck 2008: 123-124).

founded religious needs in private or outside the established churches. This approach is also relevant from the perspective of Protestantism, as it often refers to the individuality of the relationship with God. Consequently, low church attendance rates do not reflect a loss of social relevance of Protestantism but rather a measurement error which does not sufficiently take into account the particularities of Protestantism.

Chart 6: Subjective Religiosity 2006

	WG	Port	Irl	Fin	EG	Pol	Hun	Cro	Est	Rus
I am religious to the teachings of my church	16	46	34	20	9	56	21	52	14	21
I am religious in my own way	61	45	56	58	34	39	59	37	41	49
I cannot decide, whether I am a religious person or not	7	2	4	10	4	3	6	4	11	14
I am not religious	16	7	6	12	53	2	14	7	34	16

Source: Own Calculations on C&R; percent of positive answers (a lot + quite a lot).

However, this assumption does not hold against the data. In the *Protestant countries*, the statements on personal religiosity are indeed understood in an individualized sense in certain respects and the respondents state that they are religious in their own way rather than believing in the teachings of the church of which they are a member. But the percentage of those who are religiously indifferent or who categorize themselves as decidedly non-religious is (in part considerably) higher than in the non-Protestant countries of comparison, too. And the individual religious activities, like praying (Chart 4) are in protestant countries significant lower than in the other countries. From the point of view of the cultural commitment power of denominations, we cannot but consider Protestantism to be at a disadvantage as opposed to Catholicism overall. Maybe Bergers' (1967: 158) argument – which assumes that secularization is inherent and immanent in Protestantism – will prove to be true at least in part and Protestantism includes too much rationality to withstand secularization.

East Germany reports the largest percentage of those who profess to be non-religious, followed by Estonia. This is mirrored by the Catholic cultural realm. According to their replies, about half of the Portuguese, Croats and Polish are religious in accordance with the perceived rules of their church. This also implies that in a cross-country comparison, traditional religiosity is related to the organizational aspects of the church. Ireland deviates from the ‚Catholic' pattern, as more of the faithful retain a distance to the teachings of the church without lapsing into religious doubts or rejection. Nevertheless, the Irish faithful cannot be judged to be less religious than the Portuguese faithful, for example, they simply seem to interact with their religion in a more individual manner. In West Germany, Finland, Russia and Hungary, the degree of individualized religiosity is even higher. Here, they represent vast majorities of the respective populations. These cross-country results are supported by another indicator of personal religiosity – the *belief in God*. In Estonia as well as in East Germany, the statement "a personal God exists" – which is in line with the teachings of the Christian churches – was chosen by barely 14 per cent of the respondents. The majority of the East German citizens tend to consider themselves as atheists or regard themselves as non-religious.[27]

Chart 7: Forms of Belief in God

	WG	Port	Irl	Fin	EG	Pol	Hun	Cro	Est	Rus
Belief in a personal God										
2006	28	81	67	46	14	56	53	52	14	31
1999/2000	(38)	(79)	(67)	(47)	(17)	(65)	(42)	(38)	(18)	(27)
	-10	+2	0	-1	-3	-9	+11	+14	-4	+4
Belief in a higher Being										
2006	44	9	17	29	26	32	12	32	39	26
1999/2000	(36)	(15)	(23)	(34)	(16)	(23)	(17)	(51)	(45)	(32)
	+8	-6	-6	-5	+10	+9	-5	-19	-6	-6
Don't know, whether God exist	7	5	10	12	6	10	19	10	19	29
	(12)	(3)	(7)	(11)	(9)	(5)	(18)	(7)	(20)	(31)
	-5	+2	+3	+1	-3	+5	+1	+3	-1	-2
Don't believe God exist	16	1	3	10	27	1	11	2	14	4
I am an atheist	5	4	3	3	27	1	5	4	14	10
	+7	+2	+3	+5	-4	-5	-7	+2	+11	+4

Source: Own Calculations on C&R; calculations for 1999/2000 means of the results of EVS 1999/PCND 2000; percent of positive answers (a lot + quite a lot).

In Estonia, these two groups also comprise more than a quarter of the population – however, most of the Estonians believe in a higher being. Many

---

[27] The differentiation between atheists and non-religious people has proven to be useful, as it reflects different positions (see Pickel 2000: 225-232). While atheists usually explicitly or even aggressively disapprove of any kind of religion, non-religious persons do not feel compelled to take on an active opposing position against Christians or believers of other religions.

people concur with this diffuse form of faith in most of the other European countries as well. In West Germany, they represent the largest group and even in Poland and Croatia, over 30 percent profess such a general form of faith. In Portugal, we find the largest group of faithful who believe in a personal God, In Poland, Hungary and Croatia, still more than half of the population do so. Overall, it seems that a tendency toward a more *diffuse image of God* is becoming apparent in many European countries. In Hungary and Croatia, there is a trend in the opposite direction. On the one hand, this may be due to a polarization between religious and non-religious people in society, on the other hand, it may result from an increasing *interlinkage between religion and nationalist ideas* (see Nikodem/Zrinscak 2008).

Chart 8: Societal Secularization and religious vitality

	Member of a Church	Attendance at Church	Belief in a personal God	No Belief
"Religious Leaders should not try to influence government decisions"	-.11	-.11	-.11	+.12
"The constitution of European Union should make explicit reference to God"	-.30	-.34	-.35	+.29
"Scientific Research should not be restricted by religious norms and values"	-.14	-.21	-.15	+.13
"Education at school should be free from religion"	-.30	-.27	-.29	+.30

Source: Own Calculations on C6E; pearsons correlations p < .001, – = no significant correlation.

Chart 8 show clear relations between the indicators for societal secularization and individual secularization. As we expected, proximity to religion and the church causes negative replies to questions regarding the separation of the different spheres of life. This relation only holds to a moderate extent with regard to fields where the general public is largely in consensus, such as the basic principle of the segregation of religion and politics or religion and science. These are phenomena which occur across societies, which hardly cause conflicts any longer. However, when it comes to concrete questions regarding the public relevance of religion, deep rifts run through the societies. Thus, almost all of the proponents of a reference to God in the European Constitution can be found among the groups of people who are integrated in the church. These groups in particular support an incorporation of religion in the school system. It is over this issue that societies polarize. Societal secularization seems to be the first dimension of secularization that occurs in society, but individual secularization follows, because of the connection to the first with a – from country to country variable – time-lag.

Concluding these results, we can hardly say, that the individualization thesis of religion show evidence and secularization theory is lacking validity. The observable increase in *diffuse religious beliefs* and the number of religiously indifferent people does not necessarily have to be interpreted as a consequence of individualization; it can also be conceived of as a preliminary stage to secularization (see Voas 2008: 39-41). The developments in Western Europe in particular consistently indicate a gradual process of a loss of faith which unfolds in line with the secularization theory. In Eastern Europe, we find both processes of an increase as well as a decrease among the groups of indifferent and non-religious people. Due to the fact that we can hardly expect to observe an increasing individualization in these countries at present[28] and as the increase in the number of faithful is also accompanied in part by a revitalization with regard to church integration, the assumptions of the secularization theory appear to hold true more so than those of the individualization thesis.

5. Secularization, Individualization and the Market Model

The individualization thesis according to Luckmann (1967) refers to the change in the forms of religion and the loose of tights between integration in church and subjective religiosity. Due to the fact that religiosity cannot disappear, other forms have to become more important in turn when the social relevance of the traditional model of interpretation of Christian religiosity decreases. One statement of the individualization thesis refers to the dissolution of socio-structural relations of religion in modern times which liberates the individual with regard to his religiosity in the end. As a result of the loss of social control due to a separation from the social structure, the individual is provided with the chance to believe what he chooses to believe. This line of thought reflects a basic assumption of the individualization thesis – the substitution of the social norm of "heteronomy"with the new norm of "self-determination". Considering the results in Chart 9, *we cannot detect a complete detachment of religious beliefs from social structures*. Particularly in

---

[28] Thus all of the indicators of individualization, self-fulfillment and post-materialism (Norris/Inglehart 2004: 18-21) had extremely low approval rates in the East European countries. This raises the question as to why religious vitality remains so low in some Eastern European countries against this background.

rural areas, older women with a lower degree of formal education and a comparatively low income, report the highest religious vitality – but they also believe in God the most.

Chart 9: Social structural Bases of Religiosity and Relations to Values

	Member	Attend. Church	Prayer	Belief in God
Age (increasing Age)	.08	.12	.26	.11
Sex (Women)	.08	.11	.18	.11
Formal education (high education)	-.11	-.08	-.13	-.16
Urban-rural (rural)	.03	.09	.05	.08
Income (low income)	.05	.09	.16	.12

Source: Own Calculations on C&R; persons correlations p < .001, – = no significant correlation.

Even though the socio-structural foundation of religion may have gradually disintegrated in society over the last decades, the relation has not disappeared entirely.[29] The main indicators of modernization – a high degree of education reflecting a spreading rationalization as well as urbanization – have significant effects in all of the countries. In addition, the deprivation theory has to be take into account – it considers socio-economic welfare (another indicator of modernization) to be an important factor in reducing social deprivation among the people as well as the wish for compensation for all the suffering in the afterlife. And also on macro level the connection between integration in church and subjective religiosity seems high. Chart 10 shows a strong relationship between both indicators. In countries, where the belief in God is widespread, higher rates of attendance in church can be noticed. The form of the line gives the impression, that first the integration in church decline and with sometime between, also the subjective religiosity lacks over the populations.[30]

---

[29] Seperate analyses for each of the countries under research yielded only marginally different results.
[30] Another possibility of testing the individualization thesis is to consider in how far accounts of *values* of self-fulfillment are positively related to alternative forms of religiosity (Pollack/Pickel 2007). The results show a positive relation between traditional values and all types of religiosity and church integration as well as a negative relation between individualistic values and these forms. As in the previous results, there is no strong evidence for an assertion of the individualization thesis.

Chart 10: Correspondence between Attendance at Church and Belief in God

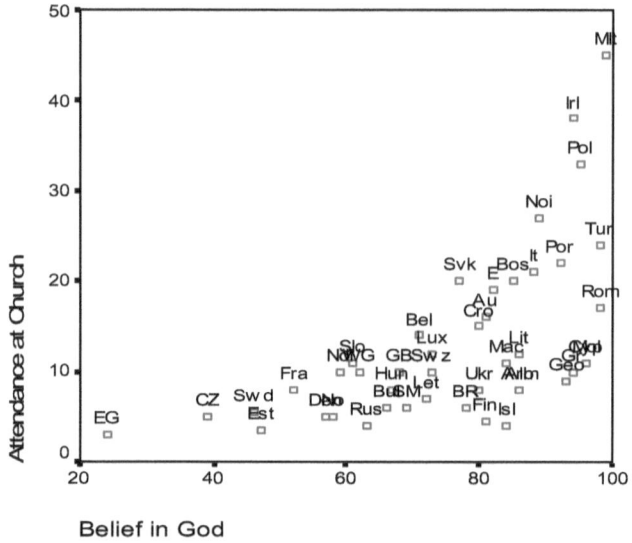

Source: Own Calculations different data-sets, 1998.

If the individualization thesis is correct, then we also should be able to observe alternatives or substitutes in the form of alternative religiosity in countries where traditional religiosity is losing its social relevance. Chart 11 lists the distribution of a number of possible functional equivalents of traditional religiosity.

Chart 11: Religiosity outside of Christianity

I believe in ...	WG	Port	Irl	Fin	EG	Pol	Hun	Cro	Est	Rus
Magic/Spirituality/Occultism	12	24	20	9	8	8	12	13	17	16
Astrology/Horoscopes	18	27	18	16	16	20	32	26	31	31
Amulets, Stones and Crystals could be helpful	25	36	20	12	16	24	26	29	38	37

Source: Own Calculations on C&R percent of positive answers (a lot + quite a lot).

However, the results clearly show that there is a rather low demand for these forms of religiosity. At most, a third of the citizens in one of the countries under research state that they have an affinity for one of the forms presented to them. More importantly, the distribution of the rates of agreement is skewed in a different direction than suggested by the individualization thesis. It is not the countries with a loss of relevance of traditional religiosity and bonding to the church which have the highest proportion of alternative religiosity but rather those countries with a strong Christian religiosity (Ireland, Portugal). Hence, if traditional religiosity is rejected, then most other forms of alternative religiosity are not accepted either. The consequences that arise from this observation are straightforward: the selected forms of alternative religiosity do not serve as substitutes for traditional religiosity.

Even this interpretation does not suffice to reject the individualization thesis as Luckmann (1967) makes allowance for a whole range of additional possibilities for an "invisible religion", which could not be taken into account in the survey at hand.[31] According to him, many of these cannot be measured by means of survey research anyway. This may be true; nevertheless, the results as presented in Chart 8 raise certain doubts with regard to the validity of religiosity rooted in anthropology which only manifests itself via a change in form. It rather appears more plausible to allow for the possibility of religiously indifferent as well as non-religious persons who will find their place next to those whose religious beliefs truly transformed into a different kind. Thus, Dobbelaere (2002: 137) allows for both a loss of faith and a transformation. However, ultimately, he considers transformation to be more of a transitional period which is often followed by a loss of faith. However, this does not mean that there is no process of individualization at all. Nevertheless, (in Europe) the influence of individualization appears to be rather consistent with the process of secularization instead of serving as a substitute

Market Model

Testing the relevance of the *market model* proves to be a bit more complicated at the individual level than testing the individualization thesis. The majority of the argumentational structure of the market model refers to the distribution of religious vitality and the macro level of observations (Iannaccone 1991; Stark/Iannaccone 1994; Fox 2008). However, since recently, the merely supply-oriented market model has been complemented

---

[31] Apart from the sphere of small and medium transcendencies in all its generality, soccer, art and other kinds of experience in everyday life are referred to. This spectrum eludes sufficient empirical testing, which is why it is more than slightly critized from different perspectives, as it renders it nearly impossible to find an intersubjectively agreed upon measure of religiosity.

by the relevance of the regulation of religious demand particularly with regard to Europe (Froese/Pfaff 2005, 2009). The quintessence of these analyses is that this type of regulation was particularly effective in Eastern Europe and is responsible for the low degree of religious vitality in East Germany for example.

In the survey at hand, we chose an approach which includes the demand aspect. It was assumed that an expanded religious supply or rather a stronger competition on the religious market would lead to an increase in religious vitality under the condition of the existence of a certain amount of interest on the demand side. Substantial groups in society would have to demand a greater plurality of religious providers in order for the market model to be successful. Simply put – those who are interested in a different religious persuasion should also plead for a larger variety of religious choices in the country. This reflects one of the core assumptions of the market model – the regulation of the religious market. The results in Chart 12 are fairly straightforward – in almost none of the European states chosen for the analysis do the citizens prefer a larger variety of possibilities in the religious realm. About three out of four persons consider religious plurality to be a cause of conflicts. Only in the Catholic countries of Ireland, Poland and Portugal, 20 per cent of the respondents voiced their support for a greater range of religious organisations and groups. Maybe this result indicates an interest in religious plurality in the presence of a religious monopoly. However, this result violates one of the basic assumptions of the religious market model – the influence of religious plurality on religious vitality – as countries with low religious vitality in particular report an exceptionally low demand for religious pluralism.

Chart 12: Demand for religious variation

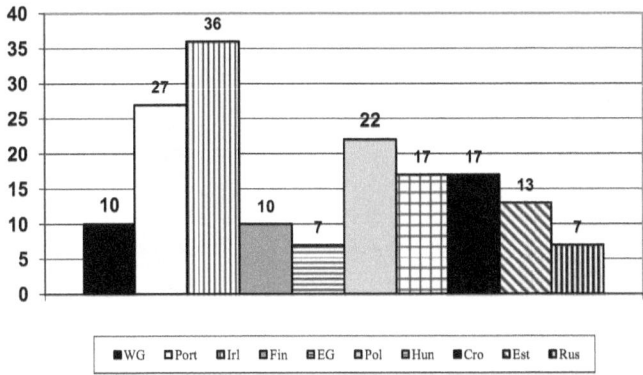

Source: Own Calculations on C&R; „I would prefer a greater variation of religious organisations and groups in my neighbourhood, because then, I could choose between different demands"; percent of positive answers (a lot + quite a lot).

Thus it is not true that religiously inactive persons are looking for a new religious place in society. Rather, they seem to take on a general non-religious or an indifferent position at most. Even though this conclusion is susceptible to several counterarguments by supporters of the market model (conflict as a substitute for competition, internal plurality of the Catholic Church, false assumption of an absence of religious interest), there appears to be only limited explanatory leeway for the religious market model in the European realm. If most people are not interested in having a larger variety of religious choices, then it is not plausible – at least in the case of Europe – to assume that a relevant increase in religious groups leads to a rise in religious vitality. This highlights a fundamental problem of the market model: it focuses on the supply side of the religious market while the religious demand is held constant. Due to the fact that economic rational choice models usually focus on the demand side, this seems to be a restriction which limits the utility of the model.

Proponents of the market model would point out that we can only derive valid conclusions with regard to the utility of the model based on concrete observations in a plural or non-plural reality. But if you test the preconditions of the market theory in the traditional way (Iannaccone 1997; Fox/Tabory 2008), the result is the same: A scatterplot combining an indicator of religious regulation (Fox 2008) and the attendance at church, show no linear correspondence or correlation for the European countries.

Chart 13: Religious regulation and religious vitality in Europe

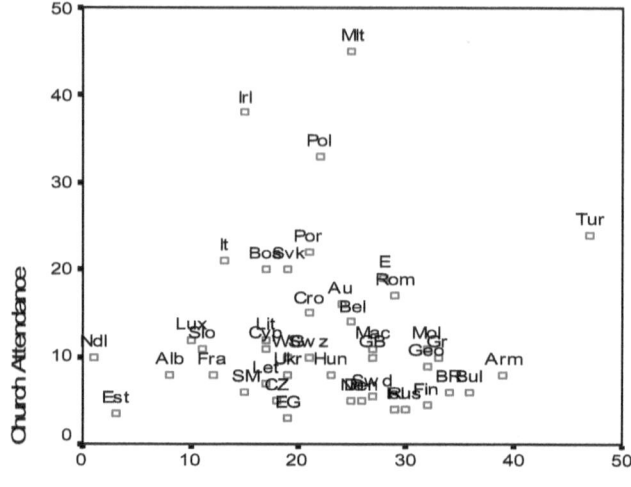

Source: Own Calculations different data-sets; Religious Regulation (Fox 2004).

This fit with other results (Pollack 2006b; Pollack/Pickel 1999, 2009) and speaks against the validity of the market model, at least within Europe. You have to remember, regulation of religion is the core part of the market model, because it is the source for religious pluralization. Even if we take into account, that religious conflict is able to substitute religious pluralism, you can say, that in Europe the market model does not fit very well for the explanation of religious vitality – until yet.

The majority of the results presented in this section support the main assumptions of the secularization theory at least as regards individual secularization. There is only sporadic evidence for the assumptions of the individualization thesis. However, we were not able to finally and categorically disprove it. The results are more straightforward with regard to the utility of the religious market model: As opposed to North America, New Zealand or Australia, this model is of little use with regard to the development in Europe. Rather, long-term cultural traditions, such as Catholicism and Protestantism, appear to be relevant in explaining the variations in the trends in the development of religiosity and religious vitality. Maybe they determine the trajectories of secularization (see Norris/Inglehart 2004).

6. Bases of Religious Vitality

What accounts for the differences in religious vitality in the countries under research? Let us systematize the observations we have made so far. The study followed a comparative design which allows us to make qualified comparisons at the macro level. In accordance with a strict application of the secularization theory, which solely takes the level of socio-economic modernization into account, Western European countries should consistently lag behind Eastern European countries. Obviously, this is not the case. To be honest, we did not expect to find evidence for this assumption as we were already aware of the fact that political repression in Eastern Europe in the times of socialism caused a loss of religious traditions. With the data at hand, we cannot definitely say whether this process represents a kind of anticipated secularization or whether it has created a state which is unnatural considering the degree of secularization which may lead to an adjustment process in the Eastern European countries in the sense of a revitalization process.

Chart 14: A comparative view on the bases of religious vitality at the macro level

	WD	Port	Irl	Fin	OD	Pol	Ung	Kro	Est	Rus
State of modernization	-	/	-	-	+	+	+	+	+	+
Political repression in the last decades (socialist)	+	+	+	+	-	-	-	-	-	-
Religious-cultural legacy	/	+	+	-	-	+	/	+	-	-
Prospected level of religious vitality	5	1	2	7	7	2	5	2	7	7
Level of religious regulation (Fox)	3	3	2	10	3	7	8	3	1	9
Indicators of religious vitality										
Integration in Church	5	3	1	7	10	1	6	3	9	8
Subjective Religiosity	7	1	2	6	9	3	5	3	9	7
Societal Secularization (reversed in antisecularization)	7	4	2	6	9	1	5	2	10	7
Religiosity outside the Church	7	1	6	10	9	7	4	4	1	1

Source: Own Calculations; negative signs stand for a disadvantageous situation for religious vitality, positive signs stand for an advantageous situation; the level of religious regulation was taken from the „Religion and State" data set by Jonathan Fox. Here, we show the overall degree of state interventions in the religious sphere and therefore the openness of the religious market. For a definition of the index see Fox/Tabory 2008: 251-255.

When combining the findings of the empirical analyses conducted before with the three basic conditions according to Martin (1978), it is possible to identify better and worse preconditions for religious vitality.[32] Portugal should record the highest level, while countries such as Estonia, Russia, Finland and East Germany should report the lowest level of religious vitality. And indeed, the actual order of the indicators of religious vitality for the countries under research is very close to the expected rank. Germany and Estonia have the highest degree of societal secularization while Ireland, Portugal and Poland record the highest degree of religious vitality. The countries' positions in the rankings do differ somewhat when comparing church integration and subjective religiosity, however, religious practices and religious beliefs highly correspond with each other.

Chart 15: Macro effects – correlation analysis

	Not member	Attendance at church	Belief in personal God	Subjective religiosity
Europe				
Socialist Past	+.30	n.s.	n.s.	n.s.
Level of Modernization (Ranking Human Development Index)	n.s.	n.s.	-.48	-.37
Catholic Heritage	n.s.	+.51	n.s.	n.s.
Protestant Heritage	n.s.	-.39	-.54	-.50
Subgroup without socialist past (*Western Europe*)				
Level of Modernization	+.50	-.54	-.65	-.73
Catholic Heritage	n.s.	+.56	+.72	+.42
Protestant Heritage	n.s.	-.53	-.63	-.47
Subgroup with socialist past (*Eastern Europe*)				
Level of Modernization	+.55	n.s.	-.60	-.43
Catholic Heritage	n.s.	+.46	n.s.	n.s.
Protestant Heritage	+.74	-.34	-.74	-.70

Source: Own Calculations; different sources.

---

[32] A combination of modernization, political repression and protestant legacy should prove to be the worst preconditions of religious vitality, a combination of low modernization, no political repression and catholic legacy the best. The assumption that the three preconditions are weighted equally is open to critical discussion.

The *religious-cultural legacy of a country* is of great importance for religious vitality with regard to religious beliefs, church integration and societal secularization. While the Catholic countries succeed in committing their church members on a long-term basis, the Protestant churches fail to do so. Apparently, Protestantism was less able to oppose the politically enforced fight against religion in the socialist countries. One of the reasons may be that Protestantism is more strongly rooted in modern-day society. Another causal characteristic – which Protestantism shares with the Orthodox Church – is the fact that they were less able to fight off political encroachments on the national level due to their organizational structure, which consists of regional churches. In this respect, Catholicism had an advantage due to the fact that its point of reference was in Rome – outside the socialist territory. The fact that processes of collective *identity building*, combining a sense of national identity and religion occur in Catholic countries in particular also certainly matters. We can observe this in Ireland as well as in Poland and Croatia. Bruce (2002a: 30-33) refers to these processes as „Cultural Defence", which could be regarded as a counter movement against comprehensive processes of globalization in accordance with Huntington's assumptions (1996), apparently presuppose a closer individual relation to the churches than envisaged by Protestantism.

While the religious-cultural heritage marks the starting point of religious vitality in a given country, the *changes in religious vitality* depend on other processes. The negative influences of rationalization and functional differentiation as propagated by the secularization theory have greatly advanced at the societal level. Even in countries with a high percentage of church members, religion is hardly accorded any influence on any other social spheres. We were not able to show whether this is directly related to a trend toward privatization. However, the communal basis of religion and the bonding to the church continue to decrease. This comes as no surprise, since people need religion less and less in order to explain the events in their surroundings. Thus it seems as if the decreasing social roots of religion would undermine subjective religiosity in the long run. In prosperous societies, religion is no longer necessary as a compensation for mundane problems (Wilson 1982; Stolz 2007). This implies that increasing material wealth contributes to the loss of relevance of religion. The determination of the dynamic effects of modernization proved to be difficult due to the fact that accelerated processes of modernization coincided with concomitantly decreasing ‚legacies' of anti-religious socialist socialization in Eastern Europe after 1989.

Chart 16: Indicators of religious vitality – correlation analysis

	Member	Attend. Church	Prayer	Belief in God
Parents brought me up in faith	.49	.43	.28	.45
I think that it is important to bring up children in faith	.53	.41	.32	.48

Source: Own Calculations on C&R; persons correlations p < .001, – = no significant correlation.

In order to enforce these rather long-term processes, *socialization* is of crucial importance. Chart 16 reflects the transgenerational transmission of Christian religiosity. Whether it is integration in church or belief in God – a lack of religious socialization undermines the religious vitality of the citizens. This holds for all European countries to the same extent. According to the main assumptions of the secularization theory, the decline in the social relevance of religion is a slow but nevertheless continuous process. This is based on cohort-specific considerations as systematized by Ronald Inglehart (1979) in his theory of value change. It is not the individual as such whose bonding to the church and maybe even to religion decreases dramatically. Rather, it is a process which goes on for generations. *Socialization* plays a particularly important role in such a developmental process. Hence, we should be able to discern differences in socialization in the countries under research which correspond to the decrease in bonding to the church and subjective religiosity. Individual religious socialization highly corresponds to the degree of religious vitality, both at the micro and macro level. The transmission of religious knowledge, religious experience and religious practices thus represents an interface to the persistence of a vital religion. It is interesting to note that the number of those who think that their own children should be raised in faith is even a bit higher than the extent of their own respective socialization suggests. This reflects a certain openness to knowledge about religious beliefs which often constitute a country's culture. However, we have to bear in mind that we cannot directly infer behaviour from these positive statements. It is often subject to additional restrictions which are likely to reduce the number of those who actually expose their children to religion and faith.

Chart 17: Religious Socialization in European comparison

	WG	Port	Irl	Fin	EG	Pol	Hun	Cro	Est	Rus
Socialization										
Parents brought me up in faith	68	94	94	59	38	96	71	85	26	30
I think that it is important to bring up children in faith (own intention)	76	88	92	78	38	90	78	81	40	50
Correlations										
Religious Socialization / own intention	.51	.50	.26	.46	.58	.49	.51	.63	.55	.51
Religious Socialization / belief in God	.21	.34	.19	.34	.31	.19	.45	.34	.33	.23

Source: Own Calculations on C&E; percent of positive answers (a lot + quite a lot).

The fact that socialization is highly relevant for the spreading of religious vitality is problematic with regard to the comparative analysis of religious vitality. Thus, in Eastern Europe, the "inertia" of family socialization causes the revitalization effect to drag on over a longer period of time. In addition to religious beliefs, non-religious or indifferent mind-sets are passed down as well. Consequently, it is even more difficult to identify for certain the conflicting dynamic developments of revitalization after 1989, due to the fact that both the cessation of political repression and secularization (which reflects increasing modernization gains) exists in parallel in Central and Eastern Europe. However, the development process of religion seems to be clear, it is a long-term reduction in religious vitality – and probably an even slower decrease in religious beliefs – which goes on for generations. Whether the process does indeed assert itself highly depends on the context and could be faced with counteracting processes, namely the revival of a national identity or an increase in social inequality which deprives certain social groups of prosperity and thus renders possible a return to religious patterns of interpretation.

7. Summary – More Secularization than Individualization or Market

Comparing the three alternative approaches, the secularization theory, the religious market model and the individualization thesis, it seems to be, that the secularization theory wins the competition. From a European perspective, the secularization theory promises to be of greater assistance in explaining religious vitality than the market model, which is the preferred model in the USA. Attempts to explain the development in Eastern Europe by the market model suffer from the fact that the assumptions upon which they are based are too vague, even though supplementing ideas which merely focus on the supply with considerations regarding the regulation of the demand has gained in substance. This neither implies that we should not take into account single elements of the market model as supplementary influential factors in addition to the secularization theory, nor that these elements cannot be of greater importance outside of Europe. However, for comparisons in Europe, the market model appears to have a limited applicability, in particular because it neglects alternative contextual elements of cultural path dependencies more than the secularization theory.

The *religious individualization thesis* only provides a limited amount of additional information for cross-country comparisons. Especially in Eastern European countries, which are most likely to report revitalization trends, increasing (subjective) religiosity is accompanied by a rise in participation in religious events. Thus, the differentiation between subjective religiosity and integration in the church as pointed out by the individualization thesis is more likely to occur in Western Europe. However, the level of faith has decreased even in this region, even though not to the same extent as in the societal sector of integration in the church. At present, we cannot say whether this represents a detachment of individualized religiosity from the socio-cultural basis or whether it is a delayed process. Regarding the trends in revitalization of religious vitality, the explanatory power of the individualization thesis remains limited as it considers new religious movements as substitutes for previous forms. We can hardly find evidence for such a development in Eastern Europe; instead, people seem to return to established forms of religion.

But an explanation, which is limited to a linear modernization or secularization, does not sufficiently do justice to the complex development of religious vitality, too. The comparative results presented here show that the different *cultural development paths* of the countries in particular are of great importance for the determinable degree of religious vitality. Especially the denominational legacy of a country affects the spreading and speed of a loss of religious traditions: Catholic countries succeed fairly well in committing their church members, effectively oppose processes of secularization and successfully maintain religious vitality; the Protestant countries do not manage to do so to the same extent. Apparently, the rationality inherent in Protestantism (Berger 1967: 111-113; Bruce 2002a: 7-8) as well as their comparatively strong integration in everyday politics through the regional churches seems to have unfavourable effects on the social relevance of Protestantism. A lot of the Christian Orthodox churches are affected by similar problems. However, in countries where the majority of the population is Orthodox Christian, we often find a close connection between the concept of the nation and religion, which involves a revitalization of religion in association with an identity-building process in the course of an emerging nationalism.

As the *cultural path dependencies determine the initial level of religious vitality* and the extent of the resistance against processes of secularization, we can hardly deny the fact that there is a dynamic process in Western Europe which can be described as a process of secularization (also Müller/Pollack 2008; Norris/Inglehart 2004; Voas 2008). At the same time, it is necessary to apply the assumptions of the secularization theory correctly, as they predict that religion will *loose its social relevance* but *will not disappear entirely*. We do find such a trend when considering the data presented in this article: it manifests itself in a process of differentiation, which is spreading across Europe, which confines religion to its core areas. The fact that many approve of a separation of religion and politics and would like to see religion abstain from influencing other spheres reflects a high degree of *societal secularization* or "compartmentalization" (Dobbelaere 2002). This is accompanied by a *decrease in bonding to the church* and decreasing membership as well as an increasing religious indifference at the individual level. Concerning religious indifference, we could point out the transformation of the forms of religion which now encompass different approaches to deal with transcendental issues. However, the fact that the number of people in Western European states who consider themselves to be non-religious is continuously increasing raises doubt as to the validity of such a theory of substitution.

In *Eastern Europe*, it is more difficult to assess the situation: *Socialist repression* of the church and the resulting ideological position against religion are additional factors in explaining regional differences in religious vitality. This complicates the identification of the degree of influence of the explanations based on the denomination and secularization theory. Thus, the processes of modernization, political repression and cultural legacy have partly counteracting or mutually increasing effects. While the tradition of regional churches of the Protestant churches in Eastern Europe provided a particularly inadvantageous basis for maintaining religious vitality especially under repressive circumstances, the Catholic churches probably managed to avoid political repressions better due to the fact that they had an external authority they could refer to in Rome.

Almost 20 years after the radical changes, the analysis of Eastern European countries suffers from an additional problem. A radical social change is occurring in the religious realm, whereby counteracting effects of a *catch-up modernization* (which subdues religious vitality) and the *withdrawal of political repressions* of the church and religion (which is favourable for religious vitality) intermingle. One could even argue that the Eastern European countries should report a far higher degree of religious vitality than they do given their degree of modernization. In comparison to the highly modernized Western European states, their level of modernization is – in part considerably – lower. Hence, according to the assumptions of the secularization theory, we would expect to find a more pronounced religious vitality, due to the fact that rationalization, differentiation as well as existential security are given to a lesser extent compared to Western Europe. However, in most of the Eastern European states, the consequences of socialist repression have caused an unnatural situation of *subdued religious vitality*, which has slowly begun to disperse after the repressions ceased. In cases where the communal basis of the religions has not been destroyed as substantially as in East Germany or in parts of Estonia and the Czech Republic, the observable *revitalization effects* do not come unexpectedly. The slow elimination of socialization effects explain the long duration of this process. This development is counteracted by continuous *increases in modernization*. When combining the two processes, there could be a *peak*, at which point the revitalization processes cease and the development joins the Western European trend toward secularization. In Slovenia (the most modernized country in Central Eastern Europe) and Poland (with it exceptionally high initial level of religious vitality), we find first indications that they have reached such a peak. The problem is that the two processes are hard to distinguish empirically, which renders difficult a clear determination of the development trends of religious vitality in Eastern and Central Eastern Europe.

As if that were not enough, *additional factors* undermine or at least moderate the universality of the secularization processes in some of the countries. They may also be assigned to the cultural path dependencies. While religiously charged political conflicts cause an above average religious vitality in Ireland (and Northern Ireland), the confluence of *religion and nation* is increasingly coming to the fore in several Eastern European states. Both patterns form and maintain *collective identity*.[33] Consequently, religion is a main resource for identity-building (Huntington 1996; Fox 2004), whereby it may be accorded social relevance in return. Examples in Europe include:

---

[33] In this regard, Bruce (2002a) refers to processes of „Cultural Defence" and „Cultural Transition", which are decisive for identity-building processes at the national as well as at the group level and which maintain religious vitality at a high level. Proponents of the market model also regard conflicts as a feasible alternative to competition, when it comes to stimulating religious vitality.

Poland, Russia and Croatia, just to name two of the countries covered in this article.

This account points to the fact that the secularization model by itself does not suffice in explaining the stock and development of religious vitality in Europe. To do justice to reality, it is obligatory to take the cultural and political *path dependencies* of the individual countries or groups of countries into account. These particularly include the historically evolved religious cultural heritage, the massive socialist political repressions but also patterns regarding the relevance of religion in society particular to the individual countries. Taking these path dependencies into account, the assumptions of the secularization theory can indeed be applied. The analysis should focus on the tension between modernity and religion and less on the assumption that secularization is irreversible.[34] Thus, on the one hand, modernization can in part proceed in the opposite direction (modernization losses affecting an entire nation or a large social group in the course of rising social inequality); on the other hand, it can be impeded by counteracting factors (political repression, processes of identity-building and identity-determination, radical social change). All in all, establishing a „*contextualized secularization theory*"as a frame of reference for empirical analyses has a lot to commend it. We can only advance the empirical interpretation of religious developments if we combine path dependencies with additional general socio-cultural explanatory models (Bruce 2002; Norris/Inglehart 2004; Stolz 2007).[35]

---

[34] By now, even dedicated proponents of explanatory models based on modernization theory (Inglehart/Welzel 2005) take path dependencies into account.

[35] Stolz (2007) suggests an alternative approach, which is also integrative in a detailed model based on action theory. He starts out from the determination of religious beliefs and practices at the micro level and considers the developments at the aggregate level as consequences of the individual processes. Stolz also points out that the pronounced mutual isolation of the three main approaches in the sociology of religion is relatively unproductive. In his opinion, the future lies in integrative explanatory models which can be tested empirically.

8. Literature

Berger, Peter L. (1967): The Sacred Canopy. Elements of a Sociological Theory of Religion. New York.

Beckford, James A. (2003): Social Theory & Religion. Cambridge.

Beck, Ulrich (2008): Der eigene Gott. Von der Friedensfähigkeit und dem Gewaltpotential von Religionen. Frankfurt/Main.

Bruce, Steve (ed.) (1992): Religion and Modernization: Sociologists and Historians Debate the Secularization Thesis. Oxford.

Bruce, Steve (1996): Religion in the Modern World: From Cathedrals to Cults. Oxford.

Bruce, Steve (1999): Choice and Religion: A Critique of Rational Choice Theory. Oxford.

Bruce, Steve (2002a): God is Dead. Secularization in the West. Oxford.

Bruce, Steve (2002b): Praying Alone? Church-Going in Britain and the Putnam Thesis. In: Journal of Contemporary Religion 17/3: 317-328.

Bruce, Steve (2006): What the Secularization Paradigm really says. In: Franzmann, Manuel/Gärtner, Christel/Köck, Nicole (eds.): Religiosität in der säkularisierten Welt. Theoretische und empirische Beiträge zur Säkularisierungsdebatte in der Religionssoziologie. Wiesbaden: 39-48.

Byrnes, Timothy A./Katzenstein, Peter J. (eds.) (2006): Religion in an Expanding Europe. Cambridge.

Casanova, Jose (1994): Public Religions in the Modern World. Chicago.

Casanova, Jose (1996): Chancen und Gefahren öffentlicher Religion. Ost- und Westeuropa im Vergleich. In: Kallscheuer, Otto (ed.): Das Europa der Religionen. Ein Kontinent zwischen Säkularisierung und Fundamentalismus. Frankfurt/Main: 181-211.

Cipriani, Roberto (2006): Secularization or „diffused religion"? In: Franzmann, Manuel/ Gärtner, Christel/Köck, Nicole (eds.): Religiosität in der säkularisierten Welt. Theoretische und empirische Beiträge zur Säkularisierungsdebatte in der Religionssoziologie. Wiesbaden: 123-142.

Chaves, Mark/Cann, David E. (1992): Regulation, Pluralism and Religious Market Structure: Explaining Religion's Vitality. In: Rationality and Society 4: 272-290.

Davie, Grace (1994): Religion in Britain since 1945: Believing without Belonging. Oxford.

Davie, Grace (2001): Patterns of Religion in Western Europe: An exceptional Case. In: Fenn, Richard K. (ed.): Sociology of Religion. Oxford: 264-278.

Davie, Grace (2002): Europe: the Exceptional Case. Parameters of Faith in the modern World. London.

Davie, Grace (2006): Religion in Europe in the 21st Century: The Factors to take into Account. In: Archive European Sociological 47/2: 271-296.

Davie, Grace (2008): From Believing without Belonging to Vicarious Religion: Understanding the Patterns of Religion in Modern Europe. In: Pollack, Detlef/Olson, Daniel V.A. (eds.): The Role of Religion in Modern Societies. New York: 165-176.

Dobbelaere, Karel (1987): Some Trends in European Sociology of Religion. In: Sociological Analysis 48: 107-137.

Dobbelaere, Karel (2002): Secularization: An Analysis on three levels. Brussels.

Dogan, Mattei/ Kazancigil, Ali, (eds.) (1994): Comparing Nations. Concepts, Strategies, Substance. Oxford.

Felling, Albert/Peters, Jan/Schreuder, Osmund, 1987: Religion im Vergleich: Bundesrepublik Deutschland und Niederlande. Frankfurt a. M.

Finke, Roger/Stark, Rodney (1988): Religious Economies and Sacred Canopies: Religious Mobilization in American Cities. In: American Sociological Review 53: 41-49.

Finke, Roger/Stark, Rodney (2003): The Dynamics of religious economies. In: Dillon, Michele (ed.): Handbook of the Sociology of Religion. Cambridge: 96-109

Finke, Roger/Stark, Rodney (2006): The Churching of America 1576-2005: Winners and Losers in our Religious Economy. New Brunswick.

Fox, Jonathan (2004): Religion, Civilization, and Civil War. Lanham.

Fox, Jonathan (2007): Do Democracies have Separation of Religion and State? In: Canadian Journal of Political Science 40/1: 1-25.

Fox, Jonathan (2008): A World Survey of Religion and the State. Cambridge.

Fox, Jonathan/Tabory, Ephraim (2008): Contemporary Evidence Regarding the Impact of State Regulation of Religion on Religious Participation and Belief. In: Sociology of Religion 69/3: 245-272.

Froese, Paul/Pfaff, Steven (2001): Replete and desolate markets: Poland, East Germany and the New Religious Paradigm. In: Social Forces 80: 481-507.

Froese, Paul/Pfaff, Steven (2005): Explaining a Religious Anomaly: A Historical Analysis of Secularization in Eastern Germany. In: Journal for the Scientific Study of Religion 44/4: 397-422.

Gabriel, Karl (Ed.) (1995): Religiöse Individualisierung oder Säkularisierung. Biographie und Gruppe als Bezugspunkte moderner Religiosität. Gütersloh.

Gill, Robin (2001): The Future of Religious Participation and Belief in Britain and Beyond. In: Fenn, Richard K. (ed.): Sociology of Religion. Oxford: 279-292.

Glock, Charles Y. (1954): Toward a typology of religious orientation. New York.

Glock, CharlesY./Stark, Rodney (1965): Religion and Society in tension. Chicago.

Haller, Max, 1988: Grenzen und Variationen gesellschaftlicher Entwicklung in Europa – eine Herausforderung und Aufgabe für die vergleichende Soziologie. In: Österreichische Zeitschrift für Soziologie 13/4: 5-19.

Huber, Stefan, 2003: Zentralität und Inhalt. Ein neues multidimensionales Messmodell der Religiosität. Opladen.

Iannaccone, Laurence R. (1991): The Consequences of Religious Market Structure: Adam Smith and the Economics of Religion. In: Rationality and Society 3: 156-177.

Iannaccone, Laurence R. (1992): Religious Market and the Economics of Religion. Social Compass 39: 123-131.

Iannaccone, Laurence R. (1998): Introduction to the Economics of Religion. Journal of Economic Literature 36: 1465-1496.

Iannacone, Laurence R./Finke, Roger/Stark, Rodney (1997): Deregulation Religion: The Economics of Church and State. In: Economic Inquiry 35: 350-364.

Inglehart, Ronald (1997): Modernization and Post modernization. Cultural, Economic and political Change in 43 Societies. Princeton.

Inglehart, Ronald/Norris, Pippa (2003): Rising Tide. Gender Equality and cultural Change around the World. Cambridge.

Jagodzinski, Wolfgang/Dobbelaere, Karel (1993): Der Wandel kirchlicher Religiosität in Westeuropa. In: Bergmann, Jörg/Hahn, Alois/Luckmann, Thomas (eds.): Religion und Kultur. Sonderheft der Kölner Zeitschrift für Soziologie und Sozialpsychologie: 69-91.

King, Gary/Keohane, Robert O./Verba, Sidney (1994) Designing Social Inquiry. Scientific Inference in Qualitative Research. Princeton.

Land, Kenneth C./Deane, Glenn /Blau, Judith R. (1991): Religious pluralism and church membership in American cities, 1906. American Sociological Review 56: 237-249.

Landman, Todd (2000): Issues and Methods in Comparative Politics. An Introduction. London.

Lauth, Hans-Joachim/Pickel, Gert/Pickel, Susanne (2008): Methoden der vergleichenden Politikwissenschaft. Eine Einführung. Wiesbaden.

Luckmann, Thomas (1967): The Invisible Religion. The problem of Religion in modern Society. New York.

Luckmann, Thomas (1991): Die unsichtbare Religion. Frankfurt/M..

Martin, David (1978): A General Theory of Secularization. New York.

Müller, Olaf (2008): Religion in Central and Eastern Europe: Was There a Re-Awakening after the Breakdown of Communism? In: Pollack, Detlef/Olson, Daniel V.A. (eds.): The Role of Religion in Modern Societies: 63-92. New York.

Müller, Olaf/Pollack, Detlef (2008): Wie religiös ist Europa? Kirchlichkeit, Religiosität und Spiritualität in West- und Osteuropa. In: BertelsmannStiftung (ed.): Religionsmonitor 2008. Gütersloh: 167-178.

Müller, Olaf/Pollack, Detlef/Pickel, Gert (2002): Werte und Wertewandel religiöser Orientierungsmuster in komparativer Perspektive: Religiosität und Individualisierung in Ostdeutschland und Osteuropa. In: Brocker, Manfred/Behr, Hartmut/Hildebrandt, Mathias (eds.): Religion und Politik. Wiesbaden: 99-125

Norris, Pippa/Inglehart, Ronald (2004): Sacred and Secular: Religion and Politics worldwide. New York.

Pickel, Gert (1998): Religiosität und Kirchlichkeit in Ost- und Westeuropa. In: Pollack, Detlef/Borowik, Irena/Jagodzinski, Wolfgang (Eds.): Religiöser Wandel in den postkommunistischen Ländern Ost- und Mitteleuropas: 55-85.

Pickel, Gert (2001): Moralische Vorstellungen und ihre religiöse Fundierung im europäischen Vergleich. In: Pickel, Gert/Krüggeler, Michael (eds.): Religion und Moral: 105-134.

Pickel, Susanne/Pickel, Gert/Lauth, Hans-Joachim/Jahn, Detlef (eds.) (2003): Methoden der vergleichenden Politikwissenschaft – Neue Entwicklungen und Diskussionen. Wiesbaden.

Pollack, Detlef (1998): Religiöser Wandel in Mittel- und Osteuropa. In: Pollack, Detlef/Borowik, Irena/Jagodzinski, Wolfgang (Eds.): Religiöser Wandel in den postkommunistischen Ländern Ost- und Mitteleuropas. Würzburg: 11-52.

Pickel, Gert (2009a): Säkularisierung, Individualisierung oder Marktmodell? Religiöse Vitalität im europäischen Vergleich. Leipzig (unpublished Manuscript).

Pickel, Gert (2009b): Secularization in an enlarged Europe – out-dated model or useful analytical frame? In: Pickel, Gert/Müller, Olaf (eds.): Church and Religion in Europe. Results from Comparative Research. Wiesbaden: 91-124

Pickel, Gert/Müller, Olaf (2009) (eds.): Church and Religion in Europe. Results from Comparative Research. Wiesbaden.

Pollack, Detlef (2001): Modifications in the religious field of Cenral and Eastern Europe. In: European Societies 3/2: 135-166.

Pollack, Detlef (2006a): Secularization revisited – eine Meistererzählung auf dem Prüfstand. Frankfurt/Oder.

Pollack, Detlef (2006b): Explaining religious vitality: Theoretical Considerations andempirical findings in Western and Eastern Europe. In: Franzmann, Manuel/Gärtner, Christel/Köck, Nicole (eds.): Religiosität in der säkularisierten Welt. Theoretische und empirische Beiträge zur Säkularisierungsdebatte in der Religionssoziologie. Wiesbaden: 83-104.

Pollack, Detlef/Pickel, Gert (2000): The Vitality of Religion-Church Integration and Politics in Eastern and Western Europe in Comparison. Arbeitsberichte des Frankfurter Institutes für Transformationsstudien 13/00.

Pollack, Detlef/Pickel, Gert (2007): Religious Individualization or Secularization? Testing hypotheses of religious change – the case of Eastern and Western Germany. In: British Journal of Sociology 58/4: 603-632.

Pollack, Detlef/Pickel, Gert (2008): Religious Individualization or Secularization: An Attempt to Evaluate the Thesis on Religious Individualization in Eastern and Western Germany. In: Pollack, Detlef/Voas, Daniel V.A. (eds.): The Role of Religion in Modern Societies. New York: 191-220.

Pollack, Detlef/Borowik, Irena/Jagodzinski, Wolfgang (eds.) (1998): Religiöser Wandel in den postkommunistischen Ländern Ost- und Mitteleuropas. Würzburg.

Przeworski, Adam/Teune, Henry (1970): The Logic of Comparative Social Inquiry. Mallabar.

Sherkat, Darren/Ellison, Christopher (1999): Recent Developments and Current Controversies in the Sociology of Religion". In: Annual Review of Sociology 25: 363-394.

Stark, Rodney (1999): Secularization, R.I.P. In: Sociology of Religion 60: 249-273.

Stark, Rodney/Bainbridge, Roger (1987): A Theory of Religion. New Brunswick.

Stark, Rodney/Finke, Roger (2000). Acts of Faith: Explaining the Human Side of Religion. Berkeley.

Stark, Rodney/Iannaccone, Laurence R. (1994): A Supply-Side Reinterpretation of the "Secularization" of Europe. Journal for the Scientific Study of Religion 33: 230-252.

Stolz, Jörg (2007): Explaining religiosity: A general sociological model. Lausanne.

Stolz, Jörg (2008): Secularization theory and rational choice. An integration of micro- and macro-theories of secularization using the example of Switzerland. In: Pollack, Detlef/Olson, Daniel V.A. (eds.): The Role of Religion in Modern Societies: 249-270. New York.

Stolz, Jörg (2009): Gods and Social Mechanisms. New Perspectives for an Explanatory Sociology of Religion. In: Cherkaoui, Mohamed/Hamilton, Peter (eds.): Raymond Boudon. A Life in Sociology. London (in print).

Swatos, William H./Olson, Daniel V. A. (2000): The Secularization Debate. Lanham.

Tomka, Miklos, 1995: The Changing Social Role of Religion in Eastern and Central Europe: Religion's Revival and ist Contradictions. In: Social Compass 42: 17-26.

Tomka, Miklos/Zulehner, Paul M. (1999): Religion in den Reformländern Ost(Mittel)-Europas. Wien.

Tomka, Miklos u.a. (2000): Religion und Kirchen in Ost(mittel)Europa: Ungarn, Litauen, Slowenien. Wien.

Voas, David (2008): The Continuing Secular Transition. In: Pollack, Detlef/OlsonDaniel V.A. (eds.): The Role of Religion in Modern Societies. New York: 25-48.

Voas, David,/Olson Daniel V.A./Crockett, Alasdair (2002): Religious Pluralism and Participation: Why Previous Research is Wrong? In: American Sociological Review 67: 212-230.

Warner, Stephen (1993): Work in Progress toward a New Paradigm for the Sociological Study of Religion in the United States. In: American Journal of Sociology 9/5: 1044-1093.

Zulehner, Paul M./Denz, Hermann (1993): Wie Europa lebt und glaubt. Europäische Wertstudie. Düsseldorf.

Zulehner, Paul M. (2002): Wiederkehr der Religion? In: Denz, Hermann (ed.): Die europäische Seele. Leben und Glauben in Europa. Wien: 23-42.

Vital coexistence: Religion and Secularism in further European integration.
Tomas Masaryk Revisited

Lucia Faltin

1. Introduction

The resurgence of religion since the 1990s, the fall of communism and further European enlargement gave religion a more prominent presence in the society. The impulse for this paper, which is a part of a wider doctoral study, came from a desire to seek further inspiration in ideas and practices that would help advance the integration of the religious and secular worlds in contemporary Europe. Further European integration requires closer interaction between the religious and secular sphere. The constructive coexistence between the two is vital for the sustainability of the peace, security and solidarity in the common Europe. I shall elaborate on this through an examination of Tomas Masaryk's religious humanism and its currency for the issue of religion in common Europe.

2. Who was TGM?

Tomáš Masaryk (1850–1937) left a lasting legacy as a humanist and democrat. The 'founding father' of the Czechoslovak Republic led his country to become one of the finest interwar democracies. His thought may not have produced any comprehensive political, philosophical or theological theory. It is rather the close connection between his thought and work that attract interest in a range of social spheres. Whether or not in agreement with Masaryk, his thought and work became seminal to his contemporaries and subsequent generations. Yet his understanding of the fundamental role of religion in a society is less known. This paper might shed some light on this subject.

TGM's religious development

Raised as a Roman Catholic, Masaryk grew increasingly aware of the difference between faith and religious structures. His reservations about the excess power of these structures resulted in his anticlericalism for which he has been often criticised. Masaryk eventually abandoned Catholicism on moral rather than dogmatic grounds and converted to the Reformed church. As he further contemplated orthodoxy and orthopraxy, he started leaning towards religious free thought. On the whole, it is difficult to identify

Masaryk with any particular denomination. Therefore his creedal and practical religiosity may be best identified as **religious humanism**.

In order to understand this concept as the foundation of Masaryk's approach to the relationship between religion and society, let us first clarify his views of God and religion.

3. Masaryk's concept of God and religion

Man – and a society – is *sub specie aeternitatis*. God is not revealed in a sense of traditional Christian theology. Human experience of God's existence comes from a combination of irrational and rational experience, what he referred to as '**metaphysical synergism**'. (Polák 2000, 30–31).

Christian monotheism understands God as just and sacred preserver of the world. In anthropomorphic sense, a belief in a loving father determines relationship between humans as through this love they all are brothers. Such theism acquires a new dimension in the Son of God. Jesus extends the unconditional love to an enemy, thus expanding human **unity**. Masaryk did not attribute a messianic purpose to Christianity. He sought inspiration in **historical** rather than Christological Jesus. Along with Moses and Mohammed, Jesus was to him a prophet and reformer; the three became the cornerstones of the main monotheistic religions. Hence religion serves as man's providential path to God and is a vital factor for the attainment of fullness of man and of his role within a society.

4. Man and society

a. Human fullness

Human fullness, according to Masaryk, consists of intellect and morality. The fullness can be attained through **education**. Human salvation therefore does not lie in the hands of the state, but in education and morality.[36] In a Platonic manner, Masaryk sees man's psychological fullness in consisting of memory and recollection. It is this inner capacity that makes man capable of active interaction with his external environment.[37] It is man's responsibility to develop this interaction alongside his own mind.

---

[36] Masaryk (*Our Current Crisis*) 2000, 273.
[37] Masaryk (*Suicide*) 2002, 182–183.

b. Religion

Religion is "**life** *sub specie aeternitatis*, an awareness of man's relationship to the world, an authenticity."[38] Religion is thus a vital part of humanity. Moral and religious life complement intellectual endeavour. Religion is to satisfy the need of the spirit and mind and to connect an individual to a wider human community.

Through the dualism of man – spirit and mind – and through the role of religion as a link between an individual and God and fellow humans, Masaryk sees the essential role of religious conviction to be **desubjectivisation** of man.

An absence of religion leads an individual to excessive egocentric perception of self, particularly in modern man who has become increasingly subjective. Furthermore, the **void** that the absence of the guiding role of religion creates, leaves an individual turned more into himself in search for an authority. Masaryk is resolute in his rejection of pansubjectivism.[39]

c. Religious humanism

This is reflected in Masaryk's religious humanism that accounts for human fullness and the interconnectedness of an individual and society as *sub specie aeternitatis*. His religious humanism thus lies in a synergy between particularism and universalism, between an individual and a community, between concrete and abstract. Whilst drawing from an inspiration of the Brethren, Masaryk emphasises that the denominational differences within Christianity and those among different faiths could have a positive effect on each tradition. He argues that the struggle between Catholicism and Protestantism ultimately proved to be mutually enriching. Along the same line of argument, he believed in the separation of Church and state what he saw as the safeguard of free development of both, yet only through their constructive interaction.

Rather than the inter-religious competition, Masaryk's greatest concern was the **absence** of religion. He was highly critical of radical secularism which drew from the Enlightenment humanism and subscribed to irreligious liberalism. Rather than calling for any radical solution, he hoped that the struggle between religion and irreligion would improve the ability of religion and its organizations to meet the needs of modern man.

---

[38] Opat 2003, 201.
[39] Masaryk (*Humanistic Ideals*) 1971, 88.

5. Religiosity and irreligiosity

Masaryk saw his times as suffering from a deep religious crisis marked by scepticism and indifferentism. He attributed Europe's moral crisis to a loss of religion, moral and spiritual authority. The crisis that brought about the Great War, meant a fiasco for the progress of secular liberalism that led modern Europe to fall into Rousseau's natural state.[40] Yet Masaryk saw the crisis not as a sign of an ultimate human and social "degeneration and decadence". He considered irreligiosity as moral and rational anarchy. He attributed the growth of indifference to the **absence of faith**, thus to the **semi-completeness of man**.[41] In order to overcome the imbalance caused by positivist scepticism, modern man needs to again acquire belief.[42] Foreseeing greater individualisation of religion as a response to people's spiritual needs, he called for a repair of the damage in human thought and deed. He trusted in the ability of educated nations to undertake this.[43]

It wasn't until after yet another world war that Masaryk's diagnosis of Europe's social malady was to be treated by the founding fathers of what was to become the European Union. In the subsequent decades, their Christian-inspired vision was overshadowed by liberal concepts of secularism.[44] Having gone through the full learning circle, our effort of the day is not entirely different from Masaryk's concept of religious humanism.

6. European integration today

When Richard Coudenhove-Kalergi suggested to Masaryk that he should to preside over the united Europe, Masaryk decided instead to direct his energy to the development of the newly-founded Czechoslovakia. He foresaw that it would take at least 50 years for democracy to grow root. Masaryk's vision of 50 years is reflected in the democratic roots of today's European Union. While some of the fundamental principles of common Europe have become enrooted, European integration is by no means a fait accompli and remains a never-ending process. The sustainability of Europe's peace, security and prosperity rely on deeper integration and social cohesion. This requires further development of the fourth fundamental principle, the principle of subsidiarity. That lays in the constructive coexistence between religious and secular spheres. It is through the perspective of the principle of subsidiarity

---

[40] Masaryk (*The World Revolution*) 1938, 426.
[41] Masaryk (*Suicide*) 2002, 140. Masaryk, however, does not altogether dismiss scepticism as a means of the search for truth, as shown in his analysis of Hume.
[42] Masaryk (*Modern Man and Religion*) 2000, 22–23.
[43] Masaryk (*The World Revolution*) 1938, 430.
[44] Adenauer, Schuman, De Gasperi

that I wish to address the role of religion and its organizations, including the Churches in further European integration. Let me focus on just three of the many issues that deserve attention: ghettoisation, migration and education, since we are meeting at the fine University of Pecs.

a. Ghettoisation

One of the main problems of the extreme forms of the religio-secular divide is ghettoisation of religious and secular communities. They tend to develop their own often mutually unconnected structures and services, such as social care, education, trade, even culture. The divide can be seen also in legislative and constitutional processes. They tend to treat religion tends as one of marginalised minorities that are merely subject to etatist protectionism. One of the problems here arises in implementation of human rights: their liberal concept emphases rights over responsibilities. Religion, with its greater accent on responsibilities, can help to restore the balance. In constitutional developments, the public debate over the preamble to the draft European Constitution has reminded Europe that its religious identity is an integral part of its current make. It brought the religious and secular public directly into mutual discussion and engaged it in the constitutional process.

The way out of the ghettos is not only a matter of further interaction between the religious and secular communities. It also requires faith communities to work together with a view of wider social interest. One of the pioneers of Jewish–Christian relations in Poland and Europe, Jesuit priest Stanislaw Musial spoke of a war about a definition of man.[45] That was in the aftermath of the Holocaust and during the Cold War. Musial's concern closely echoes Masaryk's appeal for the restoration of fullness of man. Today we face a need to redefine man's **role** in the society. Secular and religious spheres, Jews, Christians, Muslims and other faith communities and their organizations need to assume far **greater responsibility** and exert a **joint effort** in all that is required to keep our pluralistic societies **open, inclusive and civil.** Not **passive tolerance,** but only **constructive coexistence** can assure that human nature is preserved and thrives in a secular society.

---

[45] 10 Musiał 2003, 55. Musiał, S. (2003) *Black is Black.* [Czarne jest czarne]. Krakow: Wydawnictwo Literackie.

b. Migration

Ghettoisation is further exacerbated by the reduction in borders brought by the end of the fall of communism and subsequent European enlargement. In 1991, Cardinal Ratzinger wrote:

It has to be proved again whether Europe is merely an idea or a real force of reconciliation, whether it is strong enough to give the border a better significance, than a division. Borders will be the easier to respect, the more they will represent open paths: the more the minorities on either side can live their entirety within a wider unit, the less will there be exclusivity. On the contrary, lively exchange, recognized diversity and communality in difference will prevail. (Ratzinger 1993, 76.)

To a great number of migrants, religion represents a source of ethnic identification and connection to the places of their origin. Yet, to too many immigrants or migrants, cosmopolitan experience does not guarantee opening of mind, but all too often leads to extremism and indoctrination, building the walls of religious and ethnic ghettos. Masaryk's humanism that opposed ethnic and religious messianism and exclusivism made him prey to his nationalistically-oriented contemporaries. To paraphrase Timothy Radcliffe's image of pilgrimage, the mobility of Europe's populace can be seen by an individual and his interlocutors as a pilgrimage that can enrich our spiritual and intellectual wisdom.[46]

Participation in a religious community in a host country is an umbilical cord between the individual and his host and home country. Whilst it is not always possible to create multi-national or multi-ethnic religious communities within a concrete denominational group or Church, these organizations need to exert a greater effort to act as a link rather than a mere refuge which leads to immigrant exclusion and even self-isolation. A local representation of a national Church, a catholic and universal church, or a diasporic religious community – all of these are an inimitable source of interpretation of rights and responsibilities as the two sides of the same coin. These organizations need to emphasise greater civic responsibility in the context of a host country. Admittedly, Churches and religious communities strive to advance self-understanding and communal solidarity in their members. Yet, if these borders are not to grow into the walls of a ghetto, these organizations need to also build roads between an individual and the wider society. Ultimately, such borders and paths in Europe need to be placed on a map of both inter-religious as well as religio-secular world.

---

[46] Radcliffe, T. (2005) 'Christianity in Europe' in ed. C. Murphy-O'Connor *Faith in Europe?* London: Darton, Longman and Todd.

c. Education

We have seen the tragic effect of religio-secular ghettoisation in the 20th and already in the 21st century. Masaryk argues that there is something more profound that acts as a trigger for the violence, be it a suicide or murder. It is ultimately the combination of inadequate intellectual and spiritual education which aren't equally developed and unified.[47] Masaryk refers to this as **semi-education**, i.e. knowledge that cannot be practically applied and lived, what leads to existential fatigue. Europe's educational sphere is one of the areas where religio-secular ghettos thrive.

Masaryk's religious humanism understands faith as a conviction to which man arrives through reflected, critical reasoning. Following the principles of education laid down by his fellow Moravian Johannes Comenius, Masaryk believes in wisdom as intellectually and experientially processed facts of knowledge. Yet the concept of critical thinking is seen as an undesirable approach and a threat to authority not only in religious educational establishments, but in most of Europe's institutes of higher education. At the same time, the religio-secular divide in education leads to mutual ignorance of the two communities, the religious and secular. Admittedly, the same applies to mutual knowledge among faith communities. All this is not where the divide ends, but it is where the foundations of future ghettos lie.

7. Conclusion

As one of the fundamental democratic principles, the principle of subsidiarity opens further opportunities for direct and active to participation in *res publica* at all levels of social activity. Yet only a complete individual, empowered with wisdom can constructively contribute to this undertaking. With the developed principle of subsidiary based on close and constructive interaction between the religious and secular sphere, it will be less easy to blame one's maladies on Brussels, Moscow or the Vatican. The dynamics of Europe's religio-secular divide makes it an imperative that we continue to seek an optimal constitutional arrangement that is deeply rooted in and thus identified with by Europe's diverse populace. Such diversity, however, makes it impossible to offer a single theory that would resolve the problem and offer paradise on Earth. All of us have in fresh memory the lethal consequences of such experiments.

It is through religion that morality acquires a new dimension, leaving a divine imprint in man. Man's faith in God and immortality is coupled with a spiritual

---

[47] Masaryk (*Suicide*) 2002, 76.

certainty that also connects him to earth and life.[48] Masaryk's determinism does not give into fatalism, but places transcendence into the current day. More currently, this is echoed today, in Benedict XVI:

> Europe and European culture may vanish. This doesn't imply resignation, but sobriety. It is not an eschatological allusion that is significant about his statement, but it is a fact that no one can define the ultimate looks of mankind. The future remains permanently open in human freedom, and therefore it can also fail. [...] An alleged better life tomorrow is a fata morgana that takes away the strength and dignity of this day, and yet doesn't help the tomorrow.
>
> (Ratzinger 1993, 90.)

---

[48] Masaryk (*Suicide*) 2002, 77.

Religious Euro-skepticism in Hungary

János Wildmann

About the methodology

The empirical religio-sociological research project Religions and Churches in Common Europe in Hungary was a representative research with thousand people and the following independent variables:

- Sex: Fifty-two and six percent were women and forty-seven and four percent were men.

- Age: We formed four categories: Between fifteen and thirty years, from thirty-one to forty-five years, from forty-six to sixty years, and sixty-one years and older.

- Education: We had here four categories again: elementary school (Upto 8th grade), vocational school, final examination of the secondary education, college, university.

- Region: Hungary divided into seven regions

- Settlement: Here we had four categories too: Capital city, county towns, other cities and villages

- Religion: Because of the small number of samples we had to form the following categories: Catholic, Reformed (Calvinist), Other and Not belonging to any denomination

- Religiosity: Religious according with the teaching of the Church, Religious in a personal way, rather not religious, not religious at all.

Most questions were taken over from the previous research,[49] but some blocks were made by other research. The questionnaire consisted of the following chapters (Response variables):

1. The assessment of the Common Europe and the integration of Hungary
2. The role of religions and churches in the Common Europe
3. The internal situation of the Church
4. The situation of the church in today's Hungarian society

---

[49] Wildmann János: Katolikus tükör. A magyar egyház és az európai integráció. Gyakorlati teo-trilógia I. Kairológia (Catholic Mirror. The Hungarian Church and European Integration. Practical Theo-trilogy I. Kairology), Publisher Egyházfórum, Budapest 2005.

5. Church and politics
6. Church Management

All chapters had three to four blocks. The each block's had six statements that were read by the respondents. They had to decide how they agreed or disagreed with the statements. The agreement was measured on a five-point scale. During the analyses, we boiled down the two Non-Agree categories and the two Agree-categories. So now we have three response categories: I don't agree, I partly agree and I agree.

In the following I would like to introduce some results only from the first chapter. There are a lot of significant correlations, such as Sex, Age, Education, Region, and Settlement. In the following part I'm going to concentrate on the relationship between the answers and religion or religiosity. I would like to know what kind of relation Religion has to the Assessment of the European Union and the integration of Hungary.

The assessment of the European Union

We composed six kinds of statement in connection with the European Union. Two of these had relations to economy, two are cultural and the last two are related to the Christian roots of the Union. The statements were:

The European Union is

- founded mainly on religious, especially Christian values
- founded on Christian culture
- only an economic alliance
- preserves the cultural values of the nation
- represents the interest of the big capitalists and the rich
- supports the cultural and the scientific development

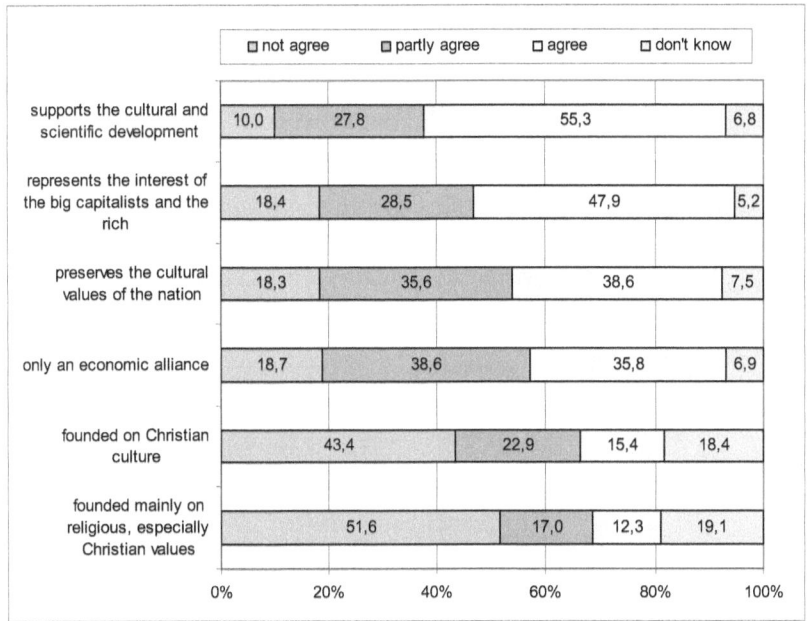

Chart 1: The European Union is (whole sample)

Chart 1 shows the results in the **whole sample**. More than half of the respondents agree with this statement: "the European Union supports the cultural and scientific development". Nearly fifty percent of these people think: „the Union represents the interest of the big capitalists and the rich". Less than forty percent of them agree with this statement: „the EU preserves the cultural values of the nation". More than a third of the respondents are of the opinion: „the EU is only an economic alliance". For these four statements the remaining thirty-forty percent of the people give the answer: "I partly agree". Considering we can realize these statements don't get a refusal even by a fifth part of the respondents. However "the Christian roots of Europe" doesn't have any meaning for the most people. On the one hand the rate of the answer "I don't know" is the highest here (18-19%); on the other hand around a half of the respondents decline both statements with reference to Christian religion. The people's opinion are the "Christian culture" is more important (15, 4%) than the "Christian values" (12, 3%) in the forming of the European Union and this result was expected. But it could be interesting that the difference between the advocacy of the two statements is only three percent.

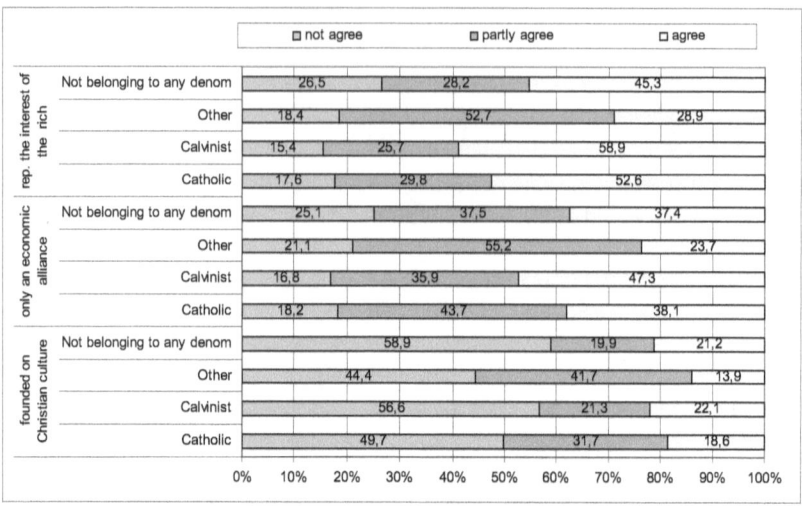

Chart 2: The European Union is (Religion)

The Religion had an influence over the answers for the statements which had relations to the economic interests and to the Christian culture (Chart 2). Without exception the Calvinists gave the decided opinion:

- "The European Union represents the interest of the big capitalists and the rich". This is according to nearly sixty percent of the Calvinist respondents and more than fifty percent of the catholic respondents. The rate of agreement is only around a half among the members of other denominations than in the case of Calvinists and Catholics. Among the members of other denominations, the rate of people who agree partly is two times higher than in the case of the other two groups.

- "The Union is only an economic alliance"; it seems clear that nearly fifty percent of the Calvinists agree with this statement and that's the highest rate here. The rate of agreement is around a quarter amongst the members of other denominations but in this instance the rate of the people who agree partly is the highest among them.

- It's interesting that the same percentage of Calvinists and non-religious people think: "The European Union is founded on Christian culture", the Catholics follow with a 2-3 percent lag, but the lag is the highest in rate of members of other denominations. The group of the non-religious people has the highest number of those who do not agree that the European Union is founded on Christian culture, followed by the Calvinists. The group with the highest rates for partly agreeing are the members of other denominations.

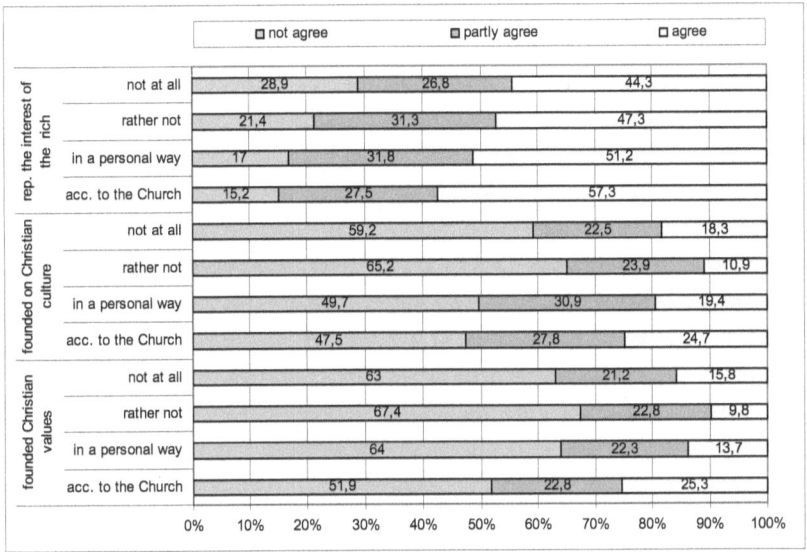

Chart 3: The European Union is (Religious)

The **religiosity** of the respondents had an influence on the answers for the statements in relation to the Christian culture/values and also in relation to capitalists. (Chart 3)

- With this statement *"the EU represents the interest of the big capitalists and the rich"* mostly agree the people according teaching of the Church with sixty percent. The Calvinists appear from them with two-thirds rate.
- Similar, but a bit smaller is the difference among the religiosity categories at the statement *"the European Union founded on Christian culture"*. However it's interesting too, the half of the religious men think that the EU has nothing to do with the Christianity neither its scale of values nor its cultural meaning.
- The respondents who are religious according teaching of the Church agree with two times higher rate that *"the European Union founded mainly on religious, especially Christian values"*, while the rate of the others are only between 9, 8 and 15, 8 percent.

The assessment of the integration of Hungary

The next block was with the following six statements:

The integration of Hungary

- leads to the disintegration of morality
- leads to a new colonization of the country
- makes the political independence of the country very vulnerable
- improves the living standards
- It is still hard to decide whether the integration is good or bad for us
- is important for the economic development of the country

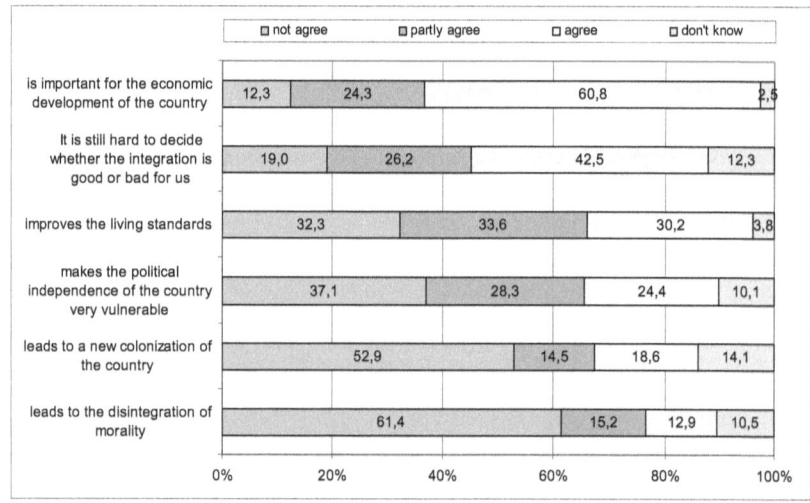

Chart 4: The integration of Hungary... (whole sample)

In the **whole sample** (Chart 4) more than sixty percent of the respondents think the next statement is generally or very important "the integration of Hungary into the European Union *is important for the economic development of the country"* and the remaining quarter of the people agree partly with it. Altogether a little more than a tenth of the respondents disagree with this statement. But it seems to be interesting, more than forty percent of the people agree fully with it: *"It is still hard to decide whether the integration is good or bad for Hungary"* and the remaining quarter of them agree partly here. It means, since the joining EU a significant part of the citizens haven't thought that this process is advantageous for them. And this appears in the estimation of the next statement: *"the integration improves the living* *standards"*, nearly a third of the respondents agree with it, but other third of them disagree and the last third of the people agree partly with this statement. A quarter of the respondents are afraid from this: *"the integration makes the political independence of the country very vulnerable"* and other thirty percent of them afraid from it partly. A fifth part of the people think: *"the integration leads to a new colonization of the country"*, little more than a tenth of the people opine: *"it leads to the disintegration of morality"*.

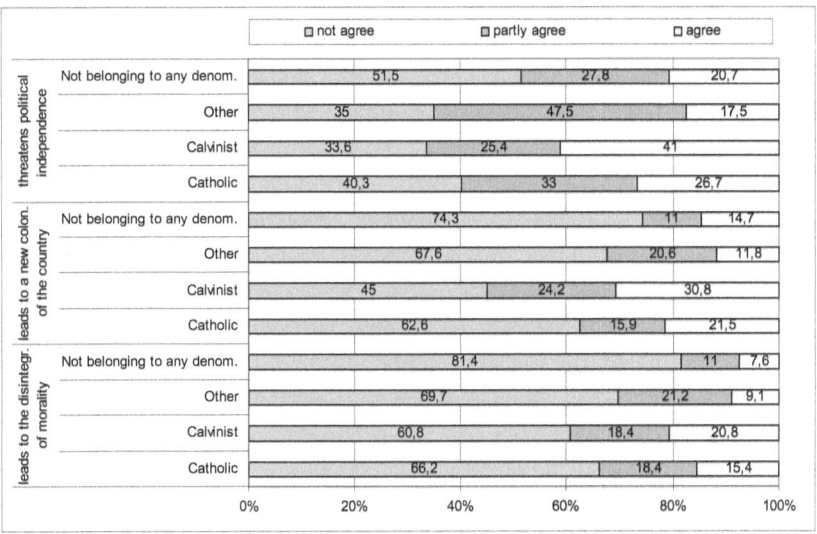

Chart 5: The integration of Hungary (Religion)

The Religion has significant connection with the next three statements (Chart 5 :):

- *"The integration of Hungary makes the political independence of the country very vulnerable"*, forty percent of the Calvinists and just half of the non-religious people agree with this. But the members of other denomination have a lowest degree of the agreement here.

- With the statement: *"the integration leads to a new colonization of Hungary"* three-quarter of the non-religious person, two-thirds of the members of other denomination and more than sixty percent of the Catholics disagree. But half of the Calvinists at least partly agree with it.

- Every fifth of the Calvinists agree also with it: *"the integration leads to the disintegration of morality"*. This rate is just fifteen percent in the

63

case of the Catholics and less than ten percent at the members of other denomination and at the non-religious person too.

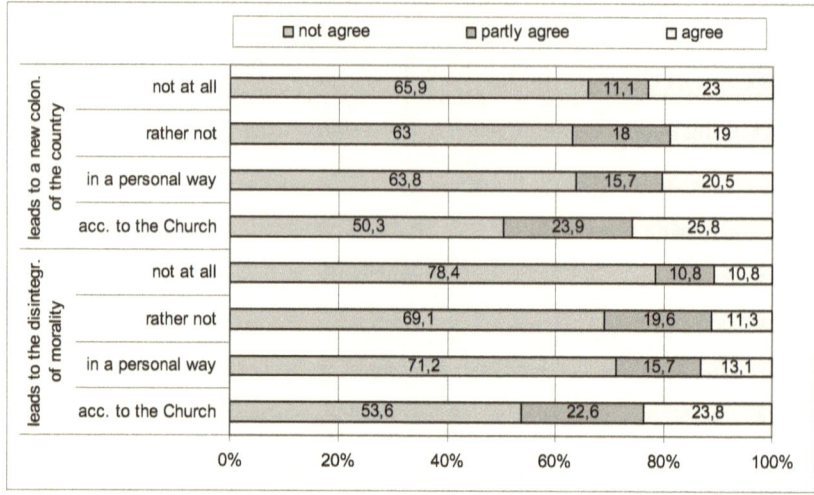

Chart 6: The integration of Hungary (Religious)

The religiosity of the respondents shows significant connection with two pessimistic statements (Chart 6).

- Respondents who are religious according to the teaching of the Church are afraid a bit more from our EU-joining means: *"the integration of Hungary leads to a new colonization of the country,"* than the others.
- The difference is bigger among the opinions in relation with *"the integration leads to the disintegration of morality"*: two times higher is the rate of the people who are religious according teaching of the Church who worry about it, than the rate of the people who are religious less.

Average of the EU-evaluation

Previously the rates of agreement were examined in connection with the individual opinions. We made a summarize index to get a comprehensive view about the assessment of the European Union and our country's integration. Here we used from the mentioned twelve statements just nine ones. The missing statements are: two in relation with the Christian religion and other talks about "the integration is good or bad for us". These statements haven't got references directly to the negative or positive assessment of the EU. The nine statements what we used were the next:

The European Union is

- only an economic alliance
- represents the interest of the big capitalists and the rich
- preserves the cultural values of the nation
- supports the cultural and scientific development

The integration of Hungary

- is important for the economic development of the country
- improves the living standards
- makes the political independence of the country very vulnerable
- leads to the disintegration of morality
- leads to a new colonization of the country.

We made our index in that way, the higher value means more positive attitude in relation with the Union and the integration. So the calculated "Average of the EU-evaluation" is the average of the agreement marks (1-5) which belong to the nine statements. As the assessment average is lower, so the opinion of the respondents is more negative in relate with the European Union, respectively the result of our integration and inversely. We could narrow down the circle of the people who were irresolute, so we used just those people's answers who answered from the nine questions at least for five.

In the following I will present the "Average of the EU-evaluation" not only in case of religion, in case of age, qualifications and settlement-type also.

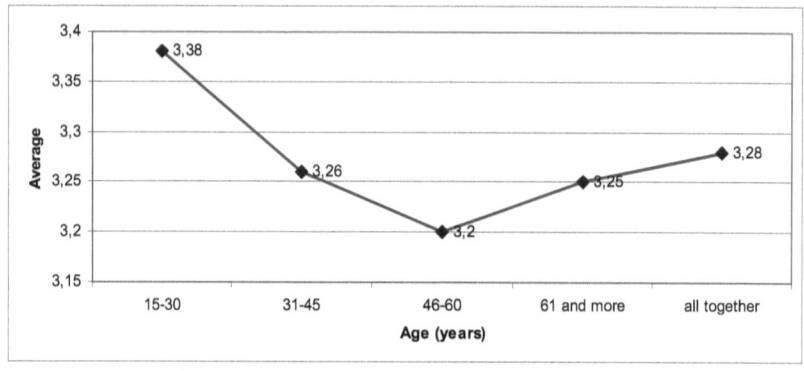

Chart 7: Average of the EU-evaluation (Age)

Chart 7 shows that the people between 15-30 years appreciate the EU and the integration of Hungary better than the others. The opinion of people with 46-60 years about the EU is the worst.

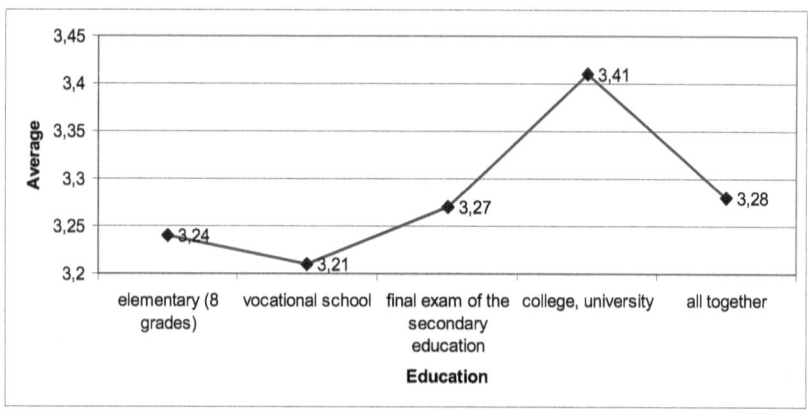

Chart 8: Average of the EU-evaluation (Education)

The graph shows that people with degree of college and university think more positive about the EU and the integration of Hungary than the other (Chart 8).

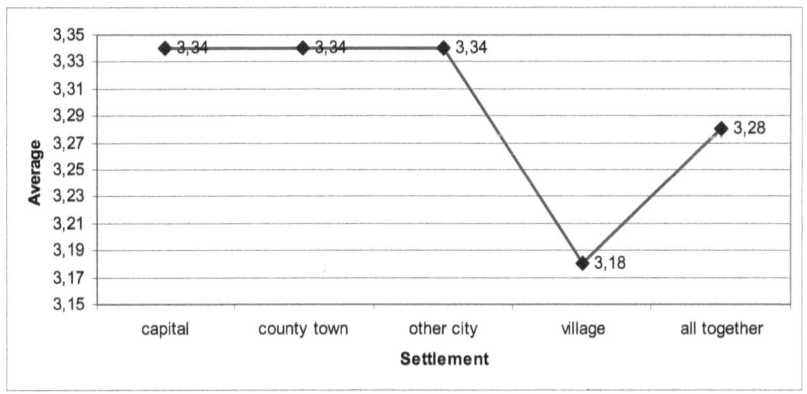

Chart 9: Average of the EU-evaluation (Settlement)

Chart 9 shows a very interesting fact, namely the people in the villages are more critical than the people in the cities.

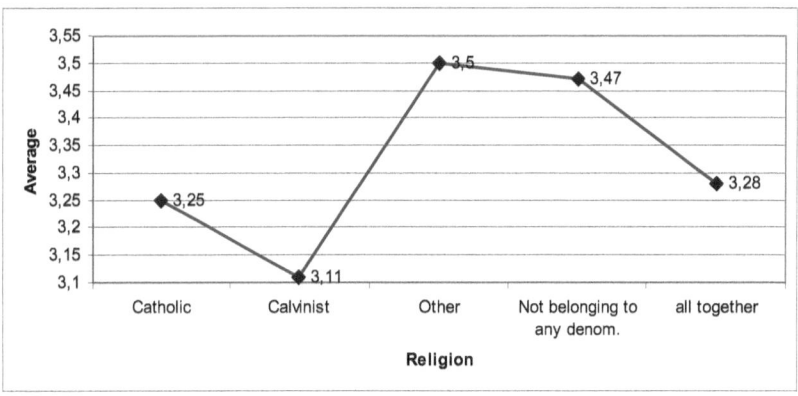

Chart 10: Average of the EU-evaluation (Religion)

Before we could see the Calvinists think more negative about the EU (*the integration leads to political independence, to new colonization of country and to the disintegration of morality*). This graph confirms this assertion. The average of the EU-evaluation is the lowest among the Calvinists (Chart 10).

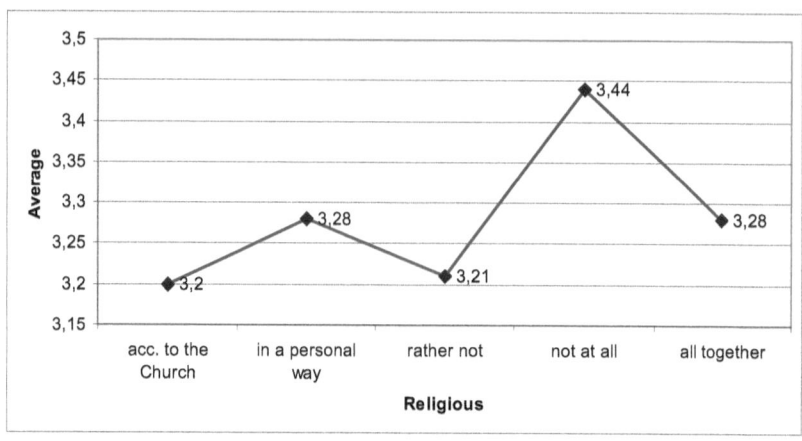

Chart 11: Average of the EU-evaluation (Religious)

We can see on the Chart 11 that religious people are more sceptical about the European Union and the integration of Hungary as a non-religious people. Obviously the rate of the EU-scepticism among religious people is the highest in Hungary.

Clusters

The interpretation of the nine or the twelve statements could be just separately. "The Average of the EU-evaluation" shows just an average but doesn't show the content behind it. The Claster-analysis makes possibly for us working with fewer categories and keeping the content information. For this reason are categorized the individual opinions.

We created six kinds of categories on the basis of people's answers.

- The first *(Loss of independence)* represents the next fears: our EU-joining risks the political and economic independent of Hungary, besides could make moral decline for the country.
- The second *(Christian values)* includes those opinions that the European Union is a kind of an organization which based on the Christian culture and values.
- The third *(Economic recovery)* includes those answers which relate to the economical consolidation and the increasing living standard of Hungary and don't relate to the getting stronger cartels and big companies.

- The fourth *(Cultural and scientific development)* means preservation the cultural values of the nation and the confidence in the cultural-scientific development.

- The fifth *(Economic Interest Groups)* contains those negative viewpoints that the European Union is only an economic alliance and behind this we can find groups with expressive economic power right now.

- Into the sixth category *(Attitude of wait)* are put those attitudes alone accordingly we are not able to seeing the consequences of our country's integration.

After we categorized the respondents on the basis of their answers and we ranked them with cluster-analysis to four homogeneous types.

- In the first type are the people who are expecting economic recovery from our EU-joining.

- The second group of the respondents are the believers in Christian culture and values.

- In the third group are the people who think the economic/political dependences are the most important result of our integration.

- The fourth type of the respondents is trusting in the cultural and scientific development.

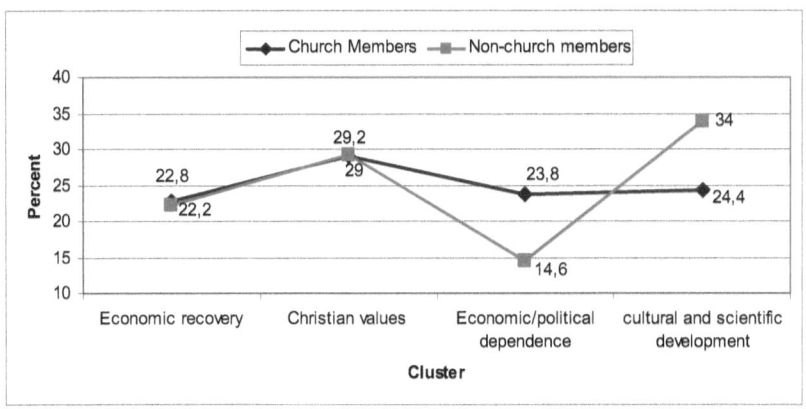

Chart 12: Cluster (Religion)

Chart 12 shows that by reason of the analyses the non-religious people to a higher degree (34,0%) belong to the fourth type (Trusting in the cultural and scientific development), than the religious people (24,4%). Among those

69

people who are afraid from the economic/political dependences are the non-religious men to a lesser degree (14, 6%).

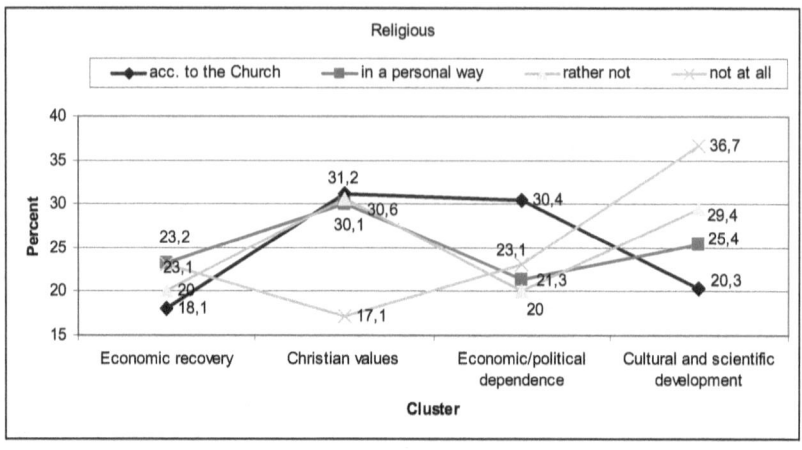

Chart 13: Cluster (Religious)

The religiosity of the respondents is an influential factor (Chart 13). The religious according to the teaching of the Church belong to the group of believers in Christian values to a higher degree (31,2%) and belong to the group of afraid from economic/political dependences also to a high degree(30,4%). The people who aren't religious at all belong to the type of trusting in cultural and scientific development with a higher rate (36, 8%). These facts make stronger our hypothesis that in Hungary the members of the churches and the religious people are more sceptical with respect to the European Union and our country's integration.

The churches in Europe

The Church as a "Creative Minority". On being church in today's Europe

Arne Rasmusson

> "Do not think that I came to bring peace on the earth; I did not come to bring peace, but a sword." (Matt 10:34).

These words of Jesus do not seem to offer a hopeful start to a talk on religion and European integration. More hopeful may be the following words: "There is neither Jew nor Greek, slave nor free, male nor female, for you are all one in Christ Jesus." (Gal. 3:27). But, in fact, these latter words have over and over again for two millennia led to intense conflicts, even wars.

I am Swedish. In a book from 1965 bearing the subtitle "The happy democracy", the leading Swedish political scientist and publicist in the 1950s and 1960s, Herbert Tingsten – also quite a militant atheist – wrote that the Scandinavian countries had succeeded in creating "the world's most perfect communities." The most important contributing factors, according to Tingsten, were high living standards and an "exceptional homogeneity about nationality, language and religion." The religious homogeneity was created when, during the Reformation of the sixteenth century, Roman Catholicism was "eradicated". In addition, he observed that religious indifference is greater and "earnest faith" more rare in Scandinavia than in other parts of the world, a fact that also contributed to the happy democracies of Scandinavia.[50] So, ethnic homogeneity and religious indifference are essential preconditions for prosperous and happy democracies. The first part of this, ethnic homogeneity, is emphatically not something that could be celebrated in current Swedish public culture, but the second part, "religious indifference", is. And that is not just a Swedish view.

If one asks about the role of religion or churches for European integration, one may inquire: Who is asking? From which perspective? For what purpose? Are Europe or the European Union the basic unit and religion and churches secondary to that entity? For many, that is simply taken for granted, just as the modern nation-state has long been the silent and taken-for-granted background for theology, political philosophy, or economics. That the European Union is the primary reality in relation to the church is, for most, a given. One might otherwise think that, at least for Roman Catholics, the question should be, what is the relevance of Europe or the European Union for the Church? Most Christians do confess that the church is catholic, ecumenical, and world-wide. The church is the wider entity, Europe is the

---

[50] Herbert Tingsten, *Från idéer till idyll: Den lyckliga demokratien*, new, enlarged edition (Stockholm: PAN/Norstedt, 1967), 9 f.

smaller. The church is universal, Europe is particular. But in fact, for most European Christians, being part of a national body is experientially more real than being part of Christ's body. The controversial issue is the relationship between the national and the European identity (which is considered weak), not the relationship between the Christian, or religious, identity and the European. For Muslims, the latter may be the more important question, but not for most Christians.

European scholars studying these issues are usually active at state universities, and they simply take the state perspective for granted; it does not matter whether the researcher is religious or not. Not only so, these scholars also tend to see the world from above, from the purported perspective of the state, even if they may adopt a critical posture and hope for a "changed state". "Seeing like a state"[51] is then construed as natural, even universal and neutral, while "seeing like a church" is construed as confessional or particular.

In her book on nationalism, Liah Greenfeld makes the beheading of Sir Thomas More in 1535, because of his refusal to accept the king's absolute supremacy, the symbolic watershed between Christendom and modern nationalism.

> Sir Thomas More was a Christian; this was his identity, and all his roles, functions, and commitments that did not derive from it (but were implied, for example, in being a subject of the king of England) were incidental to it. The view that 'one realm' could be a source of truth and claim absolute sovereignty was, to him, absurd. 'Realms' were but artificial, secondary divisions in the ultimately indivisible body of Christendom.[52]

More was unable "to deny what seemed to him plainly evident."[53] But for his judges it was different. Protestantism, in fact, often became the midwife of modern nationalism. At the other end of this development, nationalism

> acquired its own momentum; it existed in its own right; it was the only way in which people now could see reality and thus became reality itself. For nationalism was the basis of people's identity, and it was no more possible at this point to stop thinking in national terms than to cease being oneself.[54]

And that is still true. The body of the nation is now experienced as much more real than the body of Christ, the universal church. The churches thus

---

[51] Cf. James C Scott, Seeing Like a State: How Certain Schemes to Improve the Human Condition Have Failed (New Haven: Yale University Press, 1998).
[52] Liah Greenfeld, Nationalism: Five Roads to Modernity (Cambridge, Mass.: Harvard University Press, 1992), 30.
[53] Ibid., 30.
[54] Ibid., 87.

have had to understand and justify themselves in terms of the national body. And now we similarly ask how the churches can contribute to the European integration, how the churches can be *useful* for the European project, how Christians can help make the European body experientially more real.

The nationalism that the churches helped create – as well as strongly supported and legitimated – was a disaster for the churches, for Europe, for the world, and for ordinary people. Its fateful consequences culminated in the twentieth century. It created the war culture that made the First World War more or less inevitable, which was followed by the Second World War and the Holocaust, the Cold War, the many wars in the Middle East, and so on.[55] But few theologians or church leaders have seen this as a scandal, as a betrayal of baptism and of the body of Christ, because for most it has simply been self-evident that the primary body is the nation. Not many thought it strange that German Christians and French Christians could kill each other just because they happened to live on different sides of an imagined and movable border they could not see. Not even Roman Catholics found that strange. The German Roman Catholic theologian Gerhard Lohfink has written:

> The Church did not prevent the two world wars, and could not prevent them. They simply broke over it. But what is disturbing today is something beyond the mere fact of the two wars: the Church is the body of Christ, beyond all boundaries, the people of God among the nations. That in 1914 Christians went enthusiastically to war against Christians, baptized against baptized, was not seen in any way as destruction of what the Church is in and of its very nature, a destruction that cried out to heaven. That was the real catastrophe.[56]

It destroyed Europe, but it also ruined the European church. One could, of course, say that what is now the European Union was the response of Catholic politicians to this catastrophe.

However, in the dominant view in Europe today, the Christian roots not only of the European Union, but also of Europe itself, are ignored or denied; and when not denied, they are seen as negative. The recent resurgence of

---

[55] John Keegan, *A History of Warfare* (New York: Alfred A. Knopf, 1993), 3-24, 347-366; Norbert Elias, *The Germans: Power Struggles and the Development of Habitus in the Nineteenth and Twentieth Centuries* (New York: Columbia University Press, 1996); Thomas Nipperday, *Religion im Umbruch: Deutschland 1870-1918* (München: Verlag C. H. Beck, 1988), Arne Rasmusson, "Historicizing the Historicist: Ernst Troeltsch and Recent Mennonite Theology", in *The Wisdom of the Cross: Essays in Honor of John Howard Yoder*, eds. Stanley Hauerwas, Chris Huebner, Harry Huebner, and Mark Thiessen Nation. (Grand Rapids: Eerdmans, 1999), 213-248.

[56] Gerhard Lohfink, *Does God Need the Church? Toward a Theology of the People of God* (Collegeville: Liturgical Press, 1999), 315.

religion in public life is, on the whole, viewed as a problem. Modern Europe is secular, built on the values and practices of the Enlightenment. The French Revolution is regarded as the most important turning point. The Old Regime, with its alliance of throne and altar, collapsed, and a new democratic order built on reason and human rights emerged. In France, as in other countries, the revolution led to a century of struggle between the liberal secular order and a reactionary religious order, a conflict which ended with the victory of the secular order. The rise of Islam in world politics and the growing Muslim presence in Europe are thus seen as threats to the common secular public culture. So are Christian churches, insofar as they infringe on the public order by transgressing the sphere of private religion.

Behind such views we find a liberal meta-story about the secular state as savior, a sort of creation myth for modernity about Europe leaving the dark ages for enlightened modern times. It goes something like the following. Once upon a time, during the Dark Medieval Ages people lived in oppressive, unjust, unfree and intolerant societies under the umbrella of the Roman Church. The Protestant Reformation broke apart this unified Christendom and participated in the initial liberation of politics from religion, of the state from the church. One Protestant version of the story emphasizes the Reformation as the beginning of modernity, the autonomy of both politics and the individual. The Enlightenment is then just one further step, a further realization of the process that the Reformation started. But in the secular story, the Reformation led also to a period of religious wars. Precisely because there were no rational ways of deciding religious conflicts and because religion and politics were so closely connected, religious wars were the result. To create a more peaceful world one had to liberate politics from religion and instead base politics on human reason alone. This, so the story goes, is the central thrust of the Enlightenment, the French Revolution, and the increasing secularization of Europe that followed. A secular state was created, and religion was privatized and (many thought) would soon disappear completely as reason, science and democracy took over. And so peace returned to the earth – or not exactly. That lies still in the future.

This meta-story or creation myth has often been reduced and conventionalized into a set of symbols and historical clichés such as "crusades", "inquisition", "witch hunts", "religious wars", "the warfare between religion and science" (Galileo), and so on. Some of these clichés were originally part of Protestant anti-Catholic propaganda (used, for example, during the English-Spanish War in the mid-16th century) that later turned into general anti-religious propaganda, and today they still function as very influential summaries of societal images defining "us" against "them". During the referendum debate about Sweden's entry into the

European Union, these images were important on the anti-Union side. When one refers today to the Inquisition or to the Galileo affair, the interest is not Catholic history, but, say, the defense of the freedom of scientific research on embryonic stem cells against the criticism of the Roman Catholic Church or Protestant churches.[57]

Modern social science was born with this creation myth. The secularization thesis was at the heart of the rise of modern sociology. Scholarly versions of the myth shaped the very identity of the social sciences. So did nationalism. Both Durkheim and Weber were, for example, strong nationalists. As many have said, the social and economic sciences have functioned as a set of competing secular theologies. The American economist Robert Nelson, who in a couple of brilliant books has analyzed economic theory as a set of theologies promoting a secular salvation and a correlative morality, has said that the "nation-state today is in its essence the church of a secular religion" and that modern universities are serving this "progressive Gospel of efficiency."[58]

That this creation myth is a constitutive part of the self-understanding of "secular reason" may explain why it lives on in spite of the history since the French revolutions.[59] To ask about how to describe the French revolution and its legacy is to ask about how secular modernity, with all its inner contradictions, should be described. Was it about democracy against throne and altar? Defense of human rights against tyranny? Or is it also the beginning of modern nationalism and total wars? Does it not, partly because of its belief in a society built on reason, create the beginning of modern totalitarianism? The French revolution was not only about freedom and equality, democracy and human rights; it was also about the nation, national unity, and patriotism. It was hardly an accident that the French revolution, precisely in the name of the people, of human rights, of the revolution, led to

---

[57] Philip Jenkins, *The New Anti-Catholicism: The Last Acceptable Prejudice* (Oxford: Oxford University Press, 2003), esp. 177-206.

[58] Robert H. Nelson, *Economics as Religion: From Samuelson to Chicago and Beyond* (University Park: Pennsylvania State University Press, 2001). The citations come from pp. 334-336. See also idem, *Reaching for Heaven on Earth: The Theological Meaning of Economics* (Savage: Rowman & Littlefield Publishers, 1991); Christian Smith, *Moral, Believing Animals: Human Personhood and Culture* (New York: Oxford University Press, 2003); Rodney Stark and Roger Finke, *Acts of Faith: Explaining the Human Side of Religion* (Berkeley: University of California Press, 2000); and John Milbank, *Theology and Social Theory: Beyond Secular Reason*, 2nd ed. (Oxford: Blackwell, 2006).

[59] For two quite different accounts, see François Furet, *Interpreting the French Revolution* (Cambridge: Cambridge University Press, 1981) and the more apologetic Paul R. Hanson, *Contesting the French Revolution* (Chichester: Wiley-Blackwell, 2009).

years of European warfare on a scale not seen before.⁶⁰ Internally the revolution soon led to a terror system that killed tens of thousands of people, civil war, and what some historians call the first modern genocide. In the province Vendée up to a quarter of a million men, women, and children were killed in the name of the revolution.⁶¹ The Spanish Inquisition had killed three to five thousand persons during three hundred years.⁶² And this was just the beginning. The catastrophes of the twentieth century were its direct continuation.

The conflicts between the Catholic Church and the states were usually stronger than in the Protestant countries. France is again the paradigmatic example. The reasons are many. Like the Protestant national churches, the Roman Catholic Church was so closely connected to the old society and its power structures and dominating elites that change inevitably would come into conflict with the Church. The Church also had control over the educational system and the moral teaching of the society. But the Catholic Church is also, unlike national Protestant churches, supranational and has a larger independence from the state. Its international and more independent character made it more difficult to change and control. Confrontation was the result.

The French Enlightenment was also much more anti-clerical than the British and American Enlightenments. The development in Germany was again different from both the French and the British and American cases. In Britain, some of the roots of the Enlightenment, and even more, of democracy, were found in the free churches.⁶³ There was no such background in France.⁶⁴ Little of independent civil society did exist and few were trained in any democratic habits. All attempts had been suppressed by the absolute state in alliance with the church. After the end of the

---

[60] Keegan, A History of Warfare, 347-359.

[61] Michael Burleigh, Earthly Powers: The Clash of Religion and Politics in Europe from the French Revolution to the Great War (New York: HarperCollins Publishers, 2005), 96-102. Robespierre said of the Vendéens: "As long as this impure race exists the Republic will be unhappy and precarious." Cited in David A. Bell, The Cult of the Nation in France: Inventing Nationalism, 1680-1800 (Cambridge, Mass.: Harvard University Press, 2001), 101.

[62] Jenkins, The New Anti-Catholicism, 185-187.

[63] Gertrude Himmelfarb, The Roads to Modernity: The British, French, and American Enlightenments (New York: Vintage books, 2005). Cf. Peter L. Berger, Grace Davie, and Effie Fokas, Religious America, Secular Europe? A Theme and Variation (Aldershot: Ashgate, 2008).

[64] This does not mean, of course, that the French revolution had no religious sources. Cf. Dale K. Van Kley, The Religious Origins of the French Revolution: From Calvin to the Civil Constitution, 1560-1791 (New Haven: Yale University Press, 1996).

Revolution, the Catholic Church did create lay-directed ecclesial civil movements, but it still often allied itself, in reaction to the Revolution, with monarchic and non-democratic forces.

Against this background it is interesting to read Joseph Ratzinger's (now Pope Benedict XVI) reflections on the churches in Europe. After having discussed the role of Christianity in creating the idea of Europe, the different roads taken by Byzantine Christianity, the Roman Church, and the Protestants, he then points to "the difference between Christianity in the form of a State church, which became typical of Europe, and the free churches, that found refuge in North America".[65] The American Catholic Church has also, in America, become a free church. He ends this text agreeing with Toynbee that "the destiny of a society always depends on creative minorities. Believing Christians should think of themselves as one such creative minority and contribute to Europe's recovery of the best of its heritage and thus to the service of all mankind."[66] Already in 1965 he wrote:

> Few things have damaged the Church so much in the last century and a half as its stubborn clinging to antiquated state-church positions. The attempt to shelter the faith threatened by modern science with state protective measures of its very nature hollowed out that faith from within. ... That the Church's laying claim to the state ... is one of the most questionable burdens of the Church in today's world is something that those who think historically can no longer refuse to acknowledge.[67]

From this does not follow the acceptance of a privatized and individualized understanding of the role of the Church. But this role has to be understood in ways other than being a state religion.

What does it mean to be a "creative minority"? The two most famous Catholic theologians of the 20th century, Karl Rahner and Hans Urs von Balthasar, have both used the concept "diaspora" to describe the church in the world.[68] Diaspora, not Christendom, is the normal condition of the church, according to von Balthasar. I suggest that this concept is helpful for understanding not just the future of the church in Europe, but also the original nature of the church and how the churches historically have influenced the world in which they lived.

---

[65] Joseph Ratzinger, *Europe Today and Tomorrow: Addressing the Fundamental Issues* (San Francisco: Ignatius Press, 2007), 19.
[66] Ibid., 34.
[67] Ratzinger, *Ergebnisse und Probleme: Der dritten Konzilsperiode* (Köln: J. P. Bachem, 1965), 31 f. Cited in Lohfink, *Does God Need the Church?*, 118.
[68] Gerald A. McCool (ed.), *A Rahner Reader* (London: Darton, Longman & Todd, 1975), 305-309; Hans Urs von Balthasar, *Spirit and Institution (Explorations in Theology, Vol. 4)* (San Francisco: Ignatius Press, 1995), 67.

The church grew out of Judaism. It was a form of Judaism, but the Judaism in which it was shaped was diaspora Judaism. And we should remember that diaspora has been the normal form of Judaism throughout most of its history. The Mennonite theologian John Howard Yoder has developed this theme extensively; so has the Catholic Gerhard Lohfink, although he speaks of exile rather than diaspora.[69] Daniel Boyarin has, from the Jewish side, independently developed the same idea in a way remarkably similar to Yoder, a fact that Boyarin has since recognized.[70]

Boyarin, Yoder, and Lohfink all think that the exilic abandonment of ordinary "statehood" may have built on an earlier anti-royal tradition.[71] However, the experience of living within other peoples and powers and of not being in charge created, Yoder thinks, "the culturally unique traits which define 'Judaism'", a set of social innovations that shaped first Jewish identity and then also Christian identity.[72] One of his descriptions of these traits is the following:

- the phenomenon of the synagogue; a decentralized, self-sustaining, non-sacerdotal community life form capable of operating on its own wherever there are ten households.

- the phenomenon of Torah; a text around the reading and exposition of which the community is defined. This text is at once narrative and legal.

- the phenomenon of the rabbinate; a non-sacerdotal, non-hierarchical, non-violent leadership elite whose power is not civil but intellectual, validated by their identification with the Torah.[73]

This social life was and is thus possible without conventional political structures and control, a military, or cultural homogeneity. It gave space for different ways of living and different philosophical systems because "the ground floor of identity is the common life itself, the walk, *halakah*, and the shared remembering of the story behind it." The international unity "is sustained by intervisitation, by intermarriage, by commerce, and by rabbinic

---

[69] Lohfink, *Does God Need the Church?*.

[70] Daniel Boyarin, *A Radical Jew: Paul and the Politics of Identity* (Berkeley: University of California Press, 1994), 228-260; idem, *Border Lines: The Partition of Judaeo-Christianity* (Philadelphia: University of Pennsylvania Press, 2004). Boyarin discusses Yoder in "Judaism as a Free Church: Footnotes to John Howard Yoder's The Jewish-Christian Schism Revisited", *Cross Currents* 56:4 (2007), 6-21

[71] See John Howard Yoder, *The Jewish-Christian Schism Revisited*, eds. Michael G. Cartwright and Peter Ochs (Grand Rapids: Eerdmans, 2003), 70-71. Boyarin sees "the 'invention' of Diaspora" as a further advancement in a new situation of the "radical experiment of Moses". See Boyarin, *A Radical Jew*, 253-255, the citations are from 254.

[72] Yoder, *The Jewish-Christian Schism Revisited*, 171.

[73] Ibid., 171.

consultation".[74] Lohfink describes diasporic Judaism as "a federation of synagogues", a practice he describes as "one of the most creative of Israel's inventions and one with the most significant consequences."[75]

Connected to this practice is also God's command in the book of Jeremiah (29:7) to seek the welfare of and pray for the people in whose midst they live, while they at the same time should be living faithfully to God. Yoder can therefore also describe the Jewish vision as more universal than the imperial vision of Rome or of any other empire. "The Jewish world vision was *in lived experience* wider than was the Roman Empire."[76] Many Jews lived outside the Roman Empire, and Jews inside the Empire had extensive contacts with them. This is correlated with Jewish monotheism, in which God is the creator and the lord of the entire world. Justice is not the word of the king or the emperor, but transcends kingdoms and empires and is known through the Torah.

What we find here is the creation of a social life, a peoplehood, that is non-sovereign and non-territorial. It stands in sharp contrast to the type of political temple-cult that characterized the large civilizational religions. These synagogical communities were "an association of communities, each of which was a fragment of public life, each a tiny commonwealth, each a *politicum*."[77]

The early church was formed inside this social practice and continued it. As Lohfink writes:

> the association of communities discovered by Israel became the formative principle of the early Church. Here appeared with full clarity what the people of God is: a network of communities spread over the whole earth and yet existing within non-Christian society, so that each person can freely chose whether to be a Christian or not; it is a genuine community and yet not constructed on the model of pagan society, a true homeland and yet not a state.[78]

For three centuries this practice shaped the life, theology, and ethos of the church. To appreciate the radicalism of this approach, one should not just compare it with state temple religions, but also with the beginning of Islam, in which political, military, and religious power were intrinsically connected,

---

[74] Ibid., 187. "This cultural *novum* was capable of enormous flexibility. ... Wherever they went they created new trades, new arts, new literatures, even new languages, without losing their connections to Moses or one another, or their hope of return." (Ibid., 187.)
[75] Lohfink, *Does God Need the Church?*, 114.
[76] Yoder, *The Jewish-Christian Schism Revisited*, 73.
[77] Lohfink, *Does God Need the Church?*, 118.
[78] Ibid., 118.

a fact that still shapes the Islamic world. At the time of the rise of Islam the church had, of course, also changed. Christianity had become the established religion first of the Roman Empire and then of its various successors, for example in the Germanic world. Israel's short period of being a kingdom with a temple religion became the primary model for its political theology. But, as has often been noted, including by Pope Benedict, the independence of the church did not disappear. In the Byzantine world, the Empire and the church were almost identified, but in the West the church kept more of its independence. This separation or distinction of powers has had an enormous influence on the further development of Europe, not least for the emergence of a civil society alongside what became the state.

But much of the diaspora practice declined. It was the Jewish communities that lived it most faithfully. Parts of it survived in the monastic communities, which are one example of the huge influence "creative minorities" can have. They show us, as Yoder says, that "there are other more useful ways to contribute to the course of society than attempting to 'rule'." He continues: "If the history of the Middle Ages is carefully read, we shall increasingly discern that such success as there was in 'Christianizing' medieval society was obtained less by the power of the princes than by the quiet ministry of the monastic movements, in rebuilding the community from the bottom."[79]

The established national Lutheran churches of Northern Europe did not increase the independence of the church; quite the opposite. In parts of the Reformed churches the diaspora practices begin to reemerge, although they were not infrequently overwhelmed by Old testament theocratic elements. Some free church traditions that grew out of the Reformed family, as well as out of the Lutheran and Anglican churches, went much further, as did the Radical Reformation, the Anabaptists.

The politically established churches were, of course, in various ways important for the development of Europe, but these non-established minority churches were more creative. They have, without an ethos of control – and often without any idea or plan to influence the wider society – functioned as creative minorities that have shaped societies. They have been creative minorities precisely by being themselves, and not by trying to rule or be "responsible".

The picture of the Enlightenment, the French revolution, and modernity as constituting a complete break with the Christendom past is, from many perspectives, false. The very idea of "radical break" is here, as it usually is

---

[79] John Howard Yoder, *The Royal Priesthood: Essays Ecclesiological and Ecumenical* (Grand Rapids: Eerdmans, 1994), 210.

elsewhere, unhistorical: one cannot understand modernity apart from the Christian background. The depiction of the Enlightenment as one homogenous entity is misleading, for there were several roads to modernity. Moreover, describing Christianity as one thing, wholly connected to the old society, is also wrong. Indeed, it was often Christian minorities that pioneered new developments.

Let me just take a few examples. It is often said that the central practice of the church meeting contributed to Western democracy. This was one factor. How important it was relative other factors is, of course, debated. This practice goes back to the ongoing conversation around Torah in the synagogue community, which then continued in the early church and was again taken up in the dissenting Christian communities. In the Christian churches, the background is the conviction, displayed in the Pauline letters, that every Christian has received the Spirit and the gifts of the Spirit. Anyone is allowed to talk in the church and take part in the decision making. Yoder can thus write: "The multiplicity of gifts is a model for the empowerment of the humble and the end of hierarchy in social process. Dialogue under the Holy Spirit is the ground floor of the notion of democracy."[80]

In modern times, people learned what might be called "democratic" habits in the church meetings: Making and listening to arguments; being ready to accept being outvoted; the idea of one person, one vote and the view that everyone had a vote; and, not least, the right of dissent. In his classic discussion of democracy A. D. Lindsay wrote "that the inspiration of modern democracy came from men's experience of the ... character of democratic government in the Christian congregation – came therefore especially from the Independents, the Anabaptists, and the Quakers".[81] The changes involved in moving these practices to the level of national governments are a central theme in Lindsay's discussion. But he also thought that democratic politics still presupposes "a society of democratic non-political associations."[82] Most of these Christians did not think that they were part of an historical democratic project, or the Enlightenment project. They just practiced what they thought was a truthful Christian practice. But it did influence the "wider" society; the practice was taken up by others, and it has shaped how we now think. The secular German philosopher Jürgen Habermas, often described as the greatest defender of the "unfinished Enlightenment project", can say:

---

[80] Ibid., 364.
[81] A. D. Lindsay, *The Essentials of Democracy*, 2nd ed. (London: Oxford University Press, 1935), 20.
[82] Ibid., o (sic).

> I would not object if someone were to say that my conception of language and my communicative concept of action oriented to reaching understanding are nourished by the legacy of Christianity. The 'telos of reaching understanding' ... may well draw on the legacy of the Christian understanding of the logos, which is, after all, embodied in the communicative practice of religious congregations (and not just the Quakers).[83]

It can now, he thinks, be defended on secular grounds. But it may have been discovered in these congregations.

Universal human equality seems to be the central value of modern times. Christians often claim that this has its background in a Judaic and Christian understanding. So do many others. To cite Habermas again:

> Christianity has functioned for the normative self-understanding of modernity as more than a mere precursor or a catalyst. Egalitarian universalism, from which sprang the ideas of freedom and social solidarity, of an autonomous conduct of life and emancipation, of the individual morality of conscience, human rights, and democracy, is the direct heir to the Judaic ethic of justice and the Christian ethic of love. This legacy, substantially unchanged, has been the object of continual critical appropriation and reinterpretation. To this day, there is no alternative to it. And in light of the current challenges of a postnational constellation, we continue to draw on the substance of this heritage. Everything else is just idle postmodern talk.[84]

Against this, one might cite historic Christian practice that does not look egalitarian. The churches often defended a hierarchical society. Slavery returned to the colonies. Women were not seen as equal. And so on.

On the other hand, the Enlightenment idea that postulates universal equality as self-evident also has problems. It is simply not self-evident. Modern racism, based on "scientific naturalism", actually arose among Enlightenment thinkers. The liberal legal and political theorist Jeremy Waldron notes in his book about John Locke and the idea of human equality that it is very difficult to find actual arguments for equality in contemporary legal and political philosophy; it is just taken as an axiom.[85] He claims, like Habermas, that historically the idea of human equality "has been shaped and fashioned on the basis of religion",[86] and more specifically Christian theology. Waldron ends the book in the following way:

---

[83] Jürgen Habermas, *Time of Transitions* (Cambridge: Polity Press, 2006), 161.
[84] Ibid., 150 f.
[85] Jeremy Waldron, *God, Locke, and Equality: Christian Foundations of John Locke's Political Thought* (Cambridge: Cambridge University Press, 2002), 1-4.
[86] Ibid., 242.

Equality cannot do its work unless it is accepted among those whom it consecrates as equals. Locke believed this general acceptance was impossible apart from the principle's foundation in religious teaching. We believe otherwise. Locke, I suspect, would have thought we were taking a risk. And I am afraid it is not entirely clear, given our experience of a world and century in which politics and public reason have cut loose from these foundations, that his caution and suspicions were unjustified.[87]

Today it is difficult to find philosophers, scientists, or politicians who question human equality outright, but during the nineteenth and the first half of the twentieth century it was common among liberals, conservatives, and socialists, as well as among "scientifically enlightened" Christians. A frequent argument was that science (especially Darwinism) had emancipated us from dated and dangerous dogmas about human equality. This opened the way for views crucial to the legitimation of racism, colonialism and eugenics. Such views lost much of their power after 1945 because of the use fascism and Nazism made of them.[88] However, this history supports Waldron's or present Christian views that human equality is not something we can just take for granted.

When Locke made his case for social human equality, he did it with Christian arguments, but against other Christians. But he did not write in a social vacuum. What made these arguments possible was the practices of certain dissenting Christians: their practice of baptism, of the universality of the gifts, and of the church meeting.

The issue of slavery offers a related example.[89] Slavery has been a universal institution. It has existed everywhere. It was a normal and legitimate part of human society. The historically interesting issue is not how anyone could have defended slavery, but why some at some time and place started to question it and fight it. The modern struggle against slavery was not primarily driven by Enlightenment philosophers. Some of them supported

---

[87] Ibid., 243.
[88] George M. Fredrickson, *Racism: A Short History* (Princeton: Princeton University Press, 2002); George L. Mosse, *Toward the Final Solution: A History of European Racism* (London: J.M. Dent, 1978); J. Kameron Carter, *Race: A Theological Account* (Oxford: Oxford University Press, 2008); Mike Hawkins, *Social Darwinism in European and American Thought, 1860-1945: Nature as Model and Nature as Threat* (Cambridge: Cambridge University Press, 1997), Richard Weikart, *From Darwin to Hitler: Evolutionary Ethics, Eugenics, and Racism in Germany* (New York: Palgrave Macmillan, 2004), and Ian Dowbiggin, *A Concise History of Euthanasia: Life, Death, God, and Medicine* (Lanham: Rowman & Littlefield, 2005).
[89] For the following, see e.g. Rodney Stark, *For the Glory of God: How Monotheism Led to Reformations, Science, Witch-Hunts, and the End of Slavery* (Princeton: Princeton University Press, 2003), 291-365.

slavery. Thomas Jefferson, who wrote the American declaration of independence stating that everyone is created equal, owned slaves.

It was mainly Christians who worked against the slave trade and slavery, but it was not just any Christians. The first public protest against slavery in the English colonies came in 1688 from newly arrived Mennonites.[90] Later on, it was the more numerous and more centrally placed Quakers and evangelical Christians who took the lead both in America and in England. In England, Quakers, evangelical Anglicans, and Methodists were a main force behind this first modern social movement, the struggle against the slave trade and against slavery. In this social movement the network of Christian congregations, often Quakers practicing the diaspora practices, were decisive. There were others who were critical of slavery, including some Enlightenment thinkers, but they did not create a movement, and they were generally moderate in their criticism.[91] These Christians were, at the time, often seen as sectarians, religious fanatics and absolutists who harmed social unity and who did not understand economic necessities.

I could give many more examples. Some of the roots of the women's movement are in the same Christian groups.[92] There were women preachers in American already in the 18th century. The American civil rights movement had its social base in black Baptist and Methodist congregations.[93] But I will only mention one more example, taken from the Roman Catholic context.

In 1979 Pope John Paul II visited Poland. It was, in George Weigel's words, "nine days that bent the curve of modern history".[94] Weigel describes the pope as a post-Constantinian deeply critical of so-called *realpolitik*, believing

---

[90] "A Minute against Slavery, Addressed to Germantown Monthly Meeting, 1688", Quaker Heritage Press, www.qhpress.org/texts/oldqwhp/as-1688.htm. Last updated 2007. Accessed May 2, 2009.

[91] In addition to Stark, see e.g. Donald W. Dayton, *Discovering an Evangelical Heritage* (New York: Harper & Row, 1976); Adam Hochschild, *Bury the Chains: Prophets and Rebels in the Fight to Free an Empire's Slaves* (Boston: Houghton Mifflin, 2005), and Christopher Leslie Brown, *Moral Capital: Foundations of British Abolitionism* (Chapel Hill: The University of North Carolina Press, 2006). Of course, there had been many other Christians that had condemned slavery, including several popes, but it was Quakers, Methodists, evangelicals, and their like who were crucial for creating the social movements struggling against the slave trade and slavery during the eighteenth and nineteenth centuries.

[92] Dayton, *Discovering an Evangelical Heritage*; Barbara J MacHaffie, *Her Story: Women in Christian Tradition*, 2nd ed. (Minneapolis: Fortress Press, 2006).

[93] David L. Chappell, *A Stone of Hope: Prophetic Religion and the Death of Jim Crow* (Chapel Hill: University of North Carolina Press, 2004).

[94] George Weigel, *Witness to Hope: The Biography of Pope John Paul II* (New York: Cliff Street Books, 1999), ix. See for his description and discussion of this visit pp. 295-321.

that culture finally is more important than military and economic power. "As a Christian convinced that the Gospel revealed the truth about humanity and its destiny, he believed that God was in charge of history. This freed the Church to act in a singular way."[95] John Paul II did not attack the regimes on the direct political level. He unleashed a spiritual and moral revolution. "He had begun to exorcise the fear, the anomie, and sense of hopelessness that had previously kept the 'we' of society from coalescing."[96] However – and this is the point here – John Paul II's historically momentous visit to Poland in 1979 depended on the long-time work, struggle and witness of the Polish church. Without this, the visit would not have had much effect.

If one asks about the role of religion and the churches in European integration, church leaders, politicians, theologians, and other scholars all tend to think, on the one side, in terms of common values and norms, and on the other, about the possible contribution to the common welfare project. The encounter with Islam has again raised the issue of shared European values. However, these values are often described precisely as secular values. Such a secular discourse can be supported by concepts common in traditional Protestant theology such as "the freedom of the Christian", "the two-kingdoms-doctrine", "the autonomy of the secular", "natural law", and so on. Such ideas have traditionally been used by national Protestantism for making the church an integral part of society and culture. They were, not least, employed with great effect in the period leading up to the First World War. Some of these ideas have also been used by the Catholic Church, especially natural law theory.

When Cardinal Ratzinger some years ago was discussing a possible European Constitution, he wrote that one essential "element is the 'unconditional character' of human dignity and human rights", of "liberty, equality, and solidarity".[97] This is, he argued, a crucial part of the European identity. Described in such general terms, most people agree. But when one asks exactly what this means, it leads directly to a renewed "cultural struggle" between the Catholic Church and an increasingly dominant secular liberal European culture. The struggle concerns, in part, just who is a human being. Bioethical issues are central and so, therefore, are the beginning and end of life. Likewise controversial are different understandings of family and sexuality. For secular forces in Europe as well as for parts of the Protestant community, the Roman Catholic Church is not considered as part of a common European value consensus on such issues, but rather as one of the

---

[95] Ibid., 296.
[96] Ibid., 321.
[97] Ratzinger, *Europe Today and Tomorrow*, 30.

principal enemies of human rights. This illustrates how difficult it is to talk about social integration in this way.

If one instead takes one's starting point in the idea of creative minorities or in a Christian diaspora identity, the issue of integration can be discussed in other ways. The sociologist José Casanova tries to develop from such a perspective an understanding of social integration that might be helpful:

> According to this model, modern social integration emerges in and through the discursive and agonic participation of individuals, groups, social movements, and institutions in a public yet undifferentiated sphere of civil society where the collective construction and reconstruction, contestation, and affirmation of common normative structures – 'the common good' – takes place. Unlike functionalist theories of normative societal integration, however, such a theory does not conceptualize modern civil societies as a homogenous societal community sharing common norms and values but, rather, as a space and a process of public social interaction through which common norms and solidarities may be constructed and reconstructed. In other words, common norms cannot be presupposed as the premise and foundation of modern social order but, rather, as the potential and always fragile outcome of a process of communicative interaction.[98]

I have already given some historical examples of such a process. What it might lead to in the future, no one knows. There are no guarantees that it will lead to what one might personally consider a positive development. One can be sure that, at best, the results will be mixed. For churches that for centuries have been dominant and have seen themselves as guarantors of a society's fundamental values, it is difficult even to begin to think like this. Pope Benedict now talks about the importance of creative minorities, but the Catholic church in Europe did not for most of its existence think of itself as a minority; moreover, when it could conceptualize itself this way, it did its best to hinder other religious minorities, Christian or not. So does secular liberalism today, paradoxically often in the name not only of integration but also of multiculturalism!

One secular concern is the universal claims Christians make. This very idea of thinking about "truths" in religion, it is claimed, harms integration with secular people, other religions, and other Christians. All religious mission is viewed with deep suspicion. It leads only to divisions and conflicts. Worldwide liberal mission is, however, not only fully acceptable, but mandatory, as is the use of the coercive powers of states or international communities for the sake of this mission. The difference is, of course, that

---

[98] José Casanova, *Public Religions in the Modern World* (Chicago: University of Chicago Press, 1994), 230.

religions are regarded as all equally invalid or of only personal concern, while secular liberal values and norms are seen as universally true as well as socially and politically necessary for the good society.

However, it is important to note the practical difference status makes. Christian theology makes universal claims. But universal claims made by a diaspora community function very differently from those registered by a hegemonic church that can employ coercive means. Beliefs and practices that have one meaning for the church as "resident aliens" receive another meaning in a situation where the church belongs to the established power structures.

From a top-down perspective, from a homogenous elite perspective, it may seem threatening to integration to think in terms of diaspora, of creative minorities that differentiate themselves as groups from the "rest of society", minorities who make truth claims and who believe they have a mission to others. Minorities are not, of course, good by definition. History is full of destructive minorities, however "creative" they may have been. One of the most destructive differentiated "groups" history has seen is the modern secular nation-state. Nevertheless, discussing integration, sociologist Robert Putnam argues that empirical studies show that in-group solidarity is not negatively correlated to out-group solidarity. He thinks rather that strong religious communities are one important factor behind integration between communities, and he gives many examples from the American context.[99] The results of the French or Turkish secularist "anti-communitarian" approaches to civil integration are, on the other hand, not all that encouraging.

But, to conclude, from a Christian perspective one's authority concerning how to live is neither the secular state nor social science. The primary question is another: how to live as faithful followers of Jesus Christ.

---

[99] Robert D. Putnam, "E Pluribus Unum: Diversity and Community in the Twenty-First Century", *Scandinavian Political Studies* 30:2 (2007), 137-174. In their recent book, *American Grace: How Religion is Reshaping our Civic and Political Lives* (New York: Simon and Schuster, 2010), Putnam and David Campbell claim that "Having close friends at church, discussing religion frequently with your family and friends, and taking part in small groups at church are extremely powerful predictors of the entire range of generosity, good neighborliness, and civic engagement" (472). No other organisation or factor (including sex, age, education, political views, income) come close. People active in religious communities are much more likely than nonreligious Americans to work on community projects and in voluntary associations, and donate time and money, including to what Putnam and Campbell describe as secular causes (see 443-492). Cf. Arthur C. Brooks, *Who Really Cares: The Surprising Truth About Compassionate Conservatism* (New York: Basic Books, 2006).

Churches in Europe in Light of the Thoughts of Simone Weil

Endre Nagy

Lessons in the light of Simone Weil's doctrine
Sketch:
Simone Weil's challenge for Weber's theory of modernity: two forms of encountering both 1. politics (Needs for Soul) and economy (Les reflexions sur les causes de l'oppression et de la liberté...) with a radical grace, and: 2.option for poverty, and 3.the anti-ecclesiastical attitude

I. An account of her life

Simone Weil was born into an upper-middle class Jewish family in France, in 1903. However, the family was completely assimilated and secularized. Simone Weil never felt any attachment to her ancestry; in fact in her case it was the opposite. As apparent in her literary oeuvre, she was rather repugnant not only of her original background, but as though wanting to prove Sigmund Freud's tenet about "Selbsthass", she was rather repelling the Jewish embeddedness of Christianity. She grew up in a neutral spirit with regard to religion, and she also denied the problem of God as insoluble. In spite of this, she was – according her autobiography –unconsciously Christian. "I was born in it /i.e. Christian behavior/, educated and remained in this Christian inspiration for ever. Even in the time when the name of God had no significance for my thoughts I was of Christian assumption in regard to the problem of the world and life, in a determined and severe way with the most specific concepts implying in itself" (Ami személyes és ami Szent.Budapest:Vigilia. p. 186). She took into consideration of the values such as truth, beauty, virtue, poverty, love for the neighbour as well as for justice and for purity; all these compelled her to state that she was "aware of the fact that her world-view was a Christian one". Therefore it never came into her mind to become a Christian... Since she thought had been born into it.

After graduating from École Normal Superieur she went to work in a factory in order to experience the real life of the workers. But being maladroit she could hardly keep up with the working pace. She realised that the work in the factory system was humiliating for the workers. They were worth nothing in the eyes of either the "patron" or themselves. In 1935 she went to the Civil War in Spain on the side of the Anarchists, where she experienced the brutality not only of the Fascists but also of her comrades, who executed a priest and a fifteen-year-old boy. She was forced back to France by virtue of an accident where she learnt the lesson "one finds oneself in a war which resembles a war of mercenaries, only with much more cruelty and with less human respect for the enemy" (Quotation by Springsted: Introduction. P. 18).

She crossed paths with Catholicism three times through three mystical experiences in her life. Her first experience was just after the factory episode. She was living partly on teaching and on partly sick live when she went to Portugal, where in a wretched fishing village, she met a procession honouring their patron saint. She reports it in her "spiritual autobiography": "The wives of the fishermen were, in procession, making a tour of all ships, carrying candles and singing what must certainly have been very ancient hymns of heart-wrenching sadness." She says " There the conviction was suddenly borne in upon me that Christianity is preeminently the religion of slaves, that slaves cannot help belonging to it," (Springsted. P.18.). The second mystic experience occurred to her in 1937 when she was visiting Assisi, Italy. She was staying alone in the small, Roman Style chapel of Santa Maria degli Agnelli where St.Francis often prayed. There, she felt that a power that was stronger than her compelled her to go down on her knees. Her third experience was in Solesmes, France, in 1938, when she was attending the Holy Week. "I was suffering from a splitting headache, each sound hurt me like a blow; by an extreme effort of concentration I was able to rise above this wretched flesh , to leave it to suffer by itself, heaped up in a corner, and find a pure and perfect joy in the unimaginable beauty of chanting and the words" (WG. 68,6). In her wretched situation she met a young Catholic who introduced her to the English metaphysical poets, among them, George Eliot and her poem: *Love*. She quickly memorized it, and recited it, especially when she had a headache. She says: "It was during one of these recitations that Christ himself came down and took possession of me" (WG. p. 68-69). By this time she had undergone an "intellectual illumination" (which I have called 'the first stage of conversion' elsewhere): the sudden insight into the truth. The conversion is however not completed by this act. According to the great converts (included St. Augustin, Paul Claudel, et cetera), there always remains an inner resistance to be mastered. In the case of Simone Weil it was not her reason was, but her love that resisted. Her intelligence led her further – through the reading of Plato, (whom she felt to have been a Christian), the Iliad and the Bhagavad Gita – to the perfection of conversion. It took a long time for her to pray at all. It happened when she was working as a land girl for Gustave Thibon, a staunch Catholic, and learnt the Greek language. She learnt the Lord's Prayer in Greek and developed the practice of reciting it each morning "with absolute attention". And "sometimes during this recitation or at other moments,

Christ is really present with me in person...In this sudden possession of me by Christ, neither my senses nor imagination had any part; I only felt in the midst of my suffering the presence of a love, like that which one can read in a smile on a beloved face" (WG. p. 72).

Though perfectly converted she never felt invited by God to enter the Catholic Church. She refused to be baptized. After leaving France for the United States, she regularly worshipped in a church in Harlem, New York, in the black community. Thence, she returned to England. Her health deteriorated in 1943, when she suffered from tuberculosis. In an era, that did not know penicillin, she was headed for death. Furthermore, she refused to eat more than the official rations for ordinary people in France. She died on August, 1943 in Ashford, Kent.

Before taking into account the lessons she left with us, let me cite a passage of T. S. Eliot from the Preface that he wrote to the English version of the *Need for roots*: "As a political thinker, as everything else, Simone Weil is not to be classified...On one hand she was a passionate champion of common people and especially the oppressed –those oppressed by wickedness and selfishness of men and those oppressed by anonymous forces of modern society...On the other hand, she was by nature a solitary and individualist, with a horror of what she called the *collectivity* –the monster created modern totalitarianism...She cannot be classified either as a reactionary or as a socialist". And about *Need for the Roots* he makes a brief but very telling account: "This book belongs in that category of phenomena to politics which politicians seldom read, and which most of them would be unlikely to understand or to know how to apply. Such books do not influence the contemporary conduct of affairs: for the men and women already engaged in this career and committed to the jargon of market-place, always come too late" (N.R. p. XI-XII).

However, I am convinced it can be said that Simone Weil was a political thinker. As we will see in a moment, she was a moral revolutionary who disregarded the social web, and sought to better their moral basis, and by doing this hoped to better society as a whole. In contrast, the social revolutionary (like Marx, or Lenin) wants to do the contrary: "to efface the past at one blow", and abolish the old institutions and hope human beings would be changed by themselves. Simone Weil was convinced the actual political order was worse because it was based on the rights of men and not the public good. She wanted to shake the whole of the moral basis of society. She stood up against both the market-oriented economy and the so-called political democracy as practiced then and until now.

II. The great challenge: Max Weber's theory of the impossibility of any brotherhood's ethics in the modernity

The entire modern world suggests that we are living in a world with a lesser presence of God.

Max Weber already raised the question in the most radical way by suggesting that the ethics of brotherhood come in sharp contradiction with the exigencies of modern formal rational, market-oriented Capitalism. "By contrast, the sublimated religion for salvation and the rationed economy have come in a relation of more and more tension. The rationed economy means professional running. It must abide by prices in money as they are formed on the market between men in the battle of interests. No calculation is possible without any estimation in money. Money at the same time is the most abstract and most "impersonal" thing that exists in the world altogether. Thus, the more the setting (cosmos) of rational capitalist economy abides by its own laws, the more untouchable it gets for any religious ethics of brotherhood worded in any form. The more impersonal it gets, the less it does" (Weber, A világ stb. 350.) He explains to us that the relation between the feudal lord and the villain can be regulated by ethics for it is a personal one. However it cannot be pursued in the same sense and success between shareholders of banks amongst whom there is no personal connection.

He also explains in his "Economic ethics of world religion" that not only is the formal rational, impersonal economy a sharp contradiction of the brotherhood's ethics but at the same time that "the more Selbstgesätzlichkeit of the individual spheres developed with their inherent consequences and were conscious, the more the tensions between the independent spheres took shapes, the ones, that were hidden for the ancient unbiased relation to the outer world" (A világ 346). It applies to both the prophetic and mission religions of salvation, and does not hold to the "of example" religion like the Buddhism or Hinduism. For salvation in these religions was not compulsory but optional. However, there were two ways to avoid this difficulty. One was the puritan, protestant ethics as a religion for completeness that abdicates from the universal love and considers every relation between men as "thingness", and so considers this at the same time as the service for the will of the unfathomable God. It goes without saying that by doing so, Calvinism also accepts that the world has lost its values and as a pure "objectification" of economic sphere. Consequently, Calvinism abandoned salvation for a particular grace that was not underpinned. In spite of such unbrotherhood's ethics, the other solution seemed to be an extreme of brotherhood that did not question the meaning of the world but gives his/her soul for the "good" of everybody who is in need. This self-giving of the soul without any prerequisite, which is called by Baudelaire "the sacred prostitution", is not for just any man but only for the dedicated.

We will soon gain the insight that Simone Weil did not follow the first, but sought the second solution. For she did not acknowledge the world in the given, depraved state, but was eager to assist all kinds of people in need. However, before taking on this theme let's see the development of thought by Weber. After having pointed out that the market runs "without regard to the persons", i.e. it discharges the business according to calculable rules, Weber also demonstrates that the same applies for bureaucracy as well. For the peculiarity of modern culture, and specifically its technical and economic basis, demands the calculability of results. When fully developed, bureaucracy also stands in a specific sense, under the principle of *sine ira et studio*. Its specific nature, which is welcomed by capitalism, develops more perfectly. The more bureaucracy is 'dehumanised', the more it succeeds in eliminating love, hatred and all personal, irrational and emotional elements from official business. (Weber: Power and bureaucracy, In: Thompsdon, Kenneth and Tunstall, Jeremy: Sociological Perspective. Penguin Books. New York, etc.1981. p. 77). That is, both of them run on the basis of being "impersonal". The third sphere that runs parallel to brotherhood's ethics is politics and the State which is based on the legitimate use of force. Interfering with politics means – according to Weber – "an alliance with the demonic power of force". The struggle for state power, even the most developed form, or the struggle in war, brings about the community of soldiers, honoring them for their own death which sharply contradicts all kinds of brotherhood. To escape this, it is only either the radical pacifism which accepts the ethics of the Sermon of the Mount ("don't resist the force") or the Calvinist contempt of the world, on the basis of an ethics of calling, which must coerce the commands of God on the world through its own means, which is by force. But the latter cannot be considered as a kat'exochen brotherhood's ethic.

We will not to follow further Max Weber's analysis on the spheres of arts, erotic love and the intellectuality (science and philosophy) that are by profession anti-religious ones. It will suffice to quote Weber's final conclusion: "In the middle of a culture organized by the labour performed on a rational ethics of calling – disregarding any social stratum exempt from economic concern –no place remains to pursue a radical and cosmic brotherhood.: it seems so that in the circumstances of technical and social conditions of a rational culture it is destined to fail to follow Buddha, Jesus or St. Francis from a pure outer stand-point" (A világvallások. p. 385).

Similarly, the great Hungarian political thinker of the 19th century, József Eötvös conceives– in a passage where he was discussing the future of the religion – as follows: "It is not the great progress that sciences brought about in the modern time that endanger religion....Not sciences but of the industrial trend that religion can be feared. As discoveries of Copernicus, Galileo and Newton did not shake our religion, the great discoveries of our contemporaries will not do it either And that since the Church could reconcile the movement of the earth with its teachings; it will do the same with other geological discoveries as well". However, the contradiction that exists between morals as practiced and the principles of Christian religion can never be reconciled by anyone in the world". (Gondolatok. Révai testvérek 2.kiadás. 1908. p. 21) We can see a great mind, who came half a century or so before Max Weber, could conceive the same trouble with capitalism.

It is very likely that Max Weber was right to say that, although it seems to us for the domain of economy as well it holds only to some extent. For him, there were some tacit assumptions that he was not aware of, since they were taken for granted during the period of capitalism, when he lived. For Capitalism the primary precondition is the trust that must be imbued by all the business line. It presupposes partners trust one another before entering into bargain. Further, from the Stoic up until nowadays there has been a law in force in Europe which came from the natural law theories, declaring: "Pacta sunt servanda"! There are external factors (as the economists call them) that play an important part in an economic process. There are sentiments that also play a part when someone enters into business talks. Even small entrepreneurs are welded by their behavior: not motivated by harsh profit maximizing, but rather mutual aid. That is, there have been tacit, moral commands and external effects underpinning the whole economy. We only enlist some elements that demonstrate how the formal rational economy does not work in a pure ideal political form (as Max Weber described it). It is not by the "invisible hand" but many other factors like international differences between countries with divergent interests, even by multinational agencies that deceive about their real budget as happened with some big banks, or in Russia, where the Mafiosi privatized former state-owned factories on artificially low prices and enriched themselves very highly. Thus, looking at both the world market and the former Socialist countries one must stress that all capitalism has the underlying moral basis that was tacitly supposed by Max Weber. However, we have already learned that these prerequisites became explicit, and without taking note of them, capitalism cannot run in a pure form. In principle one can assume that capitalism can run pure form when the invisible hand settles the integration of economic process: in theory but not in reality.

This is the proof of reality. But there are also theoretical tenets, not to enumerate here, that speak of the collapse of Neo-liberal economic theories, and need "new axiomatisation" of economic principle.

III. Simone Weil's defiance of Weber's theory

Simone Weil did not know of these new developments of both experience and economic theories. But her theory is nothing other than a radical and swaying intrusion into the terrain of Max Weber's anti-brotherhood teachings both in the domain of politics, bureaucracy and economy. With a firm stand-point, a mystic one if you like, she lays down the fundamental principle: "There is a reality outside the world, that is to say, outside space and time, outside man's mental universe, outside any sphere whatsoever that is accessible to human faculties. Corresponding to this reality, at the center of human heart, is the longing for an absolute good, a longing which is always there and never is appeased by any object of this world...Just as the reality is the sole foundation of facts, so that other reality is the sole foundation of good. That reality is the unique source of all the good that can exist in this world: that is to say, all beauty, all truth, all justice, all legitimacy, all order, and all human behavior that is mindful of obligation." Springsted p. 132). This statement takes a central place as it penetrates all details of her theory.

(Here is: Simone Weil's defiance of the formal rational economy).

At the outset of the Need for Roots, as a special kind of introduction she conceives a crucial tenet as follows: "The notion of obligation comes before that of rights which is subordinate and relative to the former. A right is not effectual by itself, but only in relation to the obligation to which it corresponds, the effective exercise of a right springing not from the individual who possesses it, but from other men who consider themselves as being under a certain obligation towards him. Recognition of an obligation makes it effectual. An obligation which goes unrecognized by anybody loses none of the full force of its existence. A right which goes unrecognized by anybody is not worth very much". (Need for Roots. p. 3)

I remember how much I was struck when I read these statements for the first time. I studied law and we were educated that rights always come with obligations and vice versa: a teaching that seemed quite understandable by itself without any doubt. Learning that obligation now "comes first before the right" was for us, lawyers, a real iconoclastic assumption, a sacrilege.

Furthermore, reading that "A man left alone in the universe would have no rights whatsoever, but he would have obligations" was first unfathomable. However, it became understandable after considering Simone Weil's school of thought. It is clear that being alone in the universe means being obligated for one's own life and at the same time to God.

This tenet has a political assumption as well. Simone Weil developed it further by accusing the "men of 1789", who did not recognize that they were bound to the "human plane" and wanted to postulate the absolute principle. That's why they "started off with the idea of rights" (p. 4.). The same applies nowadays to political constitutions over the entire world which place emphasis on political rights instead of obligations. Don't we speak about the rights of minorities, of the youth and even of animals? But what about their obligations?

So, there are fancy fallcies in the theories of Simone Weil. Let's follow her school of thought. The obligations are coextensive with the eternal destiny of the human being, and they are unconditional. Even a positive right that contradicts them should be illegitimate. Simone Weil bases this on moral considerations. The root leads back to the saying of Jesus Christ: "I was hungered, and ye gave me no meal". From this comes the eternal obligation towards the human being, not to let him suffer from hunger when one can come to his assistance. As in the case of physical needs, (e.g. protection against violence, housing, clothing, heating, hygiene and medical care in illness) one has to assist, as these obligations correspond with the moral side (that is, that of the soul) and this deserves as much respect as the physical needs. "They are much more difficult to recognize and to enumerate than are the needs of the body" (p. 7). She tries to list the needs of the soul. But before we list them, let's recollect the needs as listed by Maslow(see. MasslowAbraham: A lét pszichológiája felé. Budapest Ursus Libris: pl. 159) and compare them those of Simone Weil. We will then have an insight into how much the latter's are more sophisticated and stand closer to reality than those by Maslow. Thus, Simone Weil does not list them as Maslow did, but puts them "in pairs of opposites which balance and complete one another" (Simone Weil /Writings Selected and Introduction by Eric O. Springsted. Modern Spiritual Master Series. Orbis Books., Maryknoll, New York.1998. p. 139) as follows: equality versus hierarchy, obedience versus liberty, truth versus freedom of expression, solitude and privacy versus social life, personal property versus collective property, punishment versus honour, disciplined participation in common task of public values versus personal initiative within this participation, security versus risk, rootedness in several kinds of natural environments versus making contact with the universe. Due to time constraints I am not able to discuss all of them so I will focus on just one.

Equality versus hierarchy: Equality "consists in a recognition public, general, effective and genuinely expressed in institutions and customs that the same amount of respect and consideration is due to human being as such and is not to a matter of degree." (The Need for Roots. Prelude to a Declaration of Duties towards Mankind. Ark. London and New York. 1987. p. 15). She explains that a certain balance is needed between equality and inequality. For, example what equality of opportunity means ("prospects for each man are the same as for the other man indiscriminately at birth. Education is so generalized that no one is prevented from developing to any capacity simply on account of his birth") needed a counterbalance as well. "To the extent to which it is really possible for the son of a farm labourer to become one day a minister, is it reallky be possible for the son of minister become one day a farm labourer." But she marks: "This second possibility could never assume any noticeable proportions without a very dangerous degree of social constraint" (P. 16). After listing several examples she concludes: "The balance of equality "would mean honouring each human condition and not just a hollow pretence" (p. 18). However, at the same time, a human being needs a hierarchy, i.e. "a certain veneration, a certain devotion towards superiors". But how? –The answer is: One should owe respect to other persons not because they are in power. The devotion should not be for the individuals but to symbols of their positions, because they symbolize high positions, thus assuming obligations towards fellow-men. "A veritable hierarchy presupposes a consciousness on the part of superiors of this symbolic function and a realization that it forms the only legitimate object of devotion among their subordinates" (p. 18). It is evident, that according to Simone Weil, that every human being in a society whether in a higher or lower position needs and deserves respect. Simone Weil –as we have seen above –considers herself a slave forever. Anyway, this is character of a just society. (What is a just society? Answer: Springsted)

Another pair of opposites is the freedom of opinion versus truth. In the case of freedom she mostly dwells on art and publications. Without going into details of what she developed, let us confine ourselves to just one topic. Intelligence needs to be expressed without control by any authority but not without any limit, because: "repression could be exercised against the press, radio broadcast, or else of a similar kind, not only for offences against moral principle that are publicly recognized, but also for baseness of tone and thought, bad taste, vulgarity or a subtly corrupting moral atmosphere. This sort of repression could take place in any moral atmosphere" (The Need for...p. 25). One can imagine what would happen if any government were to implement this rule. But it becomes more complex when she becomes concerned with the truth, that is "more sacred than any other need" (p. 35).

Nonetheless all of us know she remarks that "journalism becomes indistinguishable from organized lying", that constitutes a crime. But we think it is impossible to punish it.

Church and State Relations in Portugal

Alejandro Torres Gutiérrez

I. Introduction

The relationship between Church and State in Portugal influenced Portuguese history from the very beginning, to be precise; from the same day that Pope Alexander III awarded the title of "King" to Afonso Henriques, through the bull *Manifestis probatum*, on 23 March 1179.

The history of the relationship between Church and State in Portugal has had a very clear parallelism with Spanish history. There are many examples:

1) The tension between Church and State during the Middle Ages.

   The third king of Portugal, Afonso II,[100] was excommunicated by bull of Honorio III, because of his attacks on ecclesiastical privileges, during the 13th century.

   This tension was reproduced between Pope Boniface VIII and Philippe, *le bel*, King of France.[101] The same problems existed between Boniface VIII and Ferdinand IV, King of Castile, who was threatened with excommunication on 28 January 1301, accused of imposing taxes on the Church, without papal authorization.[102]

2) Lights and shadows were also coincident.

   The Church contributed to the formation of the Portuguese and Spanish Empires with more humanitarian methods, decreasing the brutality of the conquest.

   Nevertheless, the Inquisition was a dark chapter in the history of freedom of conscience in both countries. Neither Evangelicals nor Jews were a threat to religious unity in either country.

3) Royal interventionism in ecclesiastical matters was coincided during the 18th century. Jesuits were expulsed in both countries.

---

[100] Born in 1185, died in 1223.
[101] The tension was reflected in the bull *Clericis Laicos*. He was finally excommunicated by the bull *Super Petri Solio*. TORRES GUTIÉRREZ, ALEJANDRO. *Iglesia y Fisco en la Historia de España*. Servicio de Publicaciones de la Facultad de Derecho de la U.C.M. Madrid. 2000. Pages 57 to 60.
[102] TORRES GUTIÉRREZ, ALEJANDRO. *Op. Cit.* Pages 60 y 61.

4) *Liberal* policies in the 19th century, with a clear anticlerical accent, were reproduced in Portugal and Spain:[103]

   a) The abolition of tithes in the first half of the 19th century and land confiscation were a heavy penalty for the ecclesiastical economy.

   b) The freedoms of press and expression and the relaxation of censorship reduced Church control over society.

   c) The dissolution of religious orders was also a common chapter in both countries.[104]

   The three Portuguese 19th century constitutions, of 1822, 1826 and 1838, reserved a privileged role for the Catholic Church.

II. Close Antecedents

II. 1. The law of separation of 1911

On 5 October 1910, the 1st Portuguese Republic was proclaimed.

In 1911 the Register of births, marriages and deaths was secularized. Its supervisors would be public employees in the future.[105] Religious education in schools was eliminated.[106]

The Law of Separation of 20 April 1911, strongly anticlerical, and clearly inspired by its French antecedent of 1905, was a strong attack against the interests of the Catholic Church in Portugal. It was the triumph of secularism.

II. 2. The estado novo: the new state during Salazar

António Oliveira Salazar was concerned by the idea of a *strong regime*. This new regime, the so called *Estado Novo*, gave enough guarantees to the Catholic Church. The new Concordat of 1940,[107] restored the good relationship between Church and State, and remained in force for more than half a century, until 2004, with the single amendment of the Agreement of

---

[103] OLIVEIRA MARQUES, A. H. *História de Portugal*. Vol. III. Palas Editores. Lisboa. 1981. Page 114.

[104] OLIVEIRA MARQUES, A. H. *History of Portugal*. Imprensa Nacional – Casa da Moeda. Lisboa. 1991. Pages 117 y 118.

[105] OLIVEIRA MARQUES, A. H. *Op. Cit.* Page 139.

[106] MARCADÉ, JACQUES. *Le Portugal au XXe siècle 1910-1985*. Presses Universitaires de France. París. 1988. Pages 96 y 97.

[107] *Acta Apostolica Sedis* 32. 1940. Pages 217 to 233. *Diário do Governo*, of July 10, 1940. 1st Series. Number 158.

15 February 1975.[108] This second agreement of 1975, changed article XXIV of the Concordat of 1940, and allowed divorce for Catholics.

The Concordat of 1940 did not establish the Catholic faith as official, but it was very useful for the Catholic Church:

1) It recognized the legal personality of the Catholic Church,[109] full freedom of action in the sphere of its competences,[110] full autonomy of internal organization in accordance with Canon Law regulations,[111] and freedom of worship in public and in the private sphere.[112]

2) The Catholic Church received full capacity of acquisition and disposal of goods and properties,[113] and the right to collect money from its believers.[114] The Catholic Church obtained the recognition of its property rights in relation to the goods and properties that it had had previous to the 1st Republic: churches, Episcopal palaces, parochial residences, seminars, etc. The only exception was represented by the properties that were converted into *national monuments* or *properties of public interest*.[115] Churches were not to be demolished without the previous agreement of the religious authorities,[116] and were exempted from taxes.[117]

3) Catholic ministers had to be Portuguese citizens.[118] The highest Catholic hierarchies had to have at least the *nihil obstat* from the Portuguese Government. This consent was tacit after 30 days without any opposition.[119]

Ecclesiastics had the same protection as the public authorities, during the exercise of their functions.[120] They enjoyed the professional secret,[121] were exempted from the position of jury or any another

---

[108] *Acta Apostolica Sedis* 67. 1975. Pages 435 to 436. *Diário do Governo*, of April 4, 1975. 1st Series. Number 79.
[109] Article I, Concordat 1940.
[110] Article II, Concordat 1940.
[111] Article III, Concordat 1940.
[112] Article XVI, Concordat 1940.
[113] Article IV, Concordat 1940.
[114] Article V, Concordat 1940.
[115] Article VI, Concordat 1940.
[116] Article VII, Concordat 1940.
[117] Article VIII, Concordat 1940.
[118] Article IX, Concordat 1940.
[119] Article X, Concordat 1940.
[120] Article XI, Concordat 1940.
[121] Article XII, Concordat 1940.

activity which was incompatible with Canon Law,[122] and they had to perform military service giving religious assistance in the Portuguese army.[123] The fraudulent use of ecclesiastical habits was condemned with the same penalties as the illegal use of the uniform of public employees.[124]

4) The Catholic Church had full freedom to establish schools and seminars. These schools were financed with public funds.[125]

Education in all kinds of state schools should be oriented according to the principles of the Catholic doctrine and morals, traditional in the country. Catholic religious education was offered to all students if parents did not say anything to the contrary.[126]

5) The Concordat recognized full civil effects for Catholic marriage.[127] Its article XXIV imposed the renouncing of divorce in the case of Catholic marriages. This restriction disappeared in 1975.

In the case of Catholic marriages, the ecclesiastical tribunals had exclusive competence in the procedures of nullity. These sentences, pronounced by the religious tribunals had automatic civil effects, with the only requirement being its communication to the territorially competent *Tribunal da Relação do Estado*.[128]

III. The constitution of 2 April 1976

After the so called *Revolution of Carnations* of 2 April 1974, a new democratic Constitution was enforced two years later, on 2 April 1976, which is still in force. This Constitution has coexisted with the Concordat of 1940, (with the only modification of 1975), for almost three decades.

This Constitution established:

1) The principle of equality and non-discrimination for religious ideas.[129]

2) The recognition of the freedom of conscience, religion and worship:[130]

   a) These rights are inviolable.

---

[122] Article XIII, Concordat 1940.
[123] Article XIV, Concordat 1940.
[124] Article XV, Concordat 1940.
[125] Article XX, Concordat 1940.
[126] Article XXI, Concordat 1940.
[127] Articles XXII and XXII, Concordat 1940.
[128] Article XXV, Concordat 1940.
[129] Article 13, Portuguese Constitution.
[130] Article 41, Portuguese Constitution.

b) Nobody may be prosecuted, deprived of rights, declared exempted of duties or civil obligations, because of his convictions or religious practices.

c) Nobody may be asked about their religious convictions by public authorities. The only exception is for statistical purposes. These statistics will not allow the individualization of results.

d) Religious groups and State were separated.

e) Freedom and religion, and the right of access to public mass media were recognized.

f) Objection of conscience, according to legal dispositions was also recognized.

3) The freedom of teaching.[131]

4) The right to found a family, marriage and divorce, independently of the form of celebration.[132]

IV. The law 16/2001, of 22 June 2001, of religious freedom

The Law 16/2001, of 22 June 2001, of religious freedom, replaced the *old* Law of 1971, from the dictatorship times.

In its first chapter this new Law proclaimed the freedom of conscience, worship and religion, and established 5 basic principles:

1) The principle of equality and non-discrimination for religious reasons.[133]

2) Separation between Church and State.

3) The State is not denominational, that means:

   a) That the State does not adopt any religion as official. The State has nothing to say about religious matters.

   b) The protocol of State should not give privileges to any religious faith.

   c) The Portugal State may not program education and culture, according to religious directives.

---

[131] Article 43, Portuguese Constitution.
[132] Article 36, Portuguese Constitution.
[133] According to MENDES MACHADO, it does not means the consolidation of the *status quo* of privilege for the Catholic Church. MENDES MACHADO, JONATAS EDUARDO. *Liberdade religiosa numa comunidade constitucional inclusiva. Dos direitos da verdade aos direitos dos ciudadãos.* Coimbra Editora. Coimbra. 1996. Pages 178 y 179.

d) Public education is denominational.

 4) The principle of cooperation with religious groups, in *consideração a sua representatividade*.

 5) Principle of tolerance. This principle should be applied for the resolution of conflicts in the exercise of the rights of freedom of conscience, religion and worship, by people of different faiths.

> Nevertheless, the dispositions contained in this Law about religious freedom concerning the Churches and Religious Communities *inscribed* or *settled*[134] in Portugal, is not applied to the Catholic Church, unless there is a special agreement with the Catholic Church.[135]

The right of freedom of religion, conscience and worship is defined with a double content:

1) A first content is *positive*. It should include the rights:[136]

   a) To have, not to have, or to leave a religion.

   b) To choose freely, to change or to abandon one's own beliefs.

   c) To practice or not to practice worship, in private or in public.

   d) To profess one's own beliefs, and to proselytize.

   e) To inform and to be informed about religion. To teach and to learn about religion.

   f) To meet, to demonstrate, and to associate with others, according to each person's religious beliefs, with the only limits contemplated in articles 45 and 46 of the Portuguese Constitution.

   g) To choose names for one's own sons and daughters, according to the religious onomastic of the professed religion.

   h) To produce scientific, literary or artistic works.

---

[134] The original Portuguese expression is with declaration of *radicação*. This declaration of *radicação* or *settlement*, may be obtained after 30 years of existence in Portugal, or 60 years in another country.
[135] Article 58, Law 16/2001.
[136] Article 8, Law 16/2001.

2) A second content is *negative*. It means that:[137]
   a) Nobody may be obliged to profess a religious belief, to practice or attend worship, or receive religious assistance or religious propaganda.
   b) Nobody may be forbidden to be member, or not, of a religious group, church or religious community.
   c) Nobody may be asked about his religious beliefs, with the only exception of statistics. These statistics do not allow the individualization of results.

Parents have the right to educate their children, according to their own convictions on religious matters. The parents should respect the moral and physical integrity of their children. Minors, after the age of 16, may realize their own options about freedom of conscience, religion and worship.[138]

A religious group may teach religion in public schools, if it is demanded by a group of ten students. It is not necessary to obtain the previous administrative declaration of *settlement*, – in Portuguese: *radicação* –, or an especial agreement of cooperation, as happens in Spain.[139]

Freedom of conscience covers the right of objection of conscience against Laws in conflict with internal convictions. The only limits are the rights and obligations recognized by the Constitution, and the terms of the subsequent legislation about the exercise of that objection of conscience.[140]

The Law of religious freedom also recognizes the right of religious attendance in public institutions,[141] the right of celebrating religious festivities,[142] and a very favourable status for religious ministers.[143]

The State recognizes civil effects to religious marriages celebrated by a religious minister of a church or religious group *settled* in Portugal.[144] These

---

[137] Article 9, Law 16/2001.
[138] Article 11, Law 16/2001.
[139] Law-ranking decree 329/1998, of November 2. (Diário da República, 1st Series. Number 253). Its article 6 fixed a minimum number of 10 students, and its is possible to concentrate students from different classes from the same level, and even from different levels, if it is necessary. The limit of students in class is 25. This Law-ranking decree is previous to the Law 16/2001, and for this reason the previous declaration of *settlement* or *radicação* is not required.
[140] Article 12.1, Law 16/2001.
[141] Article 13, Law 16/2001.
[142] Article 14, Law 16/2001.
[143] Article 15, Law 16/2001.
[144] Article 19.1, Law 16/2001. These provisions are developed at the Ranking-Law Decree 324/2007, of 28 September 2007.

provisions are more generous with religious minorities that the Spanish or Italian legislations, where the limit is narrower, because in Spain and Italy, the recognition of the marriage of religious minorities depends on a previous Agreement of Cooperation with the State.

The legal concept of "church" or "religious community" is deliberately wide, because it includes all forms of organization for carrying out a religious purpose.[145]

Churches and religious communities have a wide internal autonomy of organization.[146] Religious groups also have the freedom of religious teaching,[147] and the right of access to public radio and television. They should be consulted previously in the case of administrative decisions concerning territorial and urban planning.[148]

Religious groups enjoy a very generous catalogue of tax exemptions and benefits. Tax payers enjoy the possibility of a deduction of 25% of the amount of money donated to a religious group *settled* in Portugal, with the limit of 15% of the tax quota.[149]

Tax payers may assign the 0,5% of the tax quota in the Income Tax for religious purposes or charity, for a religious group or church, with a previous declaration of *settlement* in Portugal, if this religious beneficiary has previously required this possibility.[150] Article 65.1 of the Law 16/2001, establishes a condition for enjoying this 0,5% of the income tax quota, this condition consists of a previous renunciation by the religious group of its tax benefits in Value Added Tax, or VAT.

Portuguese legislation is more generous in that point than the Italian or Spanish Law, because in Italy and Spain, the church or religious group that wants to enjoy these tax benefits, needs a previous Agreement of Cooperation with the State, and this is a heavy "legal" and "political" filter, a political and discretional decision. In Portugal that Agreement it is not necessary, because it is enough with the *settlement* recognition.

A Commission of Religious Freedom was also created. It is an independent and advisory institution of the Government and the Parliament.[151]

---

[145] Article 20, Law 16/2001.
[146] Article 22, Law 16/2001.
[147] Article 24.1, Law 16/2001.
[148] Article 28, Law 16/2001.
[149] Article 32.3, Law 16/2001.
[150] Article 32.4, Law 16/2001.
[151] Articles 52 y 53, Law 16/2001.

Commission of Religious Freedom has been integrated by prestigious members, with an open and wide way of thinking, and it has been especially flexible giving *settlement* recognitions to the Portuguese religious minorities. After less than a decade of work, the Commission has informed positively in relation to the recognition of *settlement*, for more of two dozens of religious groups and communities.

That is in contrast with the restrictive policy of the Spanish Commission of Religious Freedom that has informed positively on the recognition of *settlement* in Spain, the so called *declaración de notorio arraigo*, for only 7 religious minorities: Evangelicals, Muslims, Jews, Mormons, Jehovah Witnesses and Buddhists. In Spain there are only three religious groups with and agreement of cooperation with the State, Evangelicals, Muslims, Jews, and only they enjoy a limited catalogue of tax benefits, that do not include either VAT benefits, or a 0,5 tax quota in the Income Tax.

V. The new concordat of 2004

The new Portuguese Concordat of 2004,[152] replaced the old Concordat of 1940, from the times of Salazar's dictatorship, and entered into force on 18 December 2004.[153]

The main thematic areas of the Concordat are:

1) Recognition of legal personality and internal autonomy for the Catholic Church.

The Portuguese Republic recognizes the legal personality of the Catholic Church,[154] and its right to exercise its apostolic mission, and the public and free exercise of its activities.[155]

The appointment and removal of Catholic bishops are an exclusive competence of the Holy See. The Holy See will communicate its decision to

---

[152] ALONSO PÉREZ, JOSÉ IGNACIO. *Appunti per una prima lettura del Concordato del 18 maggio 2004 tra la Santa Sede e la Repubblica Portoghese*. In: *Ius Ecclesiae. Rivista Internazionale di Diritto Canonico*. Volume XVI. Number. 2. May-August 2004. Pages 532 to 546. CORRAL, CARLOS y SANTOS, JOSÉ LUIS. *Concordato con Portugal de 2004*. In: *Laicidad y Libertades. Escritos Jurídicos*. Number 4. December 2004. Pages 499 to 523. COSTA GOMES, MANUEL SATURINO. *A Concordata 2004: Comentário peral*. In: Estudos sobre a nova Concordata. Santa Sé – República Portuguesa. Lusitania Canonica. Number 11. Series A. Universidade Católica. Editora. Lisboa. 2006. Pages 297 to 312.
[153] *Aviso 23/2005, do Ministério dos Negócios Estrangeiros*, published in: *Diário da República*, 26 January 2005. 1st Series A.
[154] Article 1.2, of the Portuguese Concordat of 2004.
[155] Article 2, of the Portuguese Concordat of 2004.

the Portuguese Republic, but the public authorities will not enjoy any right of veto.[156]

It is recognizes also the professional secret of catholic priests.[157] Ecclesiastical individuals are exempt from the charge of jury and the condition of member of civil courts or tribunals, etc. or any civil charge incompatible with Canon Law provisions.[158]

2) Recognition of canon law marriage and the sentences of canon law tribunals.

The Portuguese Republic recognizes civil effects for marriage celebrated according to cannon law provisions, from the moment of its inscription in the Civil Register.[159]

A married couple that celebrates canon law marriage, will assume towards the Catholic Church, (not towards the State), the commitment of respecting canon law regulations about marriage, especially its essential characteristics of stability and indissolubility. The Holy See proclaims solemnly the doctrine of the Catholic Church about the indissolubility of marriage, and the Church reminds the married couple of their obligation not to use civil divorce.[160] This commitment is only in the sphere of relationships between the Church and its believers, and it does not include any effect for the State. Catholic couples may have access to divorce, without any civil restriction.

Ecclesiastic sentences and decisions about nullity of marriage, may produce civil effects after their previous *revision and confirmation*, (that means that they will not have direct and automatic civil effects), by the competent civil authority. In this sense, the civil tribunal should verify all these points:[161]

1) That the canonical sentences and resolutions are authentic.

2) That the canonical sentences and resolutions are emanated by a competent canonical court.

3) If there were full observance of the principles of contradiction and equality.

4) That the recognition is not against international public Law principles of the Portuguese Republic.

---

[156] Article 8, paragraphs 4 and 5 of the Portuguese Concordat of 2004.
[157] Article 5, of the Portuguese Concordat of 2004.
[158] Article 6, of the Portuguese Concordat of 2004.
[159] Article 13.1, of the Portuguese Concordat of 2004.
[160] Article 15, of the Portuguese Concordat of 2004.
[161] Article 16, of the Portuguese Concordat of 2004.

Points 3) and 4) are especially important, because we cannot forget the importance of the commitment included in articles 6 and 12 of the European Convention of Human Rights. We should not forget the case *Pellegrini versus Italy*, of 20 July 2001. In the *Pellegrini* case, Italy was condemned by the European Court of Human Rights because the Court of Appeal of Florence validated a canonical sentence on a marriage process in the canonical courts without the more essential warranties of procedure.[162]

3) Religious assistance.

Religious assistance for all the members of the Portuguese Army,[163] hospitals or establishments of health, assistance, education, prisons, or similar organisations, is recognized.[164]

4) Education.

The Portuguese Republic assumes the commitment of cooperation with parents in their children's instruction. Public authorities will warrant the catholic religion and moral education in public schools, and in all non-university establishments of education, without any discrimination.

Attendance of religion lectures depends on a previous declaration by the child, if he has full legal capacity. Otherwise a previous declaration is necessary in that sense from the parents, or legal representatives, of the child.

Religious teaching will be given by teachers with a previous ecclesiastical declaration of *suitability*. Teaching contents will be defined by the ecclesiastical authorities, according to the general orientations of the Portuguese educative system.[165]

The Catholic Church has the right of opening seminars and other institutions of ecclesiastical education, without state supervision. The recognition of these studies of ecclesiastical formation will be done by the State, without any discrimination regarding other studies of identical nature.[166]

---

[162] DIENI, EDOARDO. *L'arrêt Pellegrini contre Italie de la Cour Européenne des Droits de L'Homme*. In: Revue de Droit Canonique. Volume 51/1. 2001. Pages 141 to 161. TORRES GUTIÉRREZ, ALEJANDRO. *El Derecho a contraer Matrimonio*. (Artículo 12 del Convenio Europeo de Derechos Humanos). In: JAVIER GARCÍA ROCA y PABLO SANTOLAYA (Coordinadores.) La Europa de los derechos. El Convenio Europeo de Derechos Humanos. Centro de Estudios Constitucionales. Madrid. 2005. Pages 621 to 635.
[163] Article 17, of the Portuguese Concordat of 2004.
[164] Article 18, of the Portuguese Concordat of 2004.
[165] Article 19, of the Portuguese Concordat of 2004.
[166] Article 20, of the Portuguese Concordat of 2004.

The Catholic Church has a teaching right at all educative levels, without any discrimination.[167]

5) Patrimonial matters.

The properties considered by article VI of the Concordat of 7 May 1940, as national monuments or properties of public interest, continue under the use of the Catholic Church. The State assumes the commitment of their conservation, repair and restoration, in agreement with the Catholic Church. The Catholic Church will assume their custody and will determine the timetable of visits.[168]

No temple, building or object related to Catholic worship, may be demolished, occupied, transported, repaired or assigned to another purpose by the State or another public entity, without the previous agreement of the competent ecclesiastical authority, for reasons of public necessity.[169]

The objects related to worship, that are to be found in some public Museums, will always be ceded for the religious ceremonies of the temple of origin, if these temples are in the same locality as they are kept. The ecclesiastical authorities assume the responsibility for their custody. A temporary transfer of these goods may be possible, but they should be used properly.[170]

It is necessary to consult the competent ecclesiastical authorities in the case of requisition or expropriation for reasons of public utility. No act of appropriation is possible without the previous withdrawal of its sacred character by the ecclesiastical authorities.[171]

The State must reserve enough land for religious objectives and needs. For this reason, the instruments of territorial and urban development must foresee the reservation of these spaces for religious aims. The Catholic Church has the right to a previous audience.[172]

6) Economic matters.

The Concordat recognizes a wide chapter of tax benefits,[173] but the Concordat introduces the taxation of Catholic priests for their incomes obtained during the exercise of their religious functions.

---

[167] Article 21, of the Portuguese Concordat of 2004.
[168] Article 22.1, of the Portuguese Concordat of 2004.
[169] Article 24.1, of the Portuguese Concordat of 2004.
[170] Article 22, paragraphs 2 and 3 of the Portuguese Concordat of 2004.
[171] Article 24.2 of the Portuguese Concordat of 2004.
[172] Article 25 of the Portuguese Concordat of 2004.
[173] Article 26 of the Portuguese Concordat of 2004.

It is also foresees the possibility of the inclusion of the Catholic Church in the so called "tax assignation" of 0, 5% of the tax quota in the Income taxation. It requires a previous agreement with the Catholic Church.[174]

7) Interpretation and execution of the Agreement.

The Holy See and the Portuguese Republic agree on the constitution of a parity Commission, for the monitoring of the Agreement.[175]

The juridical situations and the constituted rights derived from the Concordat of 7 may 1940 and the *Acordo Missionário* are ensured.[176]

The Portuguese Republic and the Holy See will proceed to the elaboration, revision and publication of complementary legislation. To this aim, they should make the pertinent juridical consultations.[177]

If we analyze this framework, we conclude that there are many open questions. The resolution of these questions will depend not only on the broadminded approach of the public authorities, but also on the cleverness of the ecclesiastical representatives.

---

[174] Article 27 of the Portuguese Concordat of 2004.
[175] Article 29 of the Portuguese Concordat of 2004.
[176] Article 31 of the Portuguese Concordat of 2004.
[177] Article 32 of the Portuguese Concordat of 2004.

Historical Background of the Relationship between the State and Churches in Hungary

Adam Rixer

1. The beginnings

Western Christianity was adopted in Hungary in the first millennium. St Stephen, the first king of Hungary (997–1038), laid down the foundations of the Catholic Church. Although Hungary has been intensely influenced by Western Christianity throughout history, there has always been a presence of Orthodox minorities. Reformation was highly successful in the 16th century and the Reformed Church became the wellspring of national cultural development. Even though Counter-Reformation was successful, the country has preserved a high level of denominational pluralism.[178] The coexistence of Catholics and Protestants, though not wholly free of conflicts, proved to be the source of an enrichment of both national and local culture.[179]

Tensions between Catholics and Protestants were central to political conflicts between the sixteenth and nineteenth centuries,[180] although they were often combined and overshadowed by other allegiances, such as pro- and anti-Habsburg loyalty. The tradition of tolerance was also present, particularly in the politics of the Transylvanian Principality and the liberal revolution of 1848[181] served as another major historical source of the legitimacy of religious toleration.[182]

In 1895 religious freedom for all was proclaimed.[183] Public worship was nevertheless restricted to acknowledged communities. The law made it possible for religious communities to become acknowledged.[184] As a consequence of the evolution of customary law and of independent executive actions, three clusters of churches had emerged by the nineteenth century: co-opted, registered and tolerated. No explicit legal definitions

---

[178] http://www.euresisnet.eu/Pages/ReligionAndState/HUNGARY.aspx
[179] Ibid.
[180] Csizmadia Andor (ed.): Magyar állam- és jogtörténet. [Legal History of Hungary], Tankönyvkiadó, Budapest, 1991., pp. 188-190.
[181] Act 20. of 1848 on the Freedom of Religion
[182] John T. S. Madeley – Zsolt Enyedi (ed.): Special Issue on Church and State in Contemporary Europe. The Chimera of Neutrality. In: West European Politics, Vol. 26, No. 1, January 2003., A Frank Cass Journal, p. 158
[183] Act 43. of 1895
[184] http://www.euresisnet.eu/Pages/ReligionAndState/HUNGARY.aspx

were attached to these labels, but according to ministerial interpretations they referred to the level of legal state protection.[185] The co-opted churches received administrative assistance for church tax collection, and the government gave subsidies and covered part of the clergy's salaries.

In the first part of the nineteenth century the Catholic, Calvinist, Lutheran, and (since 1790) Orthodox churches were considered co-opted. There existed some room for the movement in the hierarchy of churches: the Unitarians became co-opted in 1848, and the Jews were registered in 1874 and then co-opted in 1895. In 1905 the Baptist Church, and in 1916 the Islamic religion, were accepted as registered. The anti-liberal turn in Hungarian politics at the end of the nineteenth century, and particularly after 1918-19, brought the major churches and the state into a closer union however, in both symbolic and financial terms.[186]

Since the Counter-Reformation, the Catholic Church has had unquestionable numerical and political primacy over the other denominations.

2. The era of socialism

After World War II democratic structures were abolished, e.g. human rights, when the Communists took over power. The clergy and lay believers were systematically harassed by the Communist authorities. Religious freedom ceased to exist.[187] Particularly during the early years of communist rule, the churches had faced extensive persecution by the regime. Many members of the clergy had been openly hostile to the new government at its inception. The new secular authorities, for their part, denounced such attitudes as traitorous, and they mistrusted the churches as a source of opposition. [188]

The most protracted case of tension and open conflict concerned the Roman Catholic Church. In 1945 the church was deprived of its landed property in the first postwar land reform, which occurred before the communist takeover. Most Catholic religious orders (fifty-nine of a total of sixty-three groups) were dissolved in 1948, when religious schools were also taken over by the state. Most Catholic associations and clubs, who numbered about 4000, were forced to disband. A number of the clergy were imprisoned and prosecuted for political resistance to the communist regime, most notably Cardinal Jozsef Mindszenty, primate of the Catholic Church in Hungary. In 1950 about 2500 monks and nuns, about one-quarter of the total in Hungary,

---

[185] John T. S. Madeley – Zsolt Enyedi (ed.), op. cit., p. 159.
[186] Ibid.
[187] http://www.euresisnet.eu/Pages/ReligionAndState/HUNGARY.aspx
[188] http://countrystudies.us/hungary

were deported. Authorities banned sixty-four of sixty-eight functioning religious newspapers and journals. Although in 1950 the Catholic Church accepted an agreement with the state that forced church officials to take a loyalty oath to the Constitution, relations between the church and the state remained strained throughout the decade.[189] During the 1960s, the two sides gradually reached an accommodation. In 1964 the state concluded a major agreement with the Vatican, the first of its kind in a communist state. The document ratified certain episcopal appointments already made by the church, but it did not settle Mindszenty's long-standing case. Like it had happened before in the 50s, the agreement mandated (stipulated) that certain individuals in positions in the church were obliged to take an oath of allegiance to the Constitution and the laws of the country. However, this oath was to be binding only to the extent that the country's laws were not in opposition to the tenets of the Catholic faith. The church conceded the state's right to approve the selection of high church officials. Under the agreement, the Hungarian Roman Catholic Church could staff its Papal Institute in Rome with priests endorsed by the government, and each year every diocese in the country would send a priest to Rome to attend the institute. For its part, the government promised not to interfere with the institute's work.[190]

Following the agreement, many vacant church posts were filled. Gradually, the organizational structure of the church was reestablished, and congregations became active again. The church began to take a role in the ceremonial life of the country. Relations between church and state warmed particularly after 1974, when the Vatican removed Mindszenty from his office (in 1971 Mindszenty received permission to leave the country after spending many years in the American embassy in Budapest, where he had fled to escape detention by the authorities). The new primate, Cardinal Laszlo Lekai, who held office from 1976 to 1986, sponsored a policy of "small steps," through which he sought to reconcile differences between church and state and enhance relations between the two through "quiet, peaceful dialogue." He urged Catholics to be loyal citizens of the state and simultaneously to seek personal and communal salvation through the church.[191]

Evidence suggests that a serious falling away from religion among Catholics (especially a drop in attendance at church services) occurred only during the 1960s and 1970s, ironically during the period when the government no

---

[189] Ibid.
[190] http://countrystudies.us/hungary
[191] Ibid.

longer energetically persecuted the church. Some observers have suggested that in the 1950s the church earned popularity as an anticommunist institution because of the widespread dissatisfaction with material, political, and cultural trends within the country. As conditions improved, the church no longer served as a focal point for the disaffected. Some Catholics, both lay and clerical, felt that Lekai, in his eagerness to smooth relations between church and state, went too far in compromising the church's position.[192]

The Catholic Church of the 1980s had difficulty providing adequate services to all communities. Its clergymen were aging and decreasing in number. Whereas in 1950 the church had had 3583 priests and 11.538 monks and nuns, in 1986 it had only about 2600 priests and a mere 250 monks and nuns. It was clear by this time, however, that the church was reaping tangible benefits from its relationship with the state. For example, in the 1980s the Catholic orders of the Benedictines, the Franciscans, the Piarists, and Our Lady's School Sisters were again functioning in limited numbers. A new order of nuns, the Sisters of Our Lady of Hungary, received permission to organize in 1986. In the 1980s, the Catholic Church had six seminaries for training priests and a theological academy in Budapest.[193]

After the communist takeover, the historic Protestant churches became even more thoroughly integrated into the new state system than the Catholic Church. They were not a source of organized dissent. The Reformed (Calvinist), the Unitarian, and the Lutheran churches all reached accommodation with the government in the late 1940s (so did the small Greek Orthodox and the Jewish communities). These agreements guaranteed the Protestants the right to worship and brought about some financial support (contingent after 1949 on the loyalty oath). Some Protestant leaders praised the agreements as heralding a new era in which all religions would be treated equally. However, a number of the Reformed clergy and their followers became active supporters of the Revolution of 1956.[194] After the Revolution failed, many of these people joined "free churches" (including the Baptist, the Methodist, and the Seventh-Day Adventist churches), which functioned apart from the historic Protestant churches.[195]

In 1986, *according to Western estimates*, about 67.5 percent of the population was Roman Catholic (not all of them practising believers...), 20 percent was

---

[192] http://countrystudies.us/hungary
[193] Ibid.
[194] Szathmáry Béla: Jogi és egyházjogi ismeretek. [Introduction into law and ecclesiastical law] Századvég Kiadó, Budapest, 2003., p. 106-107.
[195] http://countrystudies.us/hungary

Reformed (Calvinist), 5 percent was unaffiliated, and 5 percent was Lutheran (its members were in particular the German and Slovak minorities but also it included many ethnic Magyars). Other Christian denominations included Uniates, Orthodox, and various small Protestant groups, such as Baptists, Methodists, Seventh- Day Adventists, and Mormons. Most of these smaller groups were affiliated with the national Council of Free Churches and were dubbed free churches as a group. The country also had 65.000 to 100.000 practicing (?) Jews (according to Western estimates). The remainder of the population did not subscribe to any religious creed or organization. Nor was any single church or religion particularly associated with the national identity in the popular mind, as was the Catholic Church in Poland.[196]

Western observers concluded that although the country possessed about 1 million practicing believers, religion did not provide a viable alternative value system that could compete with the predominant secularism and materialism promoted both by the government and by trends within an increasingly modern society. Thus, religion was unlikely to become a vehicle for dissent as in Poland.[197] In consequence of the said, after 1989 – thanks to secularisation – churches operating in Hungary had/have to reconsider how to address people and proclaim the Gospel to people who were not born within the context of any church.[198]

A noteworthy phenomenon of the early 1980s was the appearance of hundreds of intensely active prayer and meditation groups within the Catholic and the Protestant congregations. Some of these groups came into conflict with the church hierarchies over military service and other aspects of cooperation with the government.[199]

The regime of the Communistic era tried to exclude churches from the spheres of social life and paralelly it made efforts to match believers of particular churches against the clergy of the same church.[200] Moreover the State Office for Church Affairs (Állami Egyházügyi Hivatal) manipulated churches and their members using the classic tool of division (*divide et impera*); for example it established (set up) the so called "békepapság" [movement of lay "peace priests"] or it tolerated the newly created Catholic

---

[196] Ibid.
[197] http://countrystudies.us/hungary
[198] Ábrahám – Egey: Learn from Me. Károli Gáspár University of the Hungarian Reformed Church, Budapest, 2001., p. 105
[199] http://countrystudies.us/hungary
[200] Tomka Miklós: Vallás és társadalom Magyarországon. [Religion and Society in Hungary] Pázmány Társadalomtudomány 4., Budapest – Piliscsaba, 2006., p. 133.

community ("Bulányisták", "Bokor Közösség") which altered in some teachings and practises from the „mainstream" Hungarian Catholic Church.

By the 1970s and 1980s, churches were free to worship within their own buildings. The situation did not change until 1989.[201]

The Constitution formally guaranteed freedom of conscience and religion even in those decades in question. Until 1989, however, these guarantees were severely circumscribed by the State Office for Church Affairs, which regulated the activities of the churches. On June 15, 1989, the government abolished this office. In its place, the government planned to establish a "National Church Council" that would act as a "consultative organization", not as an instrument for the control of the churches. In addition, the Ministry of Culture assumed responsibility for church affairs. Also in 1989, the government submitted for public debate new "Principles of a Law on Freedom of Conscience, the Right of Free Exercise of Religion, and Church Affairs." The document, prepared by representatives of the churches, banned discrimination against believers, acknowledged the churches as legal entities, and recognized their equality before the law. Yet in the late 1980s, the state's financial support of all major churches continued to give it considerable leverage in influencing church affairs.[202]

Between 1945 and 1986, religious communities erected or repaired 306 Roman Catholic, 46 Calvinist (Reformed), 33 Lutheran, and 23 Uniate churches. Congregations of the free churches built 185 new structures, and the Jewish community built a new synagogue. The various denominations maintained their own modest publishing organs that produced newspapers, periodicals, and books. Occasionally, religious services were on the radio. The various churches and denominations each supported (collectively, in the case of the free churches) at least one theological academy or college for the training of the clergy. However, the number of students was small; 75 students graduated out of a total of 648 students enrolled in such institutions in 1987.[203]

To sum it up, we have to emphasize that the very end of the '80s led to a momentous change within the state – church relationship, Those were revolutionary years – without exaggeration, as long as a revolution can be defined as "a sudden or momentous change in a situation".[204]

---

[201] http://www.euresisnet.eu/Pages/ReligionAndState/HUNGARY.aspx
[202] http://countrystudies.us/hungary
[203] Ibid.
[204] Gordon Ferguson: Revolution! The World-Changing Church in the Book of Acts. DPI, 1998., p. 14.

3. Development of the voluntary sector – historical overview

Despite the centralization of the economy and society under State socialism between 1947 and 1989, foundations and voluntary associations have a long tradition in Hungary that reaches back well into the 13th century. In contrast to most other European countries, however, religious institutions have not been the dominating force in the initial development of the Hungarian nonprofit sector,[205] though there are some authors who attach bigger importance to those religious entities, emphasizing that the lay brotherhoods maintaining different "social" institutions all pledged themselves to cooperate with the Catholic monasteries, etc.[206] The Hungarian monarchy saw its power threatened by the feudal lords and the Catholic Church alike. Challenged by the nobility as well as the clergy, the monarchy turned to the citizens of the "free royal cities" for support. Consequently, to win and maintain such support, the monarchy granted citizens numerous civic rights and privileges. These privileges to the citizens in the "free royal cities" helped the development of a citizenry that was willing and able to create social institutions outside the arena of the Catholic Church. For instance, in 1309, in Pozsony, then among the largest towns in Hungary, citizens attempted to seize ownership of a local hospital from a monastic order.[207] The secular hospitals and alms-houses in the cities of the 14th and 15th century were mostly financed by private donations, bequests, and contributions by guilds. Nevertheless all these entities had had religious goals connected with their social aims.[208] These early examples of nonprofit organizations in Hungary employed very few staff and were mostly run by volunteers. Church foundations were usually created by bequests and run by equestrian orders.[209] Secular foundations independent of the Catholic hierarchy began to appear in the 16th century. A first law regulating foundations was enacted in 1723. This law gave the King the right to control

---

[205] Kuti, Éva. "Defining the Nonprofit Sector: Hungary." *Working Papers of the Johns Hopkins Comparative Nonprofit Sector Project*, no. 13, edited by Lester M. Salamon and Helmut K. Anheier. Baltimore: The Johns Hopkins Institute for Policy Studies, 1993., p. 2.
[206] Somogyi: A középkori Magyarország szegényügye. [Poverty Affairs of the Medieval Hungary] Bp., Stephaneum, 1941, p. 20.
[207] Hahn, Géza. *A magyar egészségügy története* [The History of Health Services in Hungary]. Budapest: Medicina,1960., p. 11., quoted in Kuti 1993, p. 2.
[208] Béli Gábor: Magyar jogtörténet. A tradicionális jog. [Hungarian Legal History. The Traditional Law] Dialóg Campus Kiadó, Budapest – Pécs, 1999. – 371 p., p. 55.
[209] Bán Péter: Magyar Történelmi Fogalomtár. [Compilation of Notions of the Hungarian History] Gondolat, Budapest, 1989., p. 19.

the activities and the financial accounts of the foundations.[210] Later, this control became the task and responsibility of the central, regional and local governments.[211] Cooperation between private foundations and public institutions emerged at an early stage in the development of educational, cultural, and health services in Hungary. Moreover, In the seventeenth century, several cities mandated affluent citizens to bequest some money or property to public hospitals. Some cities (Modor, 1664; Kőszeg, 1699) declared testaments of wealthy citizens that failed to include donations to public welfare institutions as void. On the other hand, when the Jesuit order was dissolved in 1773, the government did not nationalize its properties. Instead, an Education Fund was established which worked as an independent public law foundation.[212] Similarly, when the largest Catholic university was secularized, it did not become a public institution; rather, it became a self-governing public law foundation. The city of Pest pioneered early examples of what became a common arrangement between public and private institutions in the second half of the nineteenth century. In 1842, public and private contributions co-financed the establishment of an orphanage. The building was provided by the local government (municipality), whereas the operating costs were covered by private donations.[213] Foundations contributed to the financing of public welfare institutions in various ways: there were "foundation beds" in many public hospitals, and "foundation places" in many public schools, universities, orphanages, and shelters. Other foundations were set up to provide social services from buildings donated by the government. This general pattern of cooperation between foundations and local governments functioned fairly well, and remained in effect until World War II.[214]

The development of the voluntary sector accelerated again only after the "Compromise of 1867" between Hungary and the Habsburg Court. The "Compromise" granted Hungary far-reaching independence from the

---

[210] Kecskés, László. "Az alapítványi jog fejlődése" [The Development of the Legal Regulation of Foundations]. *Magyar Jog* 2 (1988), p. 111, quoted in Kuti 1993, p. 2.

[211] Szuromi Szabolcs: A kegyes alapítványok jogállása Magyarországon a korábbi és a hatályos egyházjog, valamint az állami egyházjogi normák tükrében. [The Legal Status of Pietic Foundations in Hungary in Accordance with former and valid Ecclesiastical Law] Jogtörténeti Szemle 2004/1., p. 17.

[212] Karácsonyi, János. *Magyarország egyháztörténete főbb vonásaiban 970-től 1900-ig* [The Main Events of the History of Churches in Hungary from 970 till 1900]. Budapest: Könyvértékesítő Vállalat, 1985., p. 319-322, quoted in Kuti 1993, p. 2.

[213] Balázs, Magdolna. "Az alapítványi élet indulása Magyarországon" [The Beginnings of the Foundation Development in Hungary]. *Esély* 1 (1991), p. 85, quoted in Kuti 1993, p. 2.

[214] Kuti, Éva 1993., p 2.

Austrian crown with the exception of financial, military and foreign affairs. A Decree of 1873 regulated voluntary associations.[215] In 1912, regulations required voluntary associations to seek the approval of the Ministry of Internal Affairs for incorporation.[216] The same ministry also assumed the right to limit and even to ban voluntary associations if their activities were found detrimental to the State. This regulation remained in force until 1945. Despite these strict conditions, almost all social, professional, religious and age-related groups formed voluntary organizations. Even the worker and peasant movements and other political groups suspicious of the authorities found ways to create voluntary associations that the State could somehow "tolerate". Many associations proclaimed social and cultural aims. In some cases they served as a disguise for banned political parties, but in most cases they were a simple expression of civil society and the greater cultural variation of urban Hungary. While governments and churches tried to gain some influence over voluntary associations, neither could dominate the voluntary sector as a whole.[217]

---

[215] Dobrovits, Sándor. "Budapest egyesületei" [Voluntary Associations in Budapest]. *Statisztikai Közlemények* 74 (1936), p. 8-11., quoted in Kuti 1993, p. 3.

[216] Szabó, Lajos. *A megújuló egyesületek működésének szabályai* [Legal Rules for the Reviving Voluntary Associations],]. Budapest: Agrárinformációs vállalat, 1989., p. 5., quoted in Kuti 1993, p. 3.

[217] Kuti, Éva., 1993., p. 3.

Church and Society

Religious messages and the world of the media: Trends and experiences in Europe in the field of religious communication and information systems

Marco Ricceri

1. Introduction

In the society of global communication in which we live at present, we see the continuous innovations of information technology, the increasing flow of information, the progressive, almost dizzying growth of the communication networks, all becoming ever larger and more effective; all these factors are deeply transforming the basic life conditions of communities and individuals. In particular, what is defined as a continuous "liquid" revolution (1) is by now changing in depth the way to manage political activity (both with regard to the content of the political messages and to the consent formation), drives the economic development as well as the technological and scientific progress, transforms the social structures starting by the basic communitarian nucleus as the family and has a strong influence on the heritage of ethical values and on the cultural references and the lifestyles of people.

Understanding the nature and extent of these transformations is essential to assessing the relationship between religion and the media, as it allow us to identify those elements that can help to develop it in the most positive ways.

As an introductory remark, it must be said immediately that the complex media system, a major component of structural changes in contemporary society, shows very pronounced characteristics of ambivalence. In fact, it shows simultaneously both strong positive and negative elements, presenting significant opportunities to human progress as well as many risks of regression

To achieve the positive elements and opportunities, every individual and every community should be in the condition: a) to understand the nature and scope of new media, b) to assess with a critical attitude the communication strategies as well as the contents of messages, distinguishing what is good from what is evil and, finally, c) to play an active role in the modern communication society, that is to participate in setting the communication guidelines, political choices and specific initiatives. To understand, to assess, to participate : these are, therefore, the guidances to follow.

This is also the direction in which the European Union as well other international organizations have been working in for some time, with a set of initiatives known by the name *"media literacy"*, with the aim of spreading the practices of education and active participation to the media world. The task is to fight the main negative elements emerging in the mass communication society, especially those related to liability and a critical attitude that currently prevail in the behaviour of individuals and consumers. Initially these initiatives were for the most part dealing with studies and researches, but over time they were not only intensified but more and more combined with acts of political nature, reflecting the importance that is accorded to this area of intervention.

With "media literacy", the EU, UNESCO, and the Council of Europe (just to mention the more heavily involved international organizations) have opened a new scenario in which the final purpose is to promote policies for the correction of the most negative aspects expressed by the world of communication.

This new scenario of European and international commitment is a matter of great novelty that, objectively, is very interesting for the Churches and the possibility of an adequate transmission and understanding of their religious message. In fact, this scenario is fully open to their needs and requests, because it involves the construction of a system of safeguards and measures aimed at ensuring just a proper and positive use of the media, essential to conducting the religious mission through them.

We must, therefore, study in depth, even in terms of a short synthesis, these three aspects that are closely interconnected with each other: 1) *the main trends of change* taking place in the modern mass communication society, with reference to the ambivalence of its positive and negative elements; 2) *the awareness of this problem in the Churches*, the evolution of their thought, their process of adaptation to the new situation, the concrete actions they promoted: as examples, the position of the Catholic Church on this issue is particularly examined as well as some interesting initiatives of the Islamic world being recalled; 3) *the policies on the issue of media literacy* undertaken by EU and other international institutions, and the benefits they can bring to the religious institutions for the effectiveness of their mission.

2. The mass communication society: structural changes

For a proper assessment of the role played by the media in contemporary society, as introduction we refer to the reflections of an authoritative Italian communications sociologist, Gian Maria Fara, president of a primary research institute, Eurispes (2): "Despite the years, the comparison between what Umberto Eco described in the sixties as *apocalyptics* and *integrated*, still today is alive and vibrant. That is, the comparison between those who think the media are useful tools for growth and social and cultural promotion and those who consider them as tools in the service of power for control of the masse*s*". It deals, obviously, with two extreme positions.

2.1   Apocaliptics, Integrated, Committed

The apocalyptics: "On the one hand the apocalyptics, supporters, children and grandchildren of the 'Frankfurt School', meaning that school of thought that just from its start had to face the harshness of authoritarian and totalitarian regimes which marked the European history in the last century." (Incidentally, it should be recalled that the first television broadcast to the world was made in 1935 by Nazi Germany). The central point from which the apocalyptic thinking started was the observation of the limited capability of analysis and reaction by citizens, who were not much equipped to deal with this phenomenon. The explanations for this widespread deficiency were – and still are – of sociological, anthropological, cultural, political order. It deals with a sort of deficiency, they added, which is of a structural nature in itself. This is because the new communication and information technologies produced as a genetic modification in the individuals of our time, as a direct result of an addiction to mediocre content, which leads in turn to a sort of regression of the human species. For Adorno, Popper, Sartori, Bordieu and other thinkers, the more negative effects caused by the media world are, for instance, the strategies of social control, the opinion massification, the stimulation to false needs, the homogenisation of tastes and lifestyles. Hence the very common request among these scholars, for the support of defensive and protective interventions, especially for the most vulnerable and exposed social groups.

The integrated: An opposite position was inspired by a positive vision of the role of the media and expressed by the so-called *integrated*, for which humanity was facing with an ineluctable process, which would help individuals to develop their personal skills. "The integrated – says Fara – had the possibility to live and work within systems of strong and consolidated democracy that had just in the media its representatives and defenders of public opinion, able to influence and monitor the activity of the same governments".

The committed: In fact, the sociologist states, "media are in itself neither good nor bad; nor *is it* decisive, even if not indifferent, to know to whom they belong. Really important are the contents they transmit, the message they transfer to their users". It is not a coincidence, he adds, that "over the years, the two aforementioned positions have been joined by a third: that of so-called committed. Precisely, by people aware of the uselessness to linger the debate about the nature of the media instead to address the attention, on the one hand, on the contents of the media messages and, on the other, on the responsibility and the role of the media consumers".

The real fact which all must face – apocalyptics, integrated, committed – is the great change in the communication society and the whole media world in recent decades. At present, those who are defined as the big, traditional "agents of meaning and orientation", i.e. television, radio, newspapers, and magazines, no longer play that role of main players as they used to do on information, training and education.

Certainly, their function is always very important, especially that of television. But the progress of new information technologies as well the spread of new tools, starting from internet, led to the development of new, privileged ways for the information and knowledge dissemination. In this complex set of new instrumentation, the different systems coexist and interact with each other: the traditional communication tools ("open" television, radio, cinema, papers), personalized media (cable television, digital terrestrial, video on demand), the interactive digital media (computers, mobile phones, IPods); and all of them have their great public square on the internet.

The globalization process was built and organized just on these tools, with science and technology behind them, and, in its turn, shaped a kind of society that is increasingly interconnected and net-like, in which the information and communication paradigms are marked by freedom of access, participation, the possibility for everybody to develop, create, transmit knowledge, messages and news. The scale and the involving nature of this process are the source of the deep social and cultural changes of the modern life.

The same concepts of space and time are upset. New information technologies make any place as near as possible, the exchanges faster, the problems more shared. Incidentally, it is facing this process that Emilio Garlasco (3), an authoritative Italian expert, manager of a multinational company, proposes to substitute the term globalization, preferring to speak of the 'unification'. This is a term that includes both the geo-economic aspects of globalization and the essential aspects of a person's life with reference to the areas in which it operates and acts (home, work, school, society), its capability (intelligence, sentiment, will), its different ages (childhood, adolescence, maturity, old age). In fact, in the present communication society, all of these aspects end up being screened in a single ethical and cultural dimension, a single perceptive place, where everything is taken apart and reassembled with new form, in a process in comparison with the great, an open problem becomes the preservation of the personal and communitarian identity. In this respect, a statement made in 2004 by the American scientist Glover Ferguson, one of the most popular consultants in the world, comes to mind: "In the next few years, micro-sensors of reduced size (already baptized with the term "smart dust") will be widely available – to be planted on men and things – and able to integrate into the network. We are almost at the point of implanting intelligence on all things" (4).

2.2 The awakening of the civil society

However the real point of change, to which Gian Maria Fara draws attention, is the change of the places where mainly the opinions of every individual are formed. These places are always less represented by the traditional media, but rather more and more by the groups of reference and the networks to which he takes part.

In essence, the Italian sociologist says (5), "close to the public and traditional mass-media opinion, a new type of networking public opinion has set up in recent decades, which feeds of daily life. A public opinion which is formed from the bottom and that looks with an increasingly clear suspect at the messages and information transmitted from the top through the usual mass media system. If the tradition of sociological research has accustomed us to think that the development of sense belongs exclusively to the high levels of social organization, the experience of recent years shows, however, a difficulty in the production of meaning and orientation from the top ... free by the constraints of ideological belonging and social control, the public opinion increasingly less accepts to be driven and manipulated by outside, and recover the delegation in white that for a long time had entrusted to the subjects of political and social representation".

We are facing a sort of awakening of the civil society which forms its own opinions, its own collective intelligence, by organizing new sense agencies through the networks, personal blogs, Facebook: in short, through all the tools made available by the continuous ICT evolution. "The greatest opportunity of the network," another scholar, Esther Dyson, writes (6), "is to allow going beyond the selection and start creating. The network is incredibly malleable; allow building communities, to find ideas, to share information and to connect with other people". The result of this process is a situation in which – according to Fara – two different types of public opinion confront each other: "a mass-media and traditional public opinion, on one hand, and a network public opinion, on the other, which confront each other in the no-places of information". It is a situation in which it is difficult to identify the terms of the clash as well those of the admixture, to define the lines of influence that each one carries over the other, but it is especially difficult to draw what shall be the future development perspective of this complex system.

"At no time in history," comments Gian Maria Fara (7) "Has there been such an intensive production of knowledge, but the world does not seem have taken any particular advantage of the opportunities offered by this knowledge evolution. Having available an increasing amount of knowledge and seeing it disseminate so quickly ... let us hope for a qualitatively better world. But apparently it is not enough to be swamped daily information to be able to better define the orientation of our existence. The knowledge and information from which we expected the gift of freedom have become a dazing, confused deluge, an ungovernable ocean that leads to shore an incredible accumulation of waste. In these conditions, what seems to be less is the freedom, the conscious growth of individuals and communities. It is, then, the very large "availability" of knowledge that makes the access to it difficult and prevents that knowledge from penetrating deeply, thus forcing the society to settle for a superficial, instrumental or specialist approach". "We must all still learn – this is the conclusion of the Italian sociologist – to capitalize on the enormous wealth that new technologies make available".

To "learn" to take advantage of the great value and great opportunities offered by the global communication tools, we must first understand their nature, as well as the characteristics of the media culture they produce.

According to an effective and brief description by the Archbishop Claudio Maria Celli, president of the Pontifical Council for Social Communications of the Catholic Church, this multimedia culture is, meanwhile, "less textual and less discursive" because it is a culture in which "the narrativity is broken up into fast images and sounds". Moreover, it is a culture which may be able to be omnipresent, even intrusive, since it reaches the user anywhere through portable media. It is dynamic, as it makes any content likely to be shared, transformed, and multiplied. It is connective, reticular as it facilitates and promotes the links between users, the work by net, although this does not necessarily guarantee the quality of the relationship. It is global and local: global, as the receipt of any message extends to the whole linguistic world in which it is born and beyond; local, because in the same time it gives to the users increasing chances to strengthen at local level their relation systems as well as their identity. It is participatory, since any user is an issuer as well as a consumer. The websites of social networks, where each user enters its own content, are among the most visited in the world. (Incidentally, it is just this new situation which led some authors to speak about the end of the mass-communication, because the whole mass-culture originated by the media is based on a linear – one-way – communication model, where the center is the issuer). "This culture – Archbishop Celli concluded – also transforms the public and private dimensions of life, as it implicitly spreads the idea that everything that happens in concrete life should be transformed into a show". In addition, moreover, the present new digital revolution (digital technology opens the possibility of representing all type of information – video, audio, text, data – linked to a single numerical magnitude) often leads to confusing the real world with the virtual one, with undeniable usefulness to science and the economy (i.e. From testing to production innovation), but also with major risks to the critical spirit and original autonomy of thought of the individuals.

Father Silvio Sassi, superior general of the Catholic St. Paul Society, a religious congregation that has gained great expertise in the communication sector, highlights the very value of the possibilities opened by the particular aspect of interactivity between the issuer and the user. Till now, this relationship has been substantially uni-directional, between the issuer who produces and transmits the message and the user/consumer who is intended to receive it (incidentally, all the structuralism is based on an idea of communication in which the message is to be interpreted in its formulations, according to the intentions of the issuer). But digital revolution radically changes this one-way relationship, to a point of reverse roles, because it opens the possibility for the user to intervene at the same moment the message is formulated. To organize its own website, to be a source of information and data, testify experiences, suggest changes and alternatives; all these allow an increased and active participation by the users. "In essence," Father Sassi states, "the digital revolution lets the breakdown between the issuer and the user disappear in order to evolve the user as a single Chart of reference". In the new communication model more and more "the center becomes the recipient" because ultimately "he is the source, development and purpose of communication". (8)

We are facing, in short, a continuous evolution of technologies and languages, which are developing alongside each other, as autonomous but also complementary realities. Moreover, in the perspective, as pointed out by many experts, among whom Emilio Garlaschè is quoted (9), further radical changes are possible as a result of the present process of technological convergence. This is a convergence, they explain, that should lead to the formation of a single network of digital players, capable of elaborating, storing, reprocessing and transmitting any content, in any form, at any time, to anyone, wherever they are (be it man or machine). This process of convergence, it is stated, does not refer to the single component but the whole structure of the telecommunications system, which is intended to comply with the digital language. By this process, the world of computing and telecommunications ultimately involves and integrates the media in its operational logic. The accessibility of a player in the network is determined by two factors: by the mobility and by the possibility of getting him at a specific address. For the mobility, the comparison is between different solutions linked to different cellular networks; for addressing, internet is overcoming the limitations of the phone numbering. I have access, therefore I exist. If with the support of any interface technology, I have the possibility to access any source of information, the content becomes the central issue of the network, and the problem of ownership of the means of production, reproduction and distribution of content, as Garlaschè claims, proposes new questions of freedom and democracy: political as well economic and cultural.

For the Nobel Prize recipient Jeremy Rifkin, the issue of access is essential: "In the coming era, power will belong to the so-called gatekeepers; those who control access...Also the access relationships are made to create distinctions: distinctions between those who are connected and those who are not...In a society founded on the concept of access, the owner of the communication channels and access to the networks, will determine who plays and who remains outside". (10)

3. The position of the Catholic Church

"If you want to find the source, you have to go up, against the mainstream"

A poem from John Paul II

The Catholic Church has always followed the development of the modern communication society and has carefully considered the characteristics and implications of the new media culture. It is known that the Pope has always had keen interest in the means of mass communication – radio, television, printed paper – and their wide range of use since the beginning, being fully aware that such tools could be of great contribution to the diffusion of the religious message and the evangelization process (do not forget that the meaning of the word *"to communicate"* is *"to make unity with"*).

The documents and the concrete initiatives undertaken over the decades show a significant fact clearly: that the Catholic Church has over time had a highly diversified approach with regard to the media world and the formation of the mass communication society; the Catholic Church has learnt the importance of this phenomenon very quickly. But in the early stage, the prevailing position was mainly characterized by an attitude of great prudence, as well as being defensive. Media were evaluated in a neutral perspective – as instruments that may serve good or evil – but the emphasis was placed mainly on the aspects of danger they could pose to the conscience of the faithful. From here there were constant reminders, which are still there today, created to warn the religious and faithful and to protect them against the risks inherent in new communications media. But gradually, over the years, it has gained a very different position, which is certainly always characterized by great attention and caution, but which is also much more open, receptive and positive.

In what we might identify as a second stage, the Catholic Church, while continuing to consider the media as a neutral tool, shifted the emphasis onto responsibility for its use, calling out to specific tasks, in particular the communication producers. At the same time, the Church confirmed its role as a reference and guarantee for an adequate education to their proper use.

A further stage was marked by the explicit recognition that media was a gift from God and therefore a positive fact in itself. Only the malice of man could organize it and use it for evil. Christians were thus urged to engage in their full and proper use. "I am the voice, not the word," says John the Baptist in the Gospel. The real turning point was marked by the Second Vatican Council which took the importance of the lesson of McLuhan ("the medium is the message") in the sense that the content of the communication is influenced, adapted, modified depending on the communication medium. The Council came to indicate the new media as the "wonderful things", *Inter Mirifica*, (Council Decree), given by God to man. At the Second Vatican Council and in the following papal documents the media have increasingly been seen as a vital new tool for preaching the Gospel, as a new field of evangelization (Encyclical: *Communio et Progressio*), as an essential component of the same evangelization work that is influenced and determined by the new culture and sociality of the contemporary world (Encyclical *Aetatis Nova*).

This is a mature position that clearly recognizes communication as the constitutive factor of a new culture: a new form of civilization (Encyclical *Redemptoris Missio*) that requires not only the church's attention to the proper use of the new instruments, but also to the start of a genuine inculturation process. In summary, the evolution in the position of the Catholic Church moves from considering the media as negative tools of corruption of consciences and society, to considering them as neutral tools, useful for transmitting the Gospel message, the two admitting that they are veritable gifts of God that man should not distort but use properly, and finally, to recognizing that these resources have created a new culture and a new civilization that first should be well understood in its identity, in order to continue to better the evangelisation work.

In recent years, therefore, the Catholic Church has come to develop a position of full acceptance of these tools and has recognized explicitly their value for the progress opportunities they offer to the mankind, although it has continued to express a full awareness of their limits. It is the clear position taken recently by Pope Benedict XVI, who marked a further turning point in this evolutionary process. This happened, for example, when the Pope defined the means of mass communication as a "blessing for all." Additionally in his message for the World Day for Social Communications in 2009, for the first time, he directly addressed young people as the "digital generation", the true protagonists of the "new digital arena", those who mostly understood "the enormous potential of new media".

4. The documents of the Catholic Church. Analysis of an evolutionary process

With reference to the first stage, characterized as mentioned by a negative and defensive orientation on the subject, the first documents date back to XIX century. As an example, we quote the encyclical *"Mirari Vos"* by Pope Gregory XVI in 1832 in which, as part of a general condemnation of the liberalism principles, press freedom is expressly mentioned as one of the evils of the modern society; then the Encyclical *"Quibus Pluribus"* in 1846 in which Pope Pius IX wrote that freedom of press and expression are the basis for the dissemination of bad behaviour. Even his successor, Pope Leo XIII, points out the risks implicit in freedom of press even, as archbishop of Perugia, promoted the foundation of one of the first diocesan newspapers. For this initiative he is celebrated as the Pope of the press.

But it is in 1936 that Catholic Church published the first organic document on communication. The initiative was taken by Pope Pius XI, with the Enciclical *"Vigilanti Cura"* in which he develops a deep evaluation of positive and negative features of a powerful communication medium like the cinema, warning about the risks associated with incorrect use of this tool. Incidentally it should be remembered that Pius XI appointed Gugliemo Marconi as the first director of the Vatican Radio, organized in those days in collaboration with the Jesus Society. On 1st January 1954, Pope Pius XII published the Apostolic Exhortation to the Ordinaries of Italy with reference to another mass medium; television. The document is entitled *"The rapid progress."* Again, the assessment of risks in the use of this communication medium is one of the prevailing aspects of the message.

4.1 The Council Vatican II

The transition to a more positive stage in the evolutionary process made by the Catholic Church is reflected in the documents of the Council Vatican II and particularly in the conciliar decree *Inter Mirifica*, signed on 4th December 1963, which is an essential reference of great novelty. For the first time the Catholic Church deals exhaustively and in-depth with the complex issue of social communications, and also at an occasion of such great importance as the Ecumenic Council.

"The Church – the document states – welcomes and follows with particular attention the marvellous technical inventions that have offered new opportunities to communicate with highest ease any kind of news, ideas and teachings". Then it adds: "let us train without delay priests, religious and lay people on how to use these tools with the required expertise for apostolic purposes".

Only under the Council Vatican II, does the Catholic Church make a real turn in its approach to the media – mainly from pessimistic to optimistic – designing a more positive and receptive perspective. Media are recognized as being the true crossroads of modern social issues. Among other things it should be noted that it was under the Council that the Church, for the first time in its history, opened its doors to journalists, who were allowed in to monitor directly the performance of its work. It is with Pope John Paul II that the mass-media become tools organized and used internally by the Church to support its evangelization mission.

The Council also approved the decision to establish a regular international conference to study media – called the World Day for Social Communications – which started its activities in 1967 and was repeated every year until the 43 edition in 2009. To complete information, it should be added that the main instrument which the Catholic Church has used in the past and still uses in this area is the *P.C.C.S.-Pontifical Council for Social Communications*, which was established previously, in 1948, as the *Pontifical Commission for Consulting and Ecclesiastical Review* of the films on religious or moral issues. Currently the P.C.C.S. consists of 23 members from 21 countries: 11 are cardinals, 9 archbishops and bishops and 3 presidents of international organizations of catholic media. The Council has also 14 officials of the 5 countries and 33 advisors of 19 countries (www.pccs.it). On 27th May 1971 a Pastoral Instruction *"Communio et Progressio"* was issued, expressing strong concerns about the delays in the way the Catholic world faces the problem of the mass media. The document calls for urgent work in training religious and lay people not only on technical aspects, but above all the cultural aspects.

4.2 The Pontificate of John Paul II

In the Encyclical *"Redemptoris Missio"*, published on 7th December 1990, Pope John Paul II recognized that the communications world has become "the first aeropagus of the modern age", the instrument that is unifying humanity, making it – as it is usually put – a "global village" and thus leading to the formation of a "new culture". According to the Pope "media of social communication have become so important, that for many, they are the main tool for information and education, guidance and inspiration for the individual, family and social behaviour. The younger generation, especially, grow up dependent on them". "Perhaps – John Paul II admits – this aeropagus has been somewhat neglected" by the Church because "we generally prefer other tools to announce the Gospel and to educate people, while the mass-media is left to the individual or small groups initiatives". However, he states, "the commitment on the media ... not only has the aim of multiplying the message: There is something deeper, because the same evangelization of modern culture depends largely on their influence. Therefore, it is not enough to use them for spreading the Christian message and the Church Magisterium, but we must integrate the message into the new culture created by modern communications. It is a complex issue because this new culture comes out, even before by the contents, by the fact that there are new ways to communicate with new languages, new techniques and new psychological attitudes. My predecessor Paul VI said that "the rupture between the Gospel and culture is without any doubt the drama of our time and the scope of today's communication fully confirms this statement". It should be noted that Pope Paul VI, in the Apostolic Exhortation *"Evangeli Nuntiandi"* on 1975, highlighted a particularly important aspect of this breaking: "Contemporary man listens more willingly to witnesses than to teachers ... or if he listens to the teachers, he does so because they are witnesses".

The 22nd of February 1992 is the occasion of a new Pastoral Instruction, *"Novae Aetatis"*, which repeats the recommendations to accelerate the upgrade of the Catholic world in the field of mass media; "For many people the reality corresponds to what the media defines as such".. Faced with the spread of this phenomenon it becomes urgent to promote primarily a broad educative initiative: "the issues of mass communication deals with all levels of pastoral ministry, including education".

Two years later, in a document by the Bishops' Synod, *"Instrumentum Laboris"* (22nd February 1994) the reflection on the media world focuses, among other things, on the importance of images, which have always been a component of the transmission of the religious message: "One characteristic of our time – the document states – is the culture of images widely disseminated through the media of audio-visual communication. On the one hand, it should be appreciated as a culture close to Christianity that seeks to rise from visible to the invisible, using the liturgical signs and symbols as signs of salvation and elevating humanity through the goods of beauty and art". However, the bishops state, that this culture is often converted by modern communication media in "a culture of ephemeral and superficial show".

On Christmas 1999, the website of the Holy See opens with the personal wishes by the Pope. 1999 was also the year in which for the first time the word "Internet" is included in an official document of the Magisterium of the Church. It deals with the document *"For a Pastoral on Culture"* published by the Pontifical Council for Culture. A curiosity: John Paul II was the first pope to use internet to send a pontifical document. This happened on 22nd November 2001 when the Pope sent the post-synodal Exhortation "Ecclesia in Oceania" to the bishops of Oceania.

By the turn of the century, in 2000, the Church's attention focused mainly on issues of ethics in the mass-communications world and the great challenge-opportunity represented by the internet.

In this regard, in 2000, the Pontifical Council for Social Communications published the document *"Ethics in Social Communications"* which makes it clear that the Church considers the mass-communication media both as a product of human intelligence as well as gifts of God. Therefore, they are not blind forces of nature, but something that man can choose to use for good or evil. People who make choices – public officials, politicians, company managers, and consumers – must make them with respect for human dignity, community and the common good.

In 2002, the central consideration was concerning the function of internet to which the 36th World Day for Social Communications was dedicated. The title of the initiative, which took place on May 12, was: *"Internet, a new forum for proclaiming the Gospel"*. On that occasion, Pope John Paul II sent a message calling on Catholics not to be afraid of the internet, "to take on the network". The time had come for a face to face between Church and the internet, as some commentators note. In other words: universality against universality, message against the message. In preparation for the World Day, the Pontifical Council for Social Communications published two specific documents on 22nd February 2002: *"Ethics and Internet"* and *"The Church and Internet"* which highlight the importance of media for human promotion. "The Church – we read – has a twofold aim with regard to the communications media ... that to encourage their right evolution and – that to encourage – the right use for the good of human development, for justice and peace, for the development of the society at local, national and international level, in the light of the common good and in spirit of solidarity". But with regard to the achievement of this purpose, the Church explicitly recognizes its cognitive limitations, as stated in the second of two documents, *"The Church and the Internet"*. "Since announcing the Good News to people absorbed by the media culture requires careful consideration of – their – peculiarity. Now the Church needs to understand Internet". This understanding of the internet is also considered as the condition for allowing the Church to start taking the best possibilities of the bi-directional communication and social interaction, offered by internet. The Church, as "social community", should promote a pastoral planning to allow people to move from cyberspace to the personal community.

During a scientific conference organized in Rome by Catholic university L.U.M.S.A. (14th November 2003) Archbishop Foley, president of the Pontifical Council for Social Communications, raised the problem of teaching young people about critical use of media: "Teachers can and should help young people to be intelligent and critical consumers of mass media". At the conference, speakers underline the need "to organize education starting from primary and secondary schools and, at the same time, specific interventions by teachers". The participants reflect on the concept of the *edo-communication*, with the aim of "changing the world of communications". Media education, development of a critical attitude and a participatory approach by their users are, it should be remembered, among the main issues that at the same time the European Commission are beginning to face with the initiatives dealing with the media literacy.

In May 2004, the Italian bishops gathered in the C.E.I.-Conference of Italian Bishops, following the example of German and American bishops, to approve a theoretical and planning document, *"Communication and mission. Directory on social communications in the mission of the Church"*, in which media communication is considered an essential dimension and not "a specific sector" of the Church pastoral. The document represents the final overcoming of a pastoral approach which since then had looked more at the single instrument than at the media culture it produced. "Media – the document states – has the capacity to weigh not only on the transmission mode but also on the contents of thought. In other words, the instruments of social communication are much more than simple tools; they are real agents of a new culture. Only by transforming the spectators into protagonists – the Italian bishops say – is a penetration of the Gospel possible. Otherwise, media make possible only the loss of interiority, the superficial meeting and the replacement of truth by opinion".

On 21 February 2005 Pope John Paul II – who, as already mentioned, in the encyclical *Redemptoris Missio* (1990) defined media as the first "areopagus" of the modern era – wrote an apostolic letter significantly entitled *The rapid development* and once again urged a" pastoral and cultural revision" in the attitude of the Church towards the media, already defined as "the crossroads of the major social issues" by the II Vatican Council. In its interpretation, under the present conditions, the world too often obeys anthropological visions that are not inspired by the Christian principles, setting aside the Christian vision of man and life. The Church must be capable of facing the "epochal transition we are experiencing." For a dynamic Church, the possibility to proclaim the Gospel or to reduce it to silence in the human hearts depends, in the "global village", from its capability to implement this pastoral and cultural revision. In essence, to ignore the essential role of the media in contemporary society means, for the Church, to lose the contact with modern culture. Already in *Christifideles Laici*, (30th December 1988), John Paul II had stated: "The media world, with its capability to accelerate development and innovation as well as with its global and, at the same time, capillary influence on building the peoples' mind and attitudes, represents a new frontier for the Church mission". By now, it is up to the media to mould the cultural humus as well as the collective cultural ethos of humanity.

In the new apostolic letter, the pope recognizes that "ours is the era of global communication, in which more and more moments of human existence evolve through the media processes, or at least have to deal with them. I merely remember – he adds – the formation of personality and consciousness, the interpretation and structuring of emotional ties, the articulation of education and training phases, the processing and dissemination of cultural phenomena, the development of social, political and economic lives". But besides the great value of these resources, the emphasis is also on the need to use them with "prudence and wisdom". "Just because they affect the consciousness of individuals, form their attitudes and determine their vision of things, we must say loud and clear that the means of social communication ... – must be linked – to a framework of rights and duties, organically structured, from the point of view both of the educative and ethical responsibility as well of laws and institutional competences. The positive development of the media to serve the common good is a responsibility of everybody as well as of each single person". In this respect, the Pope recalls the need to develop: a) education and training, "to ensure that the media are known and used in an appropriate manner"; b) participation, to promote access to the media and their management, "even with appropriate rules and laws, increasing the culture of responsibility and dialogue, for mutual understanding, solidarity and peace. "Do not be afraid of new technologies – the pope concluded – they are among the wonderful things, *Inter Mirifica*, which God has made available to discover, use, and know the truth".

With regard to that, it is interesting to note that the pope's call for a law finalized to guarantee the proper use of media as well as an active participation of the citizen to them, coincides with the start of strong initiatives, taken by EU and other international institutions, to plan organic and concrete measures on media literacy, which have, substantially, a similar purpose.

By presenting the apostolic letter, the President of the Pontifical Council for Social Communications, Archbishop Foley, did not hesitate to say: "The Church is communication", while the secretary of the Council, Msgr. Boccardo, recognizes that media are a "primary good" and precisely: "just because they affect the consciousness of individuals, form their attitudes and determine their vision of things, we must say loud and clear that the means of social communication are a primary good for the individual as well as for humanity, consequently a treasure to be protected and promoted".

Finally, we remember the topic chosen by Pope John Paul II for the 2005 World Day: *Media and their service to the understanding among peoples*. There is no doubt, for the pope, that media plays a positive role in bringing people together, because communication is knowledge, confrontation, relationship with others: these are the basic conditions in order to undertake a serious way of mutual understanding. 2005 was also the year of the death of John Paul II; for the first time the Church proclaimed it to the media of all the world using the internet and the SMS system.

4.3 The Pontificate of Benedict XVI

It is especially in the recent messages of Pope Benedict XVI to the participants at the World Days for Social Communications (2007, 2008 and 2009), that it is possible to clearly grasp the elements of a completely different approach from in the past by the Catholic Church, which arrives to define the new technologies as "a real asset", "a blessing for all", "a true gift to humanity." These messages are marked, according to their presenters, "a real turning point," which follow those, – which are just as important-, promoted by the Second Vatican Council in the sixties of the twentieth century.

The papal message of 24 January 2007 is devoted to the subject *Children and Media: A Challenge for Education*. The reflection is on the question of a double need: the education of children, on one hand, and the education of the media, on the other. The children, described as "digital natives", are subjected to very different stress from that of their parents; thus they do not understand the cultural models of the past. Often, the Pope emphasizes, they are victims of what he defines as the "info-poverty" and exposed to the risks of a materialistic vision of the universe, life and human fulfilment.

This type of approach, based on children's education, it is to underline its own relevance as well as fully corresponding to that of the European Union on the subject of media literacy. Indeed, the pope states, the relationship between children, media and education can be considered from two perspectives. First, "the education of children by the media and the education of children to respond appropriately to the media"; second, "the education of the same media". There is a sort of reciprocity which points out both the responsibility of the media as an industry and the need for an active and critical participation by the readers, viewers and listeners. Within this context, an "adequate education for a proper use of the media is essential for the cultural, moral and spiritual education of children." The children, in essence, must be educated to be selective in the use of media and this is the responsibility of parents, schools and the church. The role of parents is of primary importance. "Media education – the Pope stresses – should be positive. By putting children in front of what is aesthetically and morally excellent, they are helped to develop their own original opinion, prudence and the ability of discernment". Then, children have to be educated in what is defined as the "way of beauty, truth and goodness"; and this approach should find support through the same media industry. This should be possible "only insofar as the media industry – is committed to promote – the fundamental dignity of' human beings". "In truth – the pope highlights- there are those who say that the formative influence of the media is in competition with that of the school, the Church and perhaps even the family." But those who manage the media and have "a sense of civic responsibility" have the duty to connect the media influence and education to specific ethical principles. The entire media world should be recovered to what is defined as a "human ecology".

It is interesting to note that the report written for the official presentation of the papal message highlights with particular emphasis just this aspect: for an effective child education, it is also important that parents, teachers, religious people, are able themselves to understand the new media languages.

In 2007, the authoritative voice of Archbishop John Patrick Foley, President of the Pontifical Council for Social Communications, points out that facing the media, the Catholic Church is guilty of sins of omission (plenary session of 25 March 2007). "We all have sinned ... even in the field of communications, especially with sins of omission, but also sins of action. We are guilty of sin or at least of omission for not using the *Mirifica* – the wonderful things that God gave to human beings to discover – to communicate in the best possible way his love and his goodness to the world ... Those who seek to sell products, have used media successfully to sell soap, cars, clothes and vacations, while we – we, that have the responsibility to proclaim the most important message in the history of the human race – have not often had the imagination and dedication to use media correctly in order to make known the good novel of Jesus Christ ... Sometimes we are also guilty of sins or at least of omission for the fact that more frequently we prefer to blame the use of media, than to praise it".

The new president of the Pontifical Council for Social Communications, Msgr. Celli, by commenting on a book of the authoritative Cardinal Martini (October 2007), points out the media as "a reality to understand, serve, love" and reminds us of the papal appeal on information-poverty, as the great challenge to take up: "the illiteracy of the past times ... one of the tragic consequences of the socio-economic poverty, is today extended even under the aspect of information-poverty".

In a video-message forwarded to the VI World Meeting of Families held in Mexico City (18th January 2008), again Archbishop Celli stressed the importance for the Church of taking up the challenge of educating the new generations on human and Christian values, "in a global cultural atmosphere that has been called *mediasphere*, because it has become like the air we breathe". "We, believers – this is the question – should we remain outsiders to the culture of our time, depriving it of our active participation and of our message?" The key-point is "to educate children to make a good use of the media ... in order that they are able to express serene and objective judgments, which afterwards allow them to choose or reject programs". For this reason, he points out, "the Church has for years been promoting an education aimed at increasing a critical perception of the media, also known as *edu-communication"*. Not leaving children alone but developing in them the precise criteria for choosing; this fact will serve the whole family to be "not only a group of users, but active participants and missionaries of the Word in digital culture". On another occasion, Mgr. Celli underlines the importance of addressing the so-called *digital divide*: in the present world "there are natural and virtual spaces; the last one are those divided into linguistic "galaxies" that bring all the participants – especially children and young people – into a common and shared universe. Unfortunately, there is also the new divide between those who are included in these virtual spaces and those who do not even know what a phone call is".

It is interesting to note that even in this case, the appeal for edu-communication, the strengthening of a critical thinking, an active participation of the family in digital culture, the fight against the digital divide, all these are on the same wave-length with the initiatives promoted at the same time by the European Commission and European Parliament to spread media literacy in Europe.

Info-ethics: this is the need to introduce a new ethic in the media world. This is the main and original content of the message sent by Pope Benedict XVI on January 24th 2008 announcing that the new World Communications' Day would be held next month on the topic: *"The means of social communication: at the crossroads between self-promotion and service. Seek the Truth to share."* Benedict XVI sees the enormous changes that communication is experiencing as tools of "our hope", thanks to the new technologies, and adds: "the role that the means of social communication have become in society should be now considered an integral part of the anthropological question that emerges as a key challenge of the third millennium ... In the globalization era, everybody is user and operator of social communications". The pope acknowledges that the media, with the circulation of information and dissemination of knowledge, have given a "decisive" contribution to literacy, socialization, development of democracy and dialogue among people. "The media, taken together, are not only means for dissemination of ideas, but can and should also be instruments at the service of a world of greater justice and solidarity. Not lacking, however, the risk that they may turn in systems to subjugate man to logics dictated by the dominant interests of the moment ... to impose distorted models of personal, familial, social life ... to resort to the transgression, vulgarity, violence – to encourage the audience – to propose and support some development models that increase rather than reduce the technological gap between rich and poor countries". Humanity, pontiff says, is at crossroads and must confront with "the ambiguity of progress". Even the media are at crossroads: it seems increasingly pronounced "their pretension not only to represent reality, but even to determine it thanks to the power and the capability of suggestion they have ... on some events media are not used for the proper role of information, but to create the events themselves". These trends mark a dangerous change in their functions, and because the media are "a reality that profoundly affects all the dimensions of human life (moral, intellectual, religious, relational, emotional, cultural), putting into play the real good of the person, we must stress that not everything that is technically possible is also ethically viable". It is to avoid that the media act as propagators of ethical materialism and moral relativism; hence the Pope's proposal for the definition of an "info-ethics, as there is bio-ethics in medicine and scientific research linked to life". The commitment to act in this direction is indicated as the condition of "living in this communications era not as a time of alienation and loss, but as a valuable time for the search of truth and for developing communion among individuals and peoples."

In a *Brief questionnaire on info-ethics*, distributed together with the aforementioned papal message and finalized to launch an in-depth reflection on this issue, reads: "in the field of social communication, the constitutive dimensions of man and his truth are at stake. When communication loses its ethical anchorages and avoids the social control, it ends up not maintaining the centrality and inviolable dignity of man, thus risking having a negative effect on his conscience, his choices, and ultimately affect the freedom and the same people's lives".

In May 2008, the President of the Council for Social Communications, Msgr. Celli, called on journalists of the Italian Catholic Press Union – UCSI to be aware of the on-going evolution of the internet world and the overwhelming role of users (e.g. *Facebook, YouTube, Flickr, and Twitter*). To act ethically in the contemporary society, he explains, we must look "beyond Internet", more precisely, we must go to the "heart of the digital culture" in order to find again concrete groups and people. In close relationship with the Church, the Catholic journalists were called upon to create a digital culture inspired by solidarity principles and forms of shared creativity. In today's world, a major ethical challenge is open: it deals specifically with education and its different issues. According to Msgr. Celli, even the Council of Europe, which is studying these phenomena, is struggling to find suitable answers. With particular reference to adult education, specifically parents, it would be necessary to promote a proper and widespread action of capacity-building, for an active participation in the new communication processes.

Living positively in the network: for Msgr. Celli the network can strengthen everybody, without detracting anything from anyone; it is the tool to rebuild new communions, new units.

The following year 2009, on 23rd January, on occasion of the announcement of the 43rd World Day for Social Communication', the pope, as already mentioned, did not hesitate to call directly on the young people of the "digital generation", the protagonists of "new digital arena, the so-called cyberspace", because just the young people "have grasped the enormous potential of new media in facilitating the connection, communication and mutual understanding among individuals and communities". The fact that mobile phones and computers, thanks to the global capacity and ubiquity of internet, allow people to overcome the barriers of space and time and instantly send words and pictures to the most distant corners of the world; all this represents an "unthinkable possibility for the past generations ... which brings many benefits". Young people feel "at ease in a digital world that often seems alien to those of us, adults, who have had to learn to understand and appreciate the opportunities the digital world gives for communication". The Pontiff does not hesitate to define the new technology as "a true gift to humanity" provided that "the benefits they offer are made to serve all people and all communities, especially those who are needy and vulnerable"; and then draws some of the main benefits that new technologies applied to communication are bringing to the human relations and progress. "Families can stay connected even when separated by long distances; students and researchers have an easier and immediate access to documents, the sources and scientific discoveries and may, therefore, work in team from different places; besides, the interactive nature of new media facilitates more dynamic forms of learning and communicating that contribute to social progress ... The success of these new technologies – he adds – is due to human nature itself, the desire for friendship that every man has within himself"; it deals with "modern manifestations of the fundamental and constant propensity of human beings to go beyond oneself and to enter into relationship with others". The last term for this human longing meets the divine call "engraved in our nature as beings created in the image and likeness of God, the God of communication and communion". Finally, according to the Pontiff, for the new media to express their potential in the best way, they have to provide much attention through the quality of contents and promote "a culture of respect, dialogue, friendship", active in supporting "the dignity and worth of the human person", able in "preventing the sharing of words and images degrading for human beings", and thus excluding "what feeds the hatred and intolerance, devalues the beauty and intimacy of human sexuality, exploits weak and unprotected people". January 23rd 2009, was also the day the Vatican announced an agreement with Google, the largest worldwide browser, and opened an official channel on YouTube, the most popular platform in the world for publishing videos (www.youtube.com / Vatican).

In March 2009 it was the turn of the bishops who chair the commissions for social communication all over Europe. Prepared with the special European Bishops' Commission for the Media – CEEM (which is organized under the five main European languages) and the thesis that media must be first evaluated and understood as a culture rather than as communication tools, the bishops assembly was dedicated to the topic: *The Internet culture and the Church*. Internet culture is a reticular culture, i.e. expression of a horizontal network in which individuals are increasingly encouraged to talk among themselves. Internet is defined as a "horizontal technology characterized by capillarity (single-user access), connectivity (for the option given to the individuals to enter into relationship with others) sociability (the term of reference is "social network") where the sharing of knowledge and relationships between individuals are central". The main problem is the definition of the reference values, which, like the network, are also horizontal because "the value is no longer defined by an adult as it is the network of peers". The other great, open problem is the replacement of the communicative interpersonal relations with the simple contact: "the aim is the pure contact and communication is simply a pretext, not the purpose." A specific assessment is devoted to how Church and religion are handled by the media, in the present time. In the final report, the European bishops highlight the positive signs (an increase of the Church's presence in the media and a renewed interest for the religious sphere) but also very critical signs such as: the trivialization of liturgical events often turned into real television talk show, the exploitation of the Church for political purposes especially in the debates concerning ethical problems (often the same papal messages are highlighted for their political aspect, while the true religious meaning remains hidden), the reduction of the Church as an institution committed in defending its own interests, "a vision of the religion as problem for social life"

At the end of this analysis, we can say that by now the Catholic Church, without any hesitation, recognizes the role of communication as a foundational element of the new culture and is engaged in efforts to connect this system of technologies and values to a specific project for individuals and society. It is a huge effort when we consider that in Italy, for example, more than 12 thousand Catholic websites were in operation by 2009. The Italian authoritative expert Father Silvio Sassi stresses that it is only the human intervention, "that can give guidance to the potential that the current communication has". In any case it must be clear that the communication phenomenon, by its very nature, cannot be treated in isolation because "in an extraordinary way, it is intertwined with the post-modern thought, the centrality of the subject, the sense of freedom, democracy, tolerance, with inter-culturality, with the results of scientific research, the projects of economic neo-liberalism, globalization, social mobility, migration, with the proliferation of ideologies and sects, terrorism and violence, with the poverty of the planet" (11).

5. **The Islamic world and the need for proper communication; Italian and European initiatives.**

A brief mention of some experiences in the matter, made by other religious confessions, may be useful to understand how certain basic needs that emerged clearly in the positions of the Catholic Church are, in fact, widespread throughout the world and common to other churches and religious institutions. A simple look at the websites as well as at the published documents and information, highlights that the main concern is referring to the possibility to represent and make known in the best way the heritage of their own values and the true meaning of the their initiatives. Frequent criticisms are that the way in which the media acknowledge and transmit the messages of these religious institutions is: incorrect, incomplete or distorted. This applies, for example, to the websites of Jewish religious institutions or Protestant Christian churches.

As an example, the situation of the Islamic world in Italy is mentioned. Unlike the Catholic Church and other religions, Islam has no a central structure of reference, a church in the true sense of the word that can sum up and represent a unified community. Islam is divided, however, in a very large number of communities and groups who practice their religious faith in full autonomy, its own system of social and cultural relations. There are, admittedly, some coordinating bodies, but they are never based on a pretension of an exclusive representativeness, as with other religious institutions. One needs only to look at the reports of Italy's Ministry of Interior, or even just scroll the websites of the Islamic associations in Italy, to appreciate the high complexity and vastness of this world which represents the second religion in Italy.

U.C.O.I.I. – the Union of Islamic Communities and Organizations in Italy and CO.RE.IS-Italian Islamic Religious Community are some of these institutional bodies.

U.C.O.I.I., for instance, has established itself over time as one of the most widespread Muslim communities within the Italian territory. It refers to 122 Islamic associations, with widely varying characteristics and social purposes, about 80 mosques and a large number of places of worship that still do not have the status of a mosque (data, 2009). This Union has the explicit goal of building Italian Islam and to take part in meetings and agreements with the Italian government.

CO.RE.IS also qualifies for the commitment to safeguard the religious needs of Muslims in Italy and on behalf of the Islamic community came to sign agreements with the Italian government as well as to participate in public consultations and work. The cultural activity of CO.RE.IS. is very intense. It acts with the support of a specialized institution, the *ISA Academy-Interreligious Studies Academy* which mainly disseminates the knowledge of Islam, organizes educational courses, and promotes interreligious dialogue. The online magazine *Islamic*, for instance, gives various information and details on the most controversial issues, such as the debate on the "clash of civilizations", "fundamentalism", etc. Constantly, the point being made is the effort to represent better the true nature of Islam.

In this regard, CO.RE.IS, in cooperation with the ISA Academy, also promoted the adhesion of the "Islamic" magazine to the first European network of the Muslim media, *E.M.I.N.-European Network of Islamic Media*, created in 2008, which currently operates in twelve European countries "with the aim of bringing together the mass media run by Muslims who recognize the value of an Islam integrated into the culture and the secular, multi-religious European society, far from the ideological currents of modern forms of radical Islamism". As stated at the conference of 14 November 2008 in Madrid, the will which has given rise to this initiative has the aim "to promote by Internet the knowledge of the true Islam, a religion that promotes peace and that has nothing to do with that violent and counterfeit form of Islam widespread by the fundamentalists on their websites". According to an American journalist Zahed Amanullah, editor of the Islamic website *www.altmuslim.com*, "much of the misinformation about Islam comes from the speed with which certain news are interpreted and amplified without any possibility of control". The creation of an authoritative voice of Islam in Europe, such as the network E.M.I.N., fills the serious information gap that often leads the media to commit serious mistakes when reading Islam. In fact, to quote the American journalist, "many problems have arisen from failure by the Islamic world to manage, first inside itself, the follow up of certain news, information or events, and thus to moderate the uncontrolled spread of news referring to media cases". In order for Muslims to give a positive contribution in the field of mass-media communication, it is essential that, in parallel, the media external to the Muslim world should ensure a similar seriousness and fairness in the evaluation and transmission of messages, especially religious ones, coming from that Muslim reality. This is also a very clear and explicit need, which is connected to and can find support in the specific European and international initiatives for media literacy.

6. The great opportunity of Media Literacy

With reference to the innovative processes started by the modern communication systems, media literacy represents at present one of the most important activity areas in which European Commission is committed. The E.U. is not the only international body, as already mentioned. Other international bodies are likewise committed in the same direction, for example, the Council of Europe and the United Nations with UNESCO. To understand the value of these initiatives and the contribution they can give to a positive relationship between churches and media world, it is necessary, as a preliminary, to define the terms that point out this specific field of intervention.

Media literacy is a new expression that refers to a variety of concepts and initiatives; moreover, it is also difficult to translate it from English into other languages of the Union. In general, this expression is interpreted and translated in a reductive sense, as media education. But this is a misleading translation, an error. In fact, media literacy refers to a broader concept. Surely it includes the media education of the citizens, to promote their critical attitude and an adequate capacity for understanding messages. But the real goal of media literacy is to open the media to the active participation of citizens and to contribute, in this way, to the improvement of social life and the strengthening of democracy practices.

European initiatives – as well international initiatives- for the dissemination of media literacy started just from the consideration of the serious, regressive risks to which our democratic systems are exposed because the lack of knowledge and the liability that people are facing the media world. In this situation, the media and modern communication systems are objectively in a position to develop, without major constraints, even the more negative effects of their action, like manipulation of consciences, deformation of identity, the spread of particular cultures and lifestyles; ultimately, to pass on cultures and messages that lead people to reduce their original, conscious, responsible contribution to the social, cultural and political life. The estrangement by the institutions, the weakening of community spirit and solidarity, the closure in the extreme forms of individualism: all these are, for example, some of the most significant negative consequences that may result from the activity of a self-absorbed media world, mostly committed to the promotion of own exclusive interests, not open -this is the crucial point – even to an active citizens participation.

The promotion of media literacy developed by the European institutions has just the aim of reversing this serious risk for the community and its citizens, and aims to build a different kind of relationship with the media world, characterized by greater accountability, openness, collaboration between communication producers and consumers / users, between public and private operators, between the economic players and the many subjects of the civil society, starting from private associations.

6.1   Media Literacy: a definition

The European Union officially defines media literacy as "the ability to access media, to understand and critically evaluate different aspects of the media, starting from their contents, to create communication in a variety of contexts. The media literacy relates to all media, including television and film, radio and recorded music, print, internet and other new technologies used in digital communication." (Communication 833/2007)

The term "literacy" in this case refers in practice to: a) the order in which the alphabet, the signs and symbols of writing and reading are set up and, b) the way in which the literacy process goes on, in relation to learning to read, write and perform the simple calculations necessary in daily life. Originally, therefore, the word literacy referred to the fundamental activities of reading, writing and calculation. But over time this term has taken on a much broader meaning and includes the current whole knowledge and skills that make a person a "cultivated" citizen, i.e. able to understand the world around him. It was not an easy process to achieve making it clear, that this ability directly comes from the ability to understand critically the communication messages and to evaluate them independently.

Although in the literature, the expression "media literacy" is often related to the concepts of "digital literacy", "computer literacy", "cultural literacy", "information literacy", "audio-visual literacy", "media education" – or it is used as an alternative to such concepts – media literacy in fact has a broader meaning, which implies an expansion of the role normally assigned to the basic literacy, as well as expressing an even wider idea than the simple learning of the communication and information techniques necessary for the daily use of the media (digital literacy)

Vivienne Reding, the European Commissioner for Information Society and Media, explains clearly the value of these components: "In the digital era, media literacy is crucial to achieving a full and active citizenship. The ability to read and write, according to the traditional process of literacy, is no longer sufficient. Nowadays people need a much more extensive preparation in order to express themselves effectively, to understand the messages of others, especially on blogs, in the various web sites or advertising. Everyone, young or old, has objectively an increasing need to be able to grasp the novelty of the digital world in which he lives. To achieve this purpose, a continuous process of education and training is much more important than any regulative system". (Brussels, December 2007-IP/07/1970).

6.2 Media Literacy: major components

In media literacy – which includes all the media, old and new, for their objective convergence – for scholars such as Paul Celot and José Manuel Pérez Tornero (12), there are three constituent, essential components.

The first component concerns the development of peoples' capacity: to know, understand and assess in a reflective and critical way the complex world of the media (*critical thinking*), to analyze and think in full autonomy about the logic, nature and content of messages; to know how to interpret the symbols, codes and cultural conventions used by the media. The development of this cognitive and critical approach recalls the respect of a precondition, i.e. the guarantee of a real possibility for the citizens to access the media.

The second component is the improvement in citizens of their *capability to write* with and on the media; then, *to generate content*, to use media as a platform from which *to interact* with other users.

A third component concerns the contribution that media literacy can give to the strengthening of *participatory attitude*. In this respect, it is almost obvious to remember that the complex media system is the main source of information according to which citizens build their impression of the world as well as the political processes that govern it, and if it is true that there is no democracy without participation, it is equally true that this participation can hardly be lived by those who lack a sufficient level of education and critical consciousness. Consequently, if media must also serve the democratic life and be functional to its strengthening, then they will have to "open" public participation.

These three components are generally represented by scholars with the so called 3-C and 5-C, where the letter C of the alphabet stands for: *Culture (cultural awareness), Critical (critical thinking), Creative (creative production), Comprehension (understanding), Citizenship (active citizenship)*; and this is linked to the model of interpretation which is taken as reference.

Media literacy works, therefore, in this twofold policy of democratization of society: a) from the side of citizens, by promoting the acquisition of sufficient skills to participate in the media life, it ends up reinforcing the social and political participation and thus the system of human relations as well as the functioning of institutions. Ultimately, changing the condition of individuals as passive consumers of media, the media literacy works in the construction of a fully active citizenship that has value for the individual but also for the community in which they belong; b) from the side of business and media operators, the great cultural and political initiative to spread media literacy leads to start in a continuous confrontation aimed at encouraging the adoption of behaviours, practices, organizational and governance methodologies which will be more attentive and helpful to meet the needs of modern democracies. The spread of ethical codes as well as the proliferation in Europe of collaborative experiences between people, communities and businesses in the organization of schedules and television programs, to cite some important examples, confirm the validity of the way it has been open.

6.3 UNESCO: documents and initiatives

Two important references for contextualising the media literacy concept, and, within it, media education, can be found in the initiatives of UNESCO concerning the promotion and strengthening of human rights inside the so-called knowledge society. According to the UNESCO, some of the fundamental goals of media literacy – such as to guarantee the access to contents of quality in the communication as well as to promote participation in the media planning – are related to essential elements of freedom of expression. The first definition in the matter dates back to 1982 and is written in the *Gruenwald Declaration*, a conference promoted in Germany which was attended by educators, experts and researchers from 19 countries. "Rather than condemn or praise the undoubted power of the media – it is stated in the final document – we have to accept their significant impact and penetration in the world as an indisputable fact and appreciate their importance as cultural elements of our time. The political and educational systems should be aware of their obligation to foster in citizens a critical understanding of the phenomenon of modern communications". The paper also stresses the urgent need to proceed in this direction because of the rapid technological development (satellite communication, home video, multimedia): to fill the delays in formal and informal educational systems as well as to extend the educational responsibility from teachers to parents, media professionals, and public policy makers. Since 1982, UNESCO has continued the work of deepening and promoting media literacy, even by organizing a series of periodic specific conferences on the issue, among which are: Toulouse (1990), Vienna (1998), Seville (2000), Paris 2005 and 2007), Riyadh (2006).

6.4 EUROPEAN UNION: documents and initiatives

The European Union, after having approved the Directive *Television without Frontiers* in 1989, which coordinates certain broadcasting activities of the Member States (Directive 89/552/EEC), adopted the Directive on *Media and Audiovisuals* (Directive 2007/65/CE) in December 2007, in which, among other things, it explicitly refers to media literacy, recognizing its importance: "Media education – the document states – refers to skills, knowledge and understanding that allow consumers to use media effectively and safely. Persons in possession of a media education are able to make their choices in full knowledge of the facts, to understand the nature of content and services and to use the full range of opportunities offered by new communications technologies. They are better able to protect themselves and their families from the harmful and offensive contents. For these reasons, it should be useful to promote media literacy in all sectors of society, and monitor its progress". It should be noted that previously, in 2007, the Commission sent to other EU institutions another communication, *I-2010. Annual Information Society Report 2007*, with a very precise description on the state of information society, the trends in the digital development and the indication of the main open issues, especially concerning the protection of pluralism in the media world and the dissemination of media literacy.

This line of commitment has been fully confirmed and developed in other documents elaborated by European Commission in the same period. It is the case of the Communication of 20 December 2007 entitled: *A European approach to media education in the digital environment* (COMM/2007/833), the first official document that has the value of treating this issue in a comprehensive and organic way, highlighting the importance of a European approach to media literacy. The Communication focuses in particular on three specific areas – advertising, audio-visual and internet – and reminds of the importance of developing both a critical attitude towards these media, especially in young people, and preparing the mechanisms of self and co-regulation, as well as effective codes of conduct. Member States should commit national authorities dealing with regulatory activities to work in this direction.

It is interesting to note that in these documents, regarding the spread of media literacy, the EU often refers to the co-regulation and adoption of codes of conduct by media professionals, rather than assume the use of traditional legislative activities. This means that the EU relies much more on autonomous and responsible initiatives by civil society leaders, rather than on the coercion of the law; in any case it is a trend that seems to become stronger over time.

2008 was an important year for the advancement of measures to promote media literacy. In fact, after the Communications submitted the previous year by the Commission, there is a passage to an assessment stage that is quite different from the past: that of the political assessment. At the European Parliament, on 28 July 2007, a draft resolution on *Media competences in the informatized world* was presented. The resolution was approved in December of that year (2008/2129/INI). In this document, the European Parliament, after having asked the Commission to elaborate indicators for measuring and assessing the level of diffusion of media literacy throughout Europe, confirms the importance of strengthening the citizens and their critical attitude towards media; also urges, among other things, the commitment of the Commission as well as the Member States to promote great educational programs, especially in schools, both for teachers and for students. This resolution, which is no more a study but a true political act, opens the possibility of including media literacy in the schools' and universities' curriculum, and this is, objectively, a great step forward.

On 8th October 2008 it was the turn of another communitarian institution, the Committee of Regions, which acts in the same direction by adopting a positive opinion on the Commission's documents. The opinion, in particular, calls on the states and regional and local authorities to adopt programs to promote media literacy, to be developed with the assistance of civil society organizations and the widest possible involvement of citizens, bearing in mind that the media play a decisive role in the maintenance (or lack of) of regional and local identity, intercultural dialogue and democracy.

6.5 COUNCIL OF EUROPE: documents and initiatives

The initiatives of the Council of Europe on several occasions addressed the issue of media literacy on the basis of the criteria that guide its overall action, such as, primarily: that the strengthening and safeguarding of democratic principles, human rights, freedom of expression are worthy to note. Among the key documents adopted are: the *Recommendation on media education* (n.1466/2000) which urges the governments of the Member States to promote both the practices and the spread of tools regarding media education, the *Council recommendation on the empowerment of children in the new information and communication society* (2006) which calls on Member States to develop a widespread informatics literacy ("information literacy") in parallel with in-depth educational activities for children and their teachers, for the best possible use of information and communication services and technologies; the document *Education policies relating to the media* (2007), which contains a very organic and large number of proposals, concerning the entire educational process in the field.

7. Media Literacy and religion: an objective convergence

All these efforts on the topic of media literacy, made by the European Union, UNESCO, the Council of Europe and other international organizations, both public and private, are objectively a great opportunity for the Churches. The type of approach that has been made by these institutions to the related open questions can support very much a correct dissemination of the religious message, by ensuring the churches a proper and honest representation of their role in society, enabling the conduct of their evangelization mission without distortions and misleading interpretations.

A citizen who is asked to develop his/her critical thinking of the media messages, who is educated to speak with them, and, finally, is encouraged to participate actively in the definition of communication strategies and programs, such a citizen, with such capabilities, becomes an important interlocutor for the church, since he is able to understand and assess in autonomy of thought the religious messages for what they really express. In essence, the spread of media literacy makes it easier to avoid future distortions and / or misleading interpretations of the religious message as well as distortions of the image and role of the churches. Such distortions are the greatest damage done by the modern communication society to a reflection on the true meaning of the religious dimension of life. The analysis of the documents and initiatives adopted by the Catholic Church on this communication issue confirms the existence of many elements that now show an explicit reference to the principles and guidelines assumed on media literacy by the major European and international institutions. Similar indications can be highlighted in the documentation relating to other religious confessions, starting with Islam.

We are facing, in short, a convergence of requirements, guidelines and interests that is a fact of great novelty. In this situation, starting and enhancing a more effective collaboration between religious institutions and secular public institutions, which are competent and qualified to promote joint initiatives on these communication issues, means objectively one very clear thing: put everybody in a position to live best with the present media revolution.

Notes

(1) "liquid" is the term conceived by the sociologist Zygmunt Bauman to define the contemporary society as a space with no more stable value references. See Baumann publications: *Liquid Modernity*, Ed. Laterza, Roma-Bari, 2000 and *Liquid Life*, Ed. Laterza, Roma-Bari, 2006.

(2) FARA GIAN MARIA: *Citizens, communication and institutions*, in P. Celot, JM Pérez Tornero "Media Literacy in Europe", Ed.Eurilink, Rome, 2008.

(3) GARLASCHE' EMILIO: *Consacred Life*, Ed. San Paolo, Rome, 2008. (A contradictory revolution, according to the author, because characterized by what it calls a "solitary socialization". Individuals are in the net, but at the same time they are alone. E. Garlasco is a manager of the British Communications Italy, with previous experience, always in ICT sector, in ENI, ENEL, OLIVETTI).

(4) FERGUSON GLOVER: *Consulting Magazine*, July 2004

(5) Idem – mentioned

(6) DYSON ESTHER: *Release 2.0. How to live in the digital era*, Ed. Mondadori, Milano, 1997

(7) Idem – mentioned

(8) Don SASSI SILVIO: *The culture of communication in the consecrated life*, Ed.San Paolo, Rome, 2005. (Father Silvio Sassi, ssp, is Superior General of the S.Paolo Society)

(9) Idem – mentioned

(10) RIFKIN JEREMY: in *European Consumers*, Dec. 2003

(11) Idem – mentioned

(12) CELOT PAOLO, PÉREZ TORNERO JOSÉ MARIA: *Media Literacy in Europe*, Ed. Eurilink, Roma, 2008

Bibliography

AGCOM-Italian National Authority for Guarantees in Communication sector: *Special Research Project for Children Protection*, Roma, 23 May 2003

Anderson, Craig A., Gentile Douglas A., Buckley Katherine E. : *Violent Video Game Effects on Children and Adolescents*", Ed. Oxford University Press, 2007

Arendt, Hanna : *The crise of culture*, Ed. Gallimard, Paris, 1972

Baldi, Paolo, Hasebrink Uwe: *Broadcasters and Citizens in Europe, Trends in Media Accountability and Viewers Participation*, Ed. Intellect, Bristol, 2007

Baumann, Gerd: *The Multicultural Enigma. State, Ethnicity, Religion*, Ed. Il Mulino, Bologna, 2003

Bauman, Zygmunt: *Liquid Modernity*, Ed. Laterza, Roma-Bari, 2000

Bauman, Zygmunt: *Liquid Life*, Ed. Laterza, Roma-Bari, 2006

Bauman, Zygmunt: *Consuming Life*, Ed. Polity Press, Cambridge, 2007

Bordi, Alberto: *The Italian Constitution steers the Principles of the Charter of Values*, in "Amministrazione Civile", Aug.-Sept. 2007

Cardia, Carlo: *Secularism and Religious Freedom in the Constitutional Law*, AA.VV, "60 Years after the Constitution", Ed. Chamber od Deputies, Roma, 2007

Cardia, Carlo: *The Challenges of Secularism. Ethics, Multiculturalism, Islam*, Ed.Paoline, Roma, 2007

Castells, Manuel.: *The Internet Galaxy*, Ed. Feltrinelli, Milano, 2002

EURISPES-TELEFONO AZZURRO: *9th Annual Report on Infancy and Adolescence*, Ed. Eurilink, Roma, 2008

EURISPES-TELEFONO AZZURRO: *The Dangerous Connections. Digital Youth and Social Networking. Limits and Potential*, A research published on the occasion of the Safer Internet Day, Ed. Eurispes, Roma 2009

Fumagalli Armando, Toffoletto Chiara : *Choosing TV. A Rational Map: from"Your Business" to "Wink Club"*, Ed. Ares, Milano, 2007

Morcellini, Mario: *Lesson of Communication*, Ed. Ellissi, Napoli 2003

Morcellini, Mario: *TV is Well for Children*, Ed. Meltemi, Roma, 2005

Popper, Karl: *TV Bad Teacher*, Ed. Marsilio,Venezia, 2002

Remondino ,E.: Without Rules. *The TV Empires at Conquest of Europe*, Editori Riuniti, Roma 2004; RITZER, Gorge 2004

Rifkin Jeremy: *The Age of Access: The New Culture of Hypercapitalism, Where All of Life Is a-Paid for Experience*, Ed. Tarcher, Los Angeles, 2000

Rosen, J.; Talmud, Il.: *Internet. A Jorney between Two Worlds*, Ed. Einaudi, Torino, 2001

US-Federal Trade Commission: *Marketing Violent Entertainement to Children*, Washington, Report 2007

Vanier Institute of the Family: Report *Good Servant, Bad Master: Electronic Media and the Family*, Ottawa, Canada, 2007

a) **Christian Religion**

AA.VV: *Consacred Life*, Ed, San Paolo, Roma, 2005

Appolito, A.: *Internet and the Madonna*, Ed.Feltrinelli, Milano, 2002

Arasa, Daniel: *Church Communications through Diocesan Websites. A Model of Analysis*, EDUCS, 2008 (www.pucs.it)

Assandri, Fabrizio : *When Words are Noise*, Ed. Secop, 2007

Baehr, Ted: *Movie Guide 2007* (on film productions of Christian inspiration in USA)

Benedetto XVI: *Children and Media: a Challenge for Education*, Message for the 41^ World Day of Social Communication, Vatican, 24 gennaio 2007

Benedetto XVI: *Media: at the Crossboard between Self-Promotion and Service. Look at the Truth for Share It*, Message for the 42^ World Day of Social Communication, Vatican, 24 gennaio 2008

Benedetto XVI: *New Technologies, New Relationships. Promoting a Culture of Respect, Dialogue, Friendship*, Messagge for the 43^ World Day of Social Communication, Vatican, 23 gennaio 2009

Ecumenic Council Vatican II : Decree *"Inter Mirifica"*, Vatican, 1963

European Episcopal Commission for Media – CEEM : *The Culture of Internet and the Church*, Acts, General Assembly, Vatican, 2009

Italian Episcopal Conference : *Communication and Mission. Directive (Direttorio) on Social Communication. Social Communication and the Mission of Church in Italy*, Vatican, 2004

EURISPES: *The E-Evangelization and Internet as the New Frontier of Catholic Communication*, in "20th Report on Italy", Ed. Eurilink, Roma, 2008

Giesbert Franz-Olivier : *The Church and the Media: an Unlimited Future*, in Pontifical Council for Social Communication, Symposium on the issue: "What media expect by the Church", Vatican, 2005

John Paul II : *Christifideles laici*, Post-Synodal Apostolic Exhortation, Vatican, 1988

John Paul II: *Redemptoris Missio*, Encyclical Letter, Vatican 1990

John Paul II: *Aetatis Novae*, Pastoral Recommendation, Vatican, 1992

John Paul II : *Mass Media: a Friendly Precence*, Message for the World Day of Social Communication, Vatican, 24 January 1999

John Paul II : *Internet: a New Forum for Proclaiming Gospel*, Message for the World Day of Social Comunication , Vatican, 24 January 2002

John Paul II : *The Rapid Development*, Apostolic Letter, Vatican, 2005

Hayes, Mike: *Googling God: The Religious Landscape of People in Their 20s and 30s*, Ed. Paulist Press, USA, 2007

IONA INSTITUTE, the Evangelical Alliance of Ireland: *Survey on the Knowldege of Christianism*, conducted by the Lansdowne Market Research, Dublin, april 2007

Marshall Paul, Gilbert Lela, Green Ahmanson Roberta (editors): *Blind Spot: When Journalists Don't Get Religion*, Ed. Oxford University Press, 2009

OFCOM-Office of Communications: *Report 2008*, UK, 2008

Paul VI: *Communio et Progressio*, Pastoral Recommendation, Vatican, 1971

Pio XI: *Vigilanti Cura*, Encyclical Letter, Vatican, 1936

Pio XII: *Miranda prorsus*, Encyclical Letter, Vatican, 1957

Pontificio Consiglio delle Comunicazioni Sociali: *Etica nelle Comunicazioni Sociali*, Vatican, 2000

Pontifical Council for Social Communication: *Church and Internet*, Vatican, 2002

Pontifical Council for Social Communication: *Ethics and Internet*, Vatican, 2002

Prothero Stephen : *Religious Literacy*, Ed. University of Boston, 2007

TEARFUND ASSOCIATION: *Report on Churchgoing in the U.K*, London, 2007

b) Media Literacy

Celot, Paolo; Gualtieri Fausto: *The Rights and Interests of Viewers in European Union: Policies and Tools for their Protection*, in AIART: "La Parabola", Magazine, Roma, April, 2008

Celot, Paolo; Pérez Tornero José Maria: *Media Literacy in Europe*, Ed. Eurilink, Roma, 2008

Celot Paolo: *Media Literacy in Europe*, in AIART: "La Parabola", Magazine, Roma, May, 2009

Council of Europe: *Media Education*, Doc.8753, Strasbourg, 6 June 2000,

EAVI: *Broadcasting and Citizens. Viewers participation and media accountability in Europe*, Ed. Eurispes, Roma, 2004

EU Commission: *Directive on Audiovisual Media Services*, Brussels, 11 December 2007

EU Commission: *A European Approach to Media Literacy in the Digital Envirnoment*, (COM(2007) 833 final) Brussels, dicembre 2007

EU Committee of the Regions: *Opinion on Media Literacy and Creative Content Online*, Brussels, 8 October 2008

Menduni, Enrico: *Educating in Multimedia. The School Facing Tv and Media*, Ed.Giunti, Firenze, 2000

Menduni, Enrico: *The Languages of Radio and Television: Theories, Tecniques, Formats*, Ed. Laterza, Roma-Bari, 2006

Morcellini, Mario: *Passage into the Future. Training and Socialization between Old and New Media*, Franco Angeli, Milano, 1997

Rivoltella, Pier Cesare: *Media Education. Models, Experiences, Skills'Profile*,Ed.Carocci, Roma, 2001

Rivoltella, Pier Cesare: *Realty and Challenges for Media Education in Italy*, in "Comunicare", Magazine, n.28, 2007

Tornero, Pérez José Maria: *Teacher Training. Curricula for Media and Information Literacy*, Background Strategic Paper, International Experts Group Meeting, Paris, june 2008

UNESCO: *International Symposium on Media Education*, Gruenewald-Germany, 1982

UNESCO: *Gruenewald Declaration*, Gruenewald-Germany, 1982

UNESCO: *Media education. Advances, obstacles and new trends since Gruenwald towards a scale change ?*, Paris, 21 June 2007

UNESCO: *Towards Knowledge Society*, World Report 2005, Paris, 2005

Varis, Tapio: *What is Media Competence and Why is it Necessary*, Hearing at Parliamentary Assembly of the Council of Europe, Strasbourg, 23 March 2000

Walsh, Bill: *A Brief History of Media Education*, USA, 2006a (published on the website: www.medialit.org/ReadingRoom/Walsh/Walsh1.html)

Websites

www.agcom.it

www.aiart.com

www.bibbiaedu.it
www.bible.gospelcom.net
www.bu.edu/sth/library/resouces.html
www.chiesacattolica.it
www.cinematografo.it (*Third Millennium Festival, on ethic-religious issues*)
www.clerus.org
www.cmn.ie
www.cremit.unicatt.it
www.eavi.eu
www.ec-europa.eu/policy/media_literacy/index_en.htm
www.eurispes.it
www.euromedialiteracy.eu
www.intratext.com/bri
www.ofcom.org.uk
www.paoline.it
www.paulus.net
www.pccs.it
www.qumran.net
www.religion-online.org
www.reteblu.org
www.siticattolici.it – sui siti cattolici
www.unesco.org/education/nfsunesco/pdf/MEDIA_S.PDF
www.vatican.va
www.wcpr.it – (*WCPR – World Conference Religions for Peace, Genova 2004*)
www.webcattolici.it
www.weca.it
www.zenit.org

Islamic websites

www.accademiaisa.it
www.alhuda.it
www.altmuslim.com
www.cesnur.org/religioni_italia/i/islam_04/htm
www.coreis.it
www.eminetwork.eu (*The first European network of islamic media*)
www.islamicita.it

www.islam-ucoii.it

www.lega-musulmana.it

Religious websites in USA

http//: www.CatholicRadioInternational

http//: edition.cnn.com/2009/POLITICS/04/08/1kl.osteens
    (*Column of the preacher Osteens*)

http//: www.cbn.com (*website of the preacher Pat Robertson*)

http//: edition.cnn.com/2002/US/02/25/robertson.islam (*preacher Robertson on Islam*)

http//: www.FaithMobile

http//: www.hollywoodjesus.com (*Pop culture and spiritual life*)

http//: www.google.com/search/religious+networks+USA

http//: www.LightsTogether.com

http//: www.TheMaryPage.com (*on the cult of Mary, by Univ. of Dayton, Ohio*)

http//: www.tribune.com

http//: www.tbn.org/index.php/8.html (*film producers, with Christian inspiration*)

Scenes of church communication – results of an empiric investigation

Márta Korpics

Issues of religion and religious communities can only be discussed in terms of their specific activities. When studying the participation of religious communities in social communication, it is always the particular communicating organizations (churches [218]) that are suitable as the subject of the research. Church communication takes place in three major scenes[219] (Horányi-Szilczl 2001, 83.). First, I will briefly outline the forms of communication typical of the given scene and the themes that make the particular scene eligible for analysis; then I will present some problems from a survey study conducted in the summer of 2007. The survey examined the above three scenes and asked the respondents their opinions.

Concerning the first scene, the church is active as a participant of social communication in various scenes of social communication. In the second case the church itself can be considered a specific scene of social communication. The third scene is one where communication of the transcendent domain takes place: this is a scene for sacral communication.

Communications and actions within the first two scenes together constitute the public communication of the church. By studying these scenes, the public presence of the churches can be described. Events and actions in the third scene disclose ways of relating to the transcendent domain in the given denominations, be these individual or community forms of communication. The first scene is that of social publicity. Recently, several important themes concerning the church and publicity have been raised in Hungary. The definition of the public legal status of the church, the work and activities of the professional church organizations, and the development of the civil society were all included in the examples. From a communication perspective, issues of mass communication were in the foreground. In the scene of social communication, problems and communication acts were

---

[218] My conclusions, the research and the reference are related to Christian churches and religions.
[219] According to the participation theory of communication, scene is not merely related to the physical environment but is a more complex concept. It is not a geographical notion but a medium with many elements (space, time, and knowledge etc.) that all influence the realization of the communication event. The scene is the environment of the communication. „Communication scenes are structured aggregates of agents and their knowledge where certain institutions (codes) are valid and others are not. The structure of the scene is established by the agents and their knowledge" (Bátori-Hamp-Horányi 2007)

emphasized; whereas from the perspective of the churches, public presence and participation in the society via mass media were underscored.

The second scene is that of the internal publicity of the church. In the church as a scene of social communication, there are various characteristic forms of discourse going on. In order to be successful in the different scenes of social communication, that is, to make their external publicity correspond to the rules of such publicity, churches have to shape their internal publicity and the forums of such publicity in an adequate manner (Horányi-Tamás 1997, 11). This is difficult to achieve within the church as there are certain restrictions on communication. As Miklos Tomka asserted, internal communication in the church can be described precisely in terms of social structural categories (Tomka 1996). The publicity of the internal discussions is made up of the religious persons in the society who are loyal to the church and actively practise their religion. The most mobile and ambitious persons in the society, who are ready for innovations as a result of their social status, are not present in the church. As a consequence, they hardly participate in internal church communication. This is why internal church communication in Hungary is presently (though not inevitably) conserving the given culture. It is a conservative way of communication both in its content and for its audience.[220] In addition to issues of shaping internal publicity, communication is relevant in determining practical tasks. The question is formulated in the Christian churches as an issue of effectiveness of transferring messages and finding linguistically adequate forms of communication.

The third scene in the church is the scene for sacral communication. This is the scene where connections to the transcendent domain are determined. Observing and description of this scene is the most problematic for the communication researcher.

The communication researcher does not consider answering the questions related to God as one's task (a job for the different branches of theology). Instead, the communication researcher is interested in the ways and forms of communication by which people and communities relate to God. How can they achieve and maintain this not-everyday communication? The way

---

[220] Based on surveys in the sociology of religion, conclusions may be drawn on which social strata are affected by the internal communication of the church. (20-30% of the persons older than 50 years old; whereas only 7-8% of those who are younger; a quarter of rural population but only 10% of city people.) These data are from a 1990 survey. Recently, the data might have changed.

people talk about and qualify this form of communication is also part of the third scene.[221]

In the study conducted in 2007 ("Religions and Churches in the United Europe") a survey questionnaire was applied. Certain groups of items in the survey questionnaire contained several statements on the operation of the above scenes. Although item groups were not arranged according to the above classification of the three scenes, the data obtained can be analyzed in this theoretical framework. In the current paper the analysis of some groups of items related to the three scenes will be presented.[222] The third block of the questionnaire contained statements on the internal status of the churches.[223] In this block one group of items was specifically related to the internal communication of the churches. In the very same block respondents' opinions on sacral communication in the church were asked. This group of items asked the respondents' opinions about possible ways of enriching church life. On the one hand the structural potentials of the church, and on the other hand the potentials inherent in spirituality were asked about. There were many communication acts included in the statements related to spirituality that can be considered a form of communication taking place in the sacral domain. In the fourth block of the questionnaire statements concerning the relation between the church and the society were included. Within this block there was one question targeted on the communication between the churches and the society. In the subsequent part of the paper I will present the results related to these groups of questions according to the typology outlined in the introduction of the paper.

1. Churches in the scene of social communication

Statements concerning the relationship between churches and society were related primarily to the media presence of the church as well as to the effectiveness of the media presence. Further, they also referred to the communication taking place in the various scenes of the church (Chart 1.). Responses on the communication between the church and the society were rather diverse and the rate of "does not know" answers was also high.[224] In

---

[221] To draw a parallel, Marcel Mauss, when discussing the researchability of prayer, highlights that the prayer is a special form of conversation therefore we can not directly study the act of prayer but we can ask the person praying what s/he thinks of the very act s/he has just participated in. According to Mauss, the researcher has no other alternative. (Mauss, 1971).
[222] Other results (tables and analyses) will also be published in a different study.
[223] Respondents were always asked about their own church so this why the plural form is used.
[224] In certain groups of items a much higher ratio was found.

the group of items both negative and positive statements were included on church communication and this is why the rate of agreements is not informative in itself. The rate of disagreement was higher for all the statements. The high rate of ambivalent and does-not-know responses (with one exception, about 30%) renders interpretation more difficult. The rate of disagreement with the statement on church use of communication media was very high (nearly 50%) as compared to other statements. The rate of disagreement was also relatively high with two further statements: a higher proportion of the respondents does not agree with the statement claiming that churches use public communication in their own interest but have a negative opinion on church TV and radio programmes.

Chart 1: Communication with the society

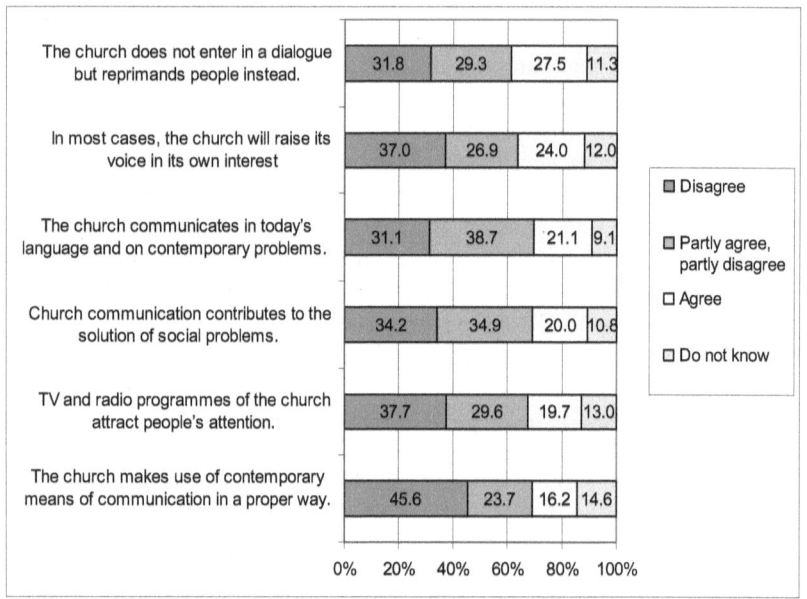

In the twenty years that have passed since the transition of the social system, the media presence of the church has been characterized by a marked increase; churches have become everyday participants in the scene of social communication. However, churches were not fully prepared for such a task. For example, there is no training for church media professionals in Hungary. Although Miklos Tomka formulated his opinion about the era of the 1990's, his claim on both internal and external church communication being relatively limited and not effective is still valid for the present situation. The issue of ineffectiveness is usually represented as a communication problem. In this scene, it is not the formulation and transfer of the message that is important but the degree of its effectiveness. Responses to his group of items in the questionnaire have revealed that the majority of the population does not have enough information on church communication. Messages sent by the church are not received by the majority of the people. Although the churches are present in social communication, they are not able to communicate effectively.

2. Internal communication of the churches

Communication in the internal scenes of the church is an important feature of the internal state of the church (Chart 2.). The rate of agreements was extremely high (50%) on the communication of the church related to scandalous events. However, rate of disagreements with the opposite statement was only about 40%. The rate of agreements on unidirectional church communication was also relatively high, about 40%; but only 32% disagreed with the opposite statement. The responses were not fully consistent at this point. The rate of does-not-know responses was very high for the whole group of items: the rate was 30% for the statement on the relational-bureaucratic system of the church. It is probable that respondents did not have any knowledge on the theme and their lack of knowledge was reflected in the responses. Responses related to the previous scene might have been influenced by general discourses about churches in the media and in the society. Responses to this group of items were determined by the lack of relevant knowledge of the respondents. This is represented in the high rate of does-not-know answers. However, the rate of agreement was unanimously high with some statements, mainly with those issues that are

not only raised in the scene of church communication but in the media as well. Respondents' opinions on internal communication were basically negative.

Chart 2: Internal communication

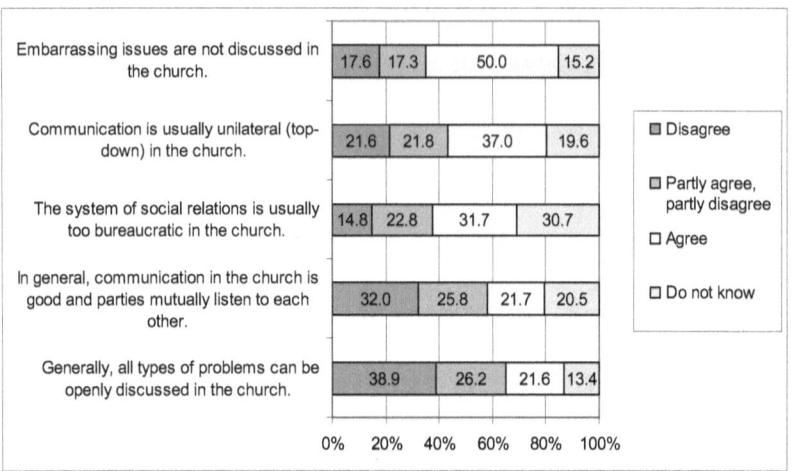

It is a commonplace in communication studies that internal publicity and its communicational features determine the external communication of the particular institution. In the past few years the Hungarian churches were criticized for both their internal and their external communication in various forums and in the media. Extreme hierarchy and bureaucratic features of the organization result dull internal communication; it is also possible that churches were not able to form a structured internal communication free of problems in the past 20 years. In many cases, the problematic nature of the internal communication of the churches manifested itself.[225] One could hardly ever encounter a proper church explanation on such cases after they were published in the mass media. This may explain the lack of information and the high rate of does-not-know responses. As a consequence, people, who obtain information from the media that screens the information, will think that the church wants to pretermit such cases. Pretermission is characteristic of both internal and external communication. The initial proposition has been confirmed: without making internal church publicity clear, transparent, structured and correct, church presence in the spheres of social communication will not be effective.

---

[225] Secret agents within the church, church and state relations in the years of state socialism and cases of pedophilia. These cases mainly affected the Catholic Church.

3. The church in the scene of sacral communication

For the previous two groups, the title of the item groups contained the scene that the questions applied to. Operation of the sacral scene of the church appeared only indirectly in some of the statements to be judged. The group of items related to the sacral scene contained statements concerning the spiritual growth of church life. Among these, mainly statements on the sacral features of church communication (liturgy, prayer, faith) were made, with two exceptions. The two statements also asked about manifestations of spirituality but their public forms. These two items were introduced to measure respondents' agreement with exemplary life of authentic Christians and agreement with charitable love. Our results show that most respondents (more than 80%; 85.5%, 81.7%, respectively) agreed that charitable love of needy persons and the exemplary life of charismatic person such as Mother Teresa enrich church life. The statement that faith enriches church life ranked third (80.2%). It is evident that respondents consider practical and public experiences of spirituality important. This is not surprising as both in Hungary and in Europe the majority of people conceive that one of the possible spheres of church activity in public life is helping the needy persons. Fewer respondents agreed, though agreements on these statements are still relatively high (64, 1%, 59, 6%, 59%, respectively) that prayer, meditation, and liturgy (the Catholic Holy Mass, the Reformed Mass) enrich the church. The rate of does-not-know answers is relatively high with these three statements and it is not surprising as these are the levels of spiritual life that are very hard to conceive even for believers.

Chart 3: Enriching church life II. Spirituality

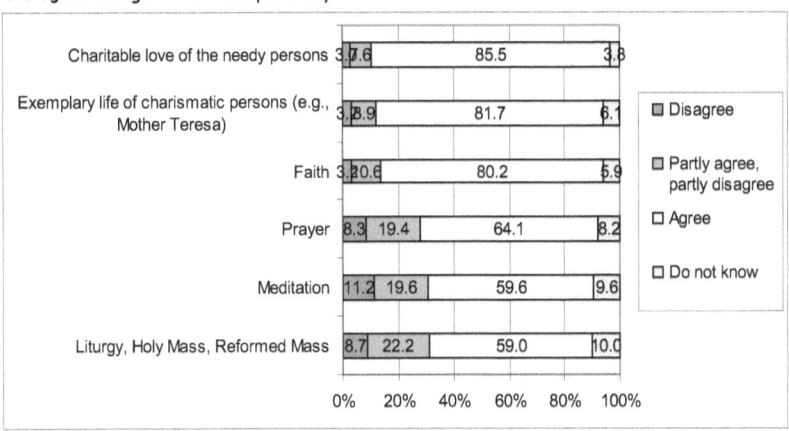

In the past twenty years since the transition of the social system the churches had to face a great number of challenges. Parallel to this, researchers of religion also had to solve their problems of the field. The current paper and other studies by the author are aimed at exploring an area of research that has not been studied extensively in Hungary. The paper represents a brief synthesis of the author's recent research.

Reference

Bátori, Zsolt- Hamp, Gábor – Horányi, Özséb 2007 *A társadalmi kommunikáció szerkezete és működése a második modernitás időszakában.* (Structure and Processes of Social Communication in the Era of Second Modernity) www.akti.hu/tanulmany/dok/horanyi.doc (2007. 06.21.)

Horányi, Özséb-P. Szilczl, Dóra 2001 Az egyházakról. (On Churches) In Buda Béla-Sárközy Erika (eds.) *Közéleti kommunikáció.* (Public Communication)

Horányi, Özséb-Tamás, Pál 1997 A társadalmi konfliktusok és az egyház. Social Conflicts and the Church. In: Horányi (ed.): *Az egyház mozgástereiről a mai Magyarországon.* On Church Scenes of Public Action in Contemporary Hungary. Budapest, Vigília, 11-19.

Mauss, Marcel 1971 Az imádság. (On Prayer) In Ferge, Zsuzsa (ed..) *Francia szociológia.* (French Sociology) Budapest, Közgazdasági és Jogi, 132-160.

Tomka, Miklós 1996 Egyház és kommunikáció. (Church and Communication) *Európai szemmel* 1996/4.

The Economic Teaching of World Religions. Cosmological and Material Beliefs

Katalin Botos

People have always had material and cosmological beliefs. The first kind of belief means how you are able to make your living, the second, how you should live. Human nature started to be established in the Stone Age. The hunter-gatherer human being was socialized (in our contemporary economic terms) according to the *repeated Prisoners Dilemma*. It resulted in a so called *"reciprocal altruism."* Archeologists state that the instinct to *"truck and barter"* is also a basic element of our human nature.

The character-lines of the Stone Age have changed in the settled agrarian civilizations. Through the widening of the market, more and more *one-shot games* were played. Merchants were suspicious and markets were seen as a necessary evil. *Cooperation* and the *adjustment to the rules* were of vital importance. Morals were built on *shame and guilt, based on tradition*. Their cosmological views were *communalist*.

Historically, those world religions which are still having believers in the population of the world today have their origins in the distant past. Judaism started 2000 –1800 years BC.

(According to the Old Testament we may position Abraham around year 1800 BC. But the written formulation of the belief is to be dated around the years 900 BC)

About 500 years BC two other important religions were formulated: Confucianism in China and Buddhism in India (the latter is to be found today in several places in Asia.). Christianity is a belief more than 2000 years old. Islam started about 500 years AC.

It is unquestionable that cultures play a very important role in economic development. In the core of the different cultures there are the religious beliefs. It is very interesting whether the cosmological beliefs are in conjunction with the material beliefs or these ideas are divided from every - day life. In other words, the question is: Do the religious teachings contain concrete prescriptions on how to live, how to produce or distribute the produced goods or they deal mostly with the „inner reality", with the soul of the human being.

According to *Depal Lal (Dunning, 2005) The Catholic Church has conjoined the material and cosmological beliefs.* In the VI century Pope Gregory I established concrete rules how to live, how to behave in the society, as a religious prescription. He significantly changed the then-existing moral norms and customs of family matters. He banned cuncubinage, transfer of children by adopting, marriage between close kins. After this radical change the Church became the beneficiary of those bequests where there was no immediate male heir. Further reforms were introduced by Pope Gregory VII in the XI century. The new church-state created an administrative and legal environment which could be seen as the forerunner of modern polity. This provided the essential infrastructure for Western the dynamic, which in time was to lead to Promethean growth.

Let us think about a bit on this expression: Promethean growth!

Depak Lal speaks about a Smithsonian and a Promethean growth. The former is based on division of labour, the growing productivity, which is a consequence of the efficient division of labour. The Promethean growth is the phenomenon where the source of the growing productivity is the injection of the fossil energy into the productive processes.

The industrial use of fossil energy in the XIX century gave a very big stimulus to the economic development in Europe. (*Maddison, 2004)* The importance of this technical innovation is to be compared to the Promethean act: stealing the fire from the Gods...

The conjoining of material and cosmological beliefs became a strength to the religious values for the economic development, too. One can see that the norms of the Christian belief positively influenced the European economic growth after the first millennium.

What can we learn from history?

According to Angus Maddison, (*Maddison, 2004*) the world per capita income was stagnating in the first millennium, but by the end of the second 1000 years it rose 13-fold.The world population grew during these 2000 years 22-fold, the world GDP 300-fold. Two distinct epochs we may find in the second millennium. The first is 1000-1820, the second is after 1820 – till today. (This second phase we may call the Promethean growth.)

Two thousand years ago the average per capita income for Group A and B (West and East) was similar. (The definition of A and B countries is to be found in *Maddison, 2004*. Countries in Group A belong today to the advanced part of the world economy measured by per capita GDP.) In the year 1000, the average for the Group A was even lower as a result of the collapse after the fall of the Roman Empire. But in the next 1000 years the Western part started to grow much quicker than the Eastern Group B. Asia was not able to produce such an efficient economic model as Western Europe and the Western Offshots. This raises the question: Why?

Why did capitalism place first only in Europe?

This question was asked by Rodney Stark as well. (*Stark, 2005*) The American sociologist put himself the following question:

Why was it that technological superiority over the rest of world emerged in Europe – after the collapse of the Roman Empire? Why did only Europeans have eyeglasses, chimneys, reliable clocks, heavy cavalry, or a system of music notation?

Why were Europeans so good in metallurgy, shipbuilding or farming?

Rodney Stark's short answer is: because of capitalism. (Weber, 2008 Stark, 2005)

Capitalism is the social order where people are interested in accumulating wealth, invest it to more production, and by this they serve the well-being of the whole society.

Two types of capital are necessary to realize this: material capital (*real capital*) and *human capital*. We have mentioned before the institutional reforms of the different popes, and the result of this: the accumulation of wealth in the Church's hands. We have to think about the rich monastic orders, where the cloisters and monasteries had a surplus of goods which made the communities fairly wealthy. This gave a basis for the establishing of universities.

The Weberian answer is that the Protestant Reformation created capitalism. Stark says it was started *much earlier*. The slow departure of the trend of growth of the European community from the Asian communities started in the first half of the second millennium.

It was really accelerated after the year 1500, and there is no question that the protestant ethic really contributed to the much quicker capital accumulation. But the basis for these processes – just as to the theoretical developments of the Enlightenment – was created in the earlier centuries. The fundamental basis of the economic results is rooted in the spiritual background which Christian belief offers to mankind from the very beginning.

The decisive element of this is – differently from other religions – the *extraordinary belief in reason*.

Religions in ancient times did not understand the World as such; they themselves felt as if gods had been playing with them. They thought they were not able to change their life, as it was determined by mystic powers, gods, who stand much above human capability. Buddhism thinks that present life is a consequence of the earlier life of the human being – he/she must endure it.

Confucionalism tries to improve the family's fortune, but thoughts about the origin of life on Earth, looking for explanations for it, or searching the destination of the living persons' lives is not in the focus of the thinking of the believers.

Christians – like Jews and Islam-followers – believe in a Creator of the Universe. The creation is a reasonable action.

As *Quintus Tertullian argued* in the second century: "Reason is a thing of God inasmuch as there is nothing which God the Maker of all has not provided, disposed, ordained by reason – nothing which He has not willed should be hand and understood by reason."

Christian belief based on reason helped a lot to accumulate knowledge, that is, "human capital", which is the most important factor of economic growth.

Judaism, too, made education a primary religious duty. Reading and writing helped to accumulate knowledge and so the possibility to transmit it to future generations. That is one of the most important factors of accumulating wealth and creating welfare.

The Judeo-Christian roots of European culture are not to be denied, (even if the EU does so in the basic legal documents of the community.) This feature of the culture is decisive for the economic development.

Morals too are having influence on economic performance. The important indirect influence we may find through the development of demography. If we look at the first millennium we can ask how was a tiny and obscure messianistic movement, Christianity, to survive on the edge of the Roman Empire. How could they dislodge paganism and become the dominant faith of Western civilisation? (*Stark, 1997)*

The answer by Rodney Stark is *the moral standard of Christianity.* Christian belief did not allow infanticide which was fairly common amongst "pagans", especially killing little girls. Christianity prohibited abortion. Consequently, sex ratio did not change so much and Christians did not have such enormous shortage of women that plagued the other part of the contemporary Roman Empire.

Christianity was socially good for women. Christian women enjoyed a substantially higher social status within the Christian subcultures than pagan women in the world. Young girls were not forced to early marriage – which led to many illnesses and early death –, and they had a voice in the choice of the future husband. Finally they had a higher fertility rate. Because of the prohibition of the infanticide of girls there were more Christian women than pagan, and more pagan non-married men. This in the end resulted in growing numbers of converts from the Roman male population. Another moral good was for the Christian religious movement that Christians did not leave ill people without care-taking, even if it put their life at risk. The Romans left those people without help who were marked by the "Black Death". As a consequence ill people who could biologically defeat their illness did not die just because there was nobody next door to give them a glass of water and a piece of bread. As a consequence the Christian population grew much quicker than the "pagan" societies.

A larger population means more consumption and stimulates production, and means more working force as well. Though Christianity was not exclusively the religion of the pure people, many members were recruited from the slaves and from layers of lower living standard.

It was an important feature of Christian beliefs that according to the religious teaching *people are created to be equal*. The roots of contemporary democratic political order one may find in the Christian belief. (This is for instance the starting point of the Constitution of the USA as well.)

Democracy is a very important prerequisite for the evolution of capitalism and, by this, of development and growth. Though not only democratic states are now functioning on market principle, the most successful countries in the recent past were democracies.

Characteristic features of world religions

Buddhism is an archetypical Eastern religion it does not believe in a personal God but it believes in *karma* and *afterlife in the form of rebirth*. In Buddhist teaching *there is not such an emphasis on social justice* as – we will see – in the Abrahamic religions. The most important virtue – according to Buddhist belief – is *compassion*. It is to be grand-hearted towards fellow human beings. But, the Buddhist generosity works in a sense of *a spiritual bank*. It is more advised to be generous towards a monk (because monks cannot earn their living by work, their duty is to pray) than to anybody else, because it "brings" the most religious „profit" for the person's afterlife. So it is an investment in a "spiritual bank" . Buddhism is much more concerned by doing such "investments" than to invest in the real world to make more capital. So, the Buddhist approach to economic life does not fit very much in contemporary capitalism. Buddhism is an individualistic, inward oriented, meditative religion.

Confucianism does not believe in a personal God either, and does not emphasize afterlife or any personal salvation. It advocates high moral standards – diligence, loyalty, reliability and reciprocity. It stresses the importance of controlling our "passionate nature." What is most important, it emphasizes one's traditional *social obligations*. The centrality of the family in Confucian culture is evident. At the same time obligations towards anyone outside the family is weak, including the state authorities. (Even the political changes after World War II made the convictions deeper; that state forms can always change but family is what you may trust- This conviction remained intact even after so much brain washing, especially among the peasants.)

Let us see an example: Confucius and a neighboring king were discussing where the moral standards are higher: "The king told Confucius that virtue in his land was such that if a father stole, his son would report the crime to the police and the criminal to the state. Confucius replied that in his state, virtue was far greater for a son would never think of treating his father so." (*Fukujama, 1994, p 86*)

The familism in China based on Confucianism failed to develop concentrated wealth that could have capitalized early industries. It is because the principle of equal male inheritance was deeply integrated in that culture, quite different from the European culture based on Christianity (let us think of the mentioned reforms of the popes.) The missing property rights in the country also strengthened family-ties in the 1980th, 1990th – you might believe only in your relatives when investing in Chinese economy after Teng Hsziao Ping reforms

The common feature of the monotheistic religions is the belief in the personal God and *accountability* in afterlife. According to the Old and New Testament, activity is men's privilege, it may result in private property, but property is a *trust*. These religions are individualistic, but all of them contain responsibility – in different extent- for the community, too.

Jewish religion teaches us that we are responsible for our activity. It demands activity and creativity. Main virtues are: *creativity, cooperation, compassion*. Because the whole world belongs to God, you may not hold forever the land you have obtained from another man; in 50 years you have to turn it back. The important feature of the religion is the *Tzedakah:* the *distributive justice.* Tzedakah combines charity and justice. According to Roman Law, what is according to the law due to you is righteous, but not charity. Charity is a voluntary, non-obligatory action. In the Jewish religion, on the contrary, charity is a must. You cannot leave your fellow believer in trouble if you are able to help him or her. In the Old Testament you find a lot of paragraphs where prescriptions tell you how to behave towards poor people, widows or orphans.

But as Johnatan Sacks mentions, it should be noted, that "Judaism embodies a dual ethic, one universal code applying to everyone, and the other a particular way of life demanded of the heirs of those who followed Moses into the wilderness ". *(Dunning 2005)*

Christianity is based on both the Old- and the New Testament. Its ethic is not dual, it is general. Christianity respects the dignity of the individual and private property. God has made us trustees of his creation. The Incarnation did not change the relevance of the moral teaching of the Old Testament. It confirms the goodness of Creation and the mandate given to men and women to exercise authority over the physical world. But, according to Christian teaching, market forces do not create autonomously a fair and just economic life. It is the *rule of law* that has to correct spontaneous economic order; the *state has to create social justice*.

Islam regards the individuum to be the cornerstone of the society too, who is personally *accountable* to God. Welfare in this world and welfare in the life-to- come are connected, co-dependent... Property is a *trust*, therefore it is subject to moral limits. All activities have to go through *a moral filter*. Justice is the criterion by which God will evaluate mankind There are some very direct *prohibitions*. Most important is *"ryba:"* i.e. usury /interest. *Islam opposes the fixed and guaranteed reward on capital.* This is really an interesting feature of the economic teaching of Islam. After the big financial crises of the 2008-2009 we have to think about the intermediary system of the contemporary world. Why? Because the greatest problem is that the creditor-debtor relationship is so very much divided. Financial innovations made the intermediary institutions irresponsible. One should think as correct if the financing is a joint venture in a certain sense, like in the Muslim banking system. Islam looks on life of the people as a network of relationships. One cannot be successful at the expense of the others.

Concerning the community the Islamic paradigm has freedom, justice, and solidarity, all rolled into one as its defining character. They think it is unique, so – according to *Kushid Amman (Dunning, 2005)* – there is no possibility to find a common denominator with other religions as an ethical basis. However, there is in the Islam a very similar institution as in the Jewish religion. *It is the zakat.* One has to pay a type of tax for helping the poor. It is obligatory, no believer can avoid it.

It is an institutional form of *distributive justice*. Something that is so often quoted by Christian theoreticians as well. As mentioned earlier, Christian social teaching stresses the importance of rule of law and the activity of every citizen in the political life to create a more just world.

Concerning distributive justice, we have to mention that the *Caritas in Veritate* papal encyclical letter contains references to the contemporary globalized world economy. It says that there is no possibility of a distribution of labour between market and state as before. Today market players are so much bigger economic units, the state is sometimes unable to correct the activity of the allocating markets by redistribution. There is no other way, the market actions are to be more ethical than before. (Very similar is the idea of the collaborative enterprise researches in contemporary non-mainstream economics. (Tencati,A -Zsolnay,L 2010)) It has to build the essence of ethical norms into functioning of the market – if this does not happen, there won't be anybody to correct the results.

Conclusions

In modern developed societies we see an economic imperialism. Everything is to be solved under market conditions, led by profit motivation. Charity is nearly suspicious. People are searching profit motivation even behind *caritative* actions. We have to explain to the public that "It is good to do good"

But it is true that world religions are against the fully (and exclusively) profit – oriented activity. However, it does not mean that they are against market mechanism. All world religions accept *private property, entrepreneurship, most of them accept profit-* though some religions only as a by- product of an activity which finally wants to achieve satisfaction of human needs (Confucionalism). Most of them stress the importance of fair and just prices (Justice is specially stressed in Islam). All world religions think about the necessity of solidarity.

The economic teaching contains in each religion a combination of competition and cooperation.

Studying the world economy and economic history, we can see some clear connections between religious background and competitiveness. In a certain sense it is indirect, rooting in traditions of the population in different parts of the world, but strong enough to influence behaviour of the participants of the market. Nowadays in Eastern societies we see the strengthening of the individual competition and improving the legal framework for market actors. Western societies – on the contrary – have to learn from the solidarity among the members of the big families in Asia. Under market conditions, often those layers or groups of society are more competitive where there is a greater solidarity (more work in the family or friends without compensation, credit based on trust without interest rates, etc.) *The overstressed individualism* costs *a lot* and makes the economies where it prevails uncompetitive in the world markets.

Literature

Dunning, J. H. : Making Globalization Good Oxford University Press, New York ,2003

Caritas in Veritate Encyclica of XVI Benedict

Fukuyama, F.: Trust The Free Press, New York, 1995

Maddison, A.: World Economic History in a Millennial Perspective. OECG, Paris, 2004

Stark, R: The Victory of Reason Random House, New York 2005

Stark, R.:The Rise of Christianity Princeton University Press, Princeton, 1997

Tencati, A-Zsolnai, L.: The collaborative Enterprise Peter Lang AG, Bern 2010

Weber, M.: Világvallások gazdasági etikája Gondolat Kiadó-ELTE TáT K Budapest, 2007

Religious Identities and Environmental Attitudes in Hungary

Benedek Jávor

Introduction

Ecological problems have become one of the most important and challenging problems of the global society by the 21st century. This issue, which needs a revaluation of the basic interactions, institutions and value priorities of the society, can't be left out of consideration any more by the churches either. In this situation there is an increasing importance of believers' relationship to environmental problems, how they see the role of the churches in managing environmental crisis, what kind of expectations they have concerning their church and to what extent and in which activities can the churches rely on their own believers during combating environmental problems.

Linking ecological problems to religions is not a brand new issue. Lynn White's provocative article, *Historical roots of our ecological crisis*, which supposed perhaps for the first time a relationship between the anthropocentrism of Christian tradition and the unconcerned or hostile approach to environment in the European culture, was published in the Science in 1967, more than 40 years ago. His theory has provoked a continuous scientific debate since then, where pro and contra argumentations fight each other, proving or disproving White's thesis. According to which the commandment in the Book of Creation: *"Be fruitful, and multiply, and replenish the earth, and subdue it: and have dominion over the fish of the sea, and over the fowl of the air, and over every living thing that moveth upon the earth."* (Gen1:28) finally became the root of an approach to nature which is based on an anthropocentric and unmerciful dominion, and which is the basis of the rejection of the intrinsic value of nature, and direct cause of the ecological crisis provoking resource depletion of modernity.

After years of theoretical debates, from the beginning of the 80s, a number of researches were started to back or disprove White's thesis, using sociological methodology to describe and survey environmental attitudes of religious communities compared to secularized social environment or to other religious communities. These studies – carried out first of all in the United States, and partly in Scandinavia – produced controversial results. Some researches seemed to find a significant connection between Christianity and a lower environmental awareness (Guth et al 1995; Greely 1993; Eckberg-Blocker 1989; etc.) Other results (Hagevi 2002; Boyd 1999; Sherkat-Ellison 2007; Biel-Nilsson 2005; Ann-Videras 2007; etc.) qualify this image, and they point out that we have to make a difference between religious denominations (in some cases the White-effect can be proved, in others not). We have to take into consideration some background variables (e.g. political commitment, see Henry Institute 2008 and Pew Forum 2004 surveys), which sometimes give a more plausible explanation to the apparent connection than the White-hypothesis, and the methodology as well, e.g. how we pose the question, also can have a strong effect on the results.

Central and Eastern European countries

Churches of the region turned to environmental issues with a strong delay compared to Western European states or overseas. First signs of opening their mind to this question appeared around the millennium, and since that gradually local churches have paid more and more attention turned to environment. Conferences, publications, youth events dealt with the issue in the last years. In the Autumn of 2008 a parallel release of a Circular Letter of the Hungarian Catholic Bishops' Conference on the ecological crisis and the publication of the important document "*Alternative globalization addressing people and Earth (AGAPE)*" of the World Council of Churches by the Luther Publishing House (official press of the Hungarian Lutheran Church) put the issue in the focus. However, there are not any known quantitative researches to study the attitudes of Hungarian churches and their believers to environmental problems. Yet, such studies would help not only Hungarian churches to map expectations of their members and those areas where churches could rely on believers' help and participation. These researches also could have an international relevance as Hungary's religious diversity – parallel with a relative cultural homogeneity – makes the country a highly appropriate field for such comparative studies. According to this, a proper survey could provide information not only on the Hungarian situation, but it could contribute also to the international discourse on the relation between religion and environmental attitudes.

The study

In this situation the Pazmany Peter Catholic University and the environmental NGO Védegylet – Protect the Future! started a joint research, which – besides providing useful information on this relationship – also can serve as a starting point for further studies. A random sample of 800 people answered a questionnaire of 23 questions. The sample was not totally representative, but it was close to this in the case of sex and domicile (education and age distribution differed more from representativeness). In the focus of our study we put four traditional Hungarian religious communities (Calvinist, Catholic, Jewish and Lutheran), the Baptist Church, which has been existing in Hungary since the 19th century, and has a close relationship with Evangelical churches of the United States, and the members of an – in Hungary relatively new –, "non-western" religious community, the Buddhists. Most of the forms (550) were filled by Catholic believers, but we also had 80 Calvinists, 40 Lutherans and 30-30 Baptists, Jews and Buddhists in our sample. A further 40 questionnaire were filled by members of other churches (Adventist, Unitarian, Mormon, Faith Church – a Hungarian evangelical church – etc.) and by people not connected to any religion or atheist. In their answers people classified themselves into one of the 10 categories describing the strength of belonging (commitment) to their church. Later these 10 categories were merged into four main categories while processing the data. The forms were filled between November 2006 and May 2007 (a further 20 forms were filled in the Buddhist community in August 2008). To process the data we used the widely known SPSS software.

The statement of the problem

In our study we wanted to find answers to three basic question groups. First, how the focus group perceives environmental problems and how they see the seriousness of the ecological crisis. In this section we posed questions to falsificate the relationship between Christian belief and White's dominion thesis, and also to back or refuse the existence of an alternative Christian view of nature, which we called the "stewardship" or the "good steward" approach. The second question group was aimed to explore believers' opinion on the role of the churches in managing environmental problems. Finally, we wanted to know what the believers' expectations are concerning their church in this issue.

Results

In the first question group we asked respondents to sign on a scale 1-5 (1: not serious at all; 5: the most serious problem) how serious they regard environmental problems. We studied how the believers of each religious group see the seriousness of the ecological crisis. (Chart 1)

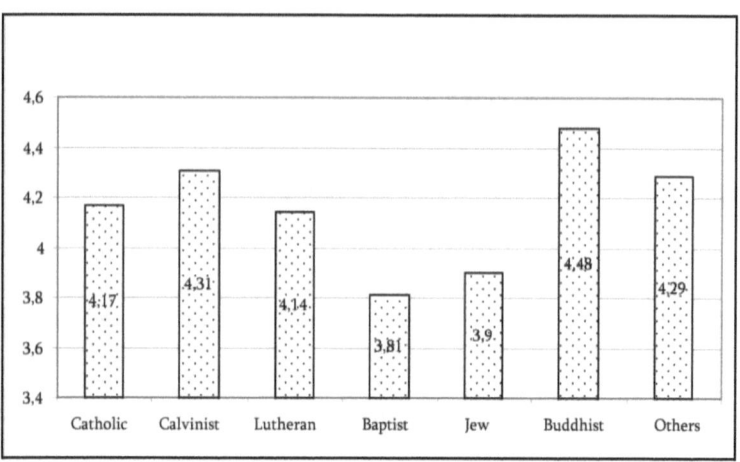

Chart 1: Perception of the seriousness of environmental problems by different religious communities, (1-5 scale)

Marks given by members of the Buddhist community are outstandingly high (mean: 4,48), this is followed by Calvinist, Catholic and Lutheran believers (the category "others" is so diverse that it is not possible to reach any conclusion). Compared to this environmental problems are regarded much less serious by members of the Jewish religious community and particularly Baptist believers.

We studied also the relationship between perception of ecological problems and the level of religious commitment. (Chart 2) Our results showed that religious commitment (active participation in the life of a church) is in inverse proportion to environmental concern (4,08–4,34 mean values in the two outermost categories).

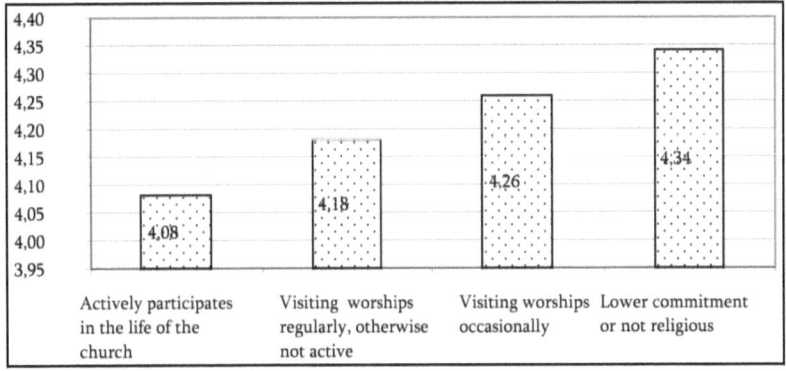

Chart 2: Judgment of the seriousness of environmental problems in relation to religious commitment, (1-5 scale)

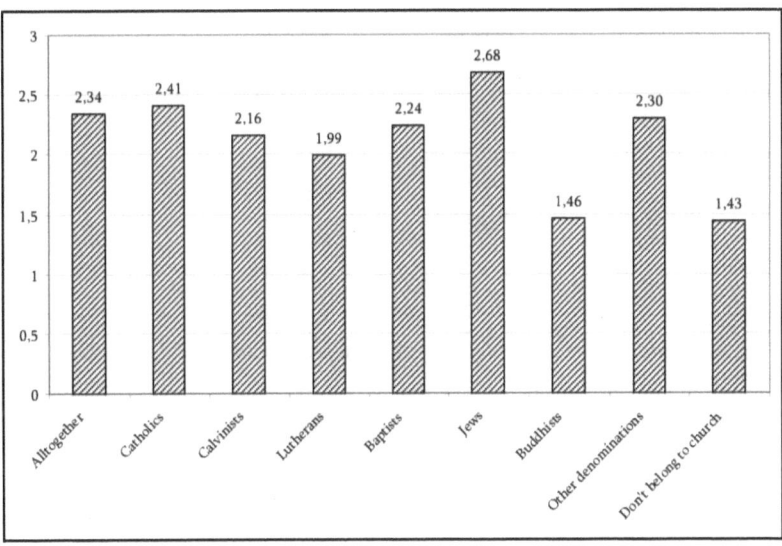

Chart 3: Acceptance of the complex „dominion thesis" (mean values of agreement by denominations)

In this section we also studied if White's "dominion thesis" is in fact more typical among those who have stronger commitment to churches, than in the less-committed or non-religious groups (Chart 3.), and whether there is any difference between different religious groups as it is shown by some international results (Hand et al. 1984; Shaiko 1987). For this we used two statements which basically describe the dominion thesis, and we asked the respondents to give 1-5 values according to the level of their agreement with the statements (1: don't agree at all; 5: totally agree). The two statements were as following:

1. World was created by God uniquely to serve aims and interests of humankind
2. Nature itself doesn't have any value, we have to protect it only to defend basic conditions of human life

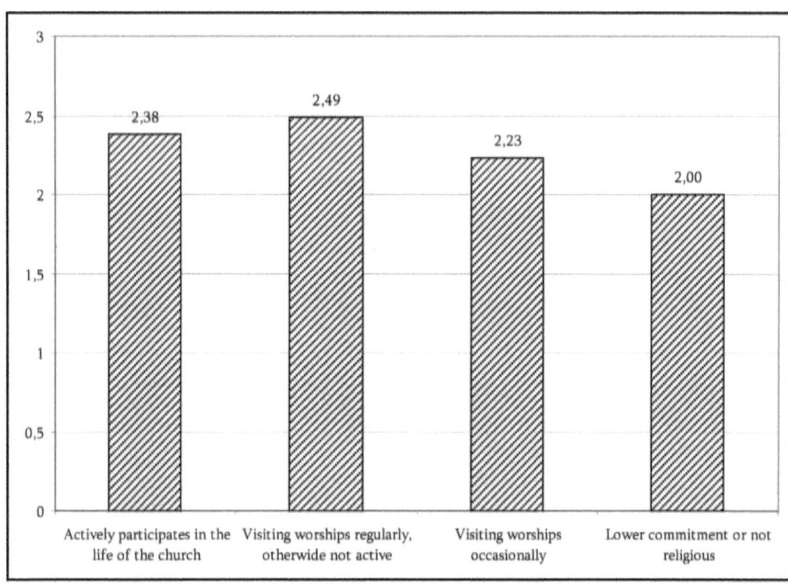

Chart 4: Acceptance of the complex „dominion thesis" (mean values of agreement by commitment groups)

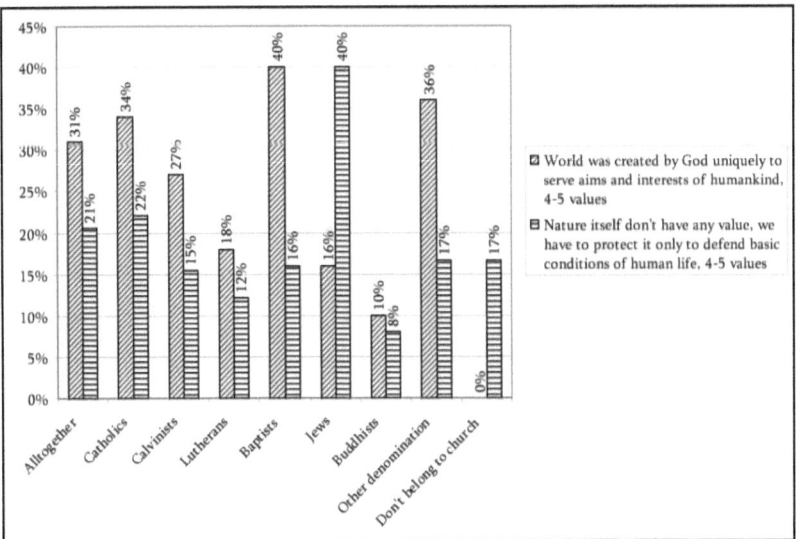

Chart 5: Agreement with the statements defining „dominion thesis" (proportion of those who gave 4 or 5 degrees) according to denominational commitment

Chart 3. shows answers to these two questions according to church commitment and Chart 4. according to the strength of belonging to each religion. There is an outstanding rejection of the two statements by members of the Buddhist community and among those who don't belong to any religion. There is a high level of agreement with the so defined dominion thesis first of all in the Jewish and Baptist community and to a bit more moderate extent among Catholics. It is interesting to see, that the judgment of the two statements, which have more or less the same meaning in our hypothesis (two definitions of the dominion thesis) is totally different among Jews and Baptists: one of the statements was widely accepted while the other was refused. (Chart 5.)

We also studied the appearance and attitudes of another possible Christianity-based nature conception and approach. The "good steward" attitude, which we identified as accepting ethical obligations and responsibility for the created world, was also defined by the agreement with two statements. These statements were:

1. Protection of the creation and the created world is an important duty of every believer

2. In our relationship with the physical world we, humans, are subjugated not only biological, but also moral laws

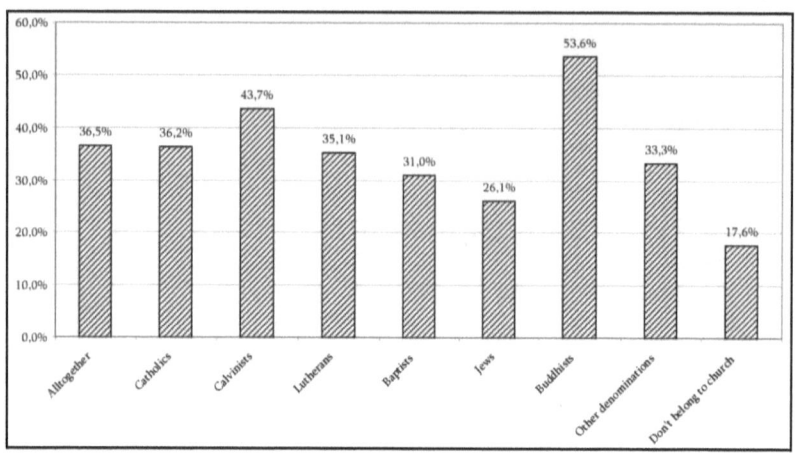

Chart 6: Proportion of „good stewards" by churches

We defined those respondents as members of the "good steward" group, who gave high (4-5) values to both questions. Proportion of "good stewards" is shown in Chart 6. and 7. according to church belonging and commitment groups. There is high proportion of "good stewards" in the Buddhist community, and slightly above the mean in the group of Calvinist respondents. Outstandingly low proportion was measured among those, who don't belong to any church, and a ratio under the mean was detected in the Jewish and the Baptist community. Conversely the ratio of "good stewards" is not in linear proportion to the strength of belonging to churches. (Chart 7.) The highest proportion was found in the group who visit worships occasionally, and the lowest value in the weakly or non-committed group.

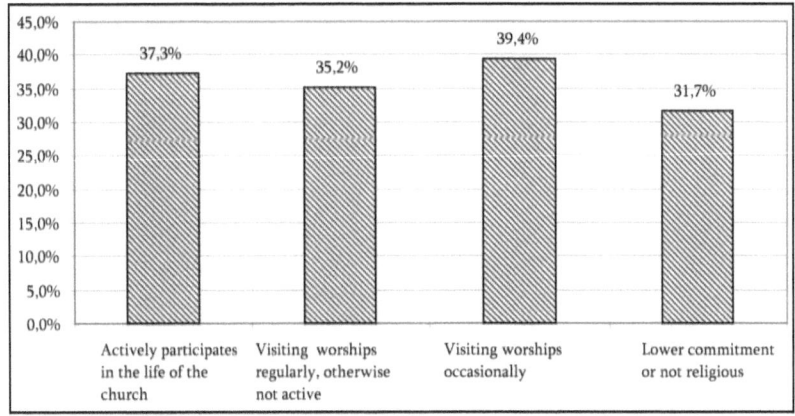

Chart 7: Proportion of „good stewards" in relation with the strength of belonging to churches

We also examined whether there is a difference between answers of "good stewards" given to other questions compared to all the other respondents. This comparison showed that "good stewards" generally consider environmental problems more serious, they attribute higher responsibility to churches and they are less satisfied with the activity of churches in this field. (Chart 8.) Also they tend to be more active in this field (Chart 9.) and they can mention church documents concerning environmental questions in a higher proportion (20%) than the mean (16%).

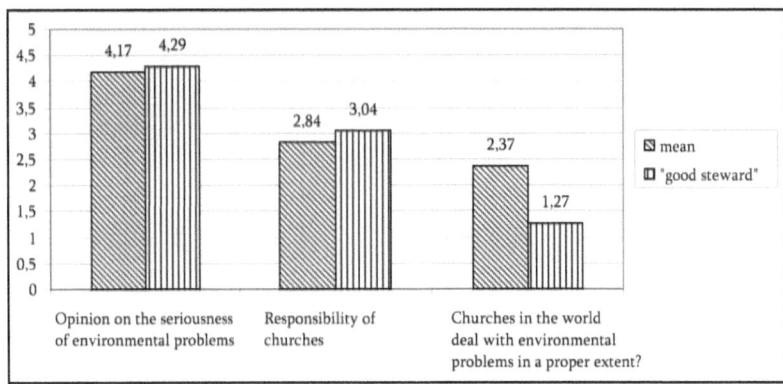

Chart 8: Opinion of „good stewards" in different questions compared to mean values

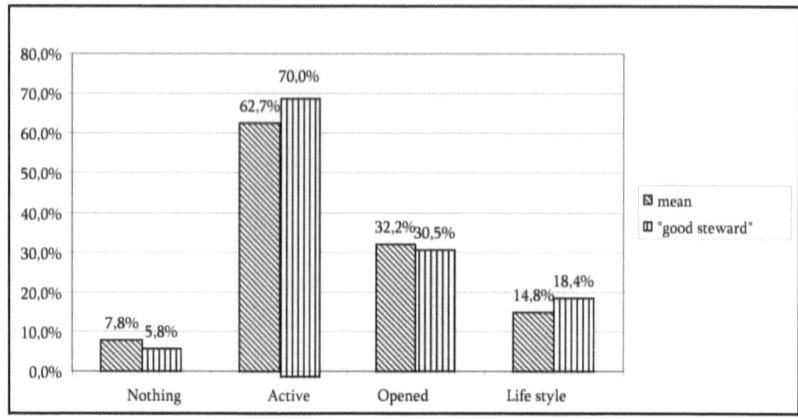

Chart 9: What would you do in your church to manage environmental problems? (Nothing = Nothing or no answer; Active = Some particular activity mentioned; Opened = Would be opened to such kind of activity, would join to them if someone started; Life style = Put in practice environmental principles not in public/church life, but in his/her own life)

In the next section of our research we studied, how believers think about responsibility of churches in managing environmental problems, if they ascribe any role or "ecological mission" to churches. How they recognize churches' activity in the topic, and to what extent they are informed about initiatives and documents of the churches?

First we asked respondents to value on a 1-5 scale the responsibility of churches in environmental field (1: no responsibility at all; 5: very high responsibility). Results showed, that highest responsibility was attributed to churches by Buddhists and those, who don't belong to any church, Calvinist, Lutheran, Baptist and Catholic respondents consider this responsibility almost the same while Jewish believers have the lowest expectations in this regard. (Chart 10.)

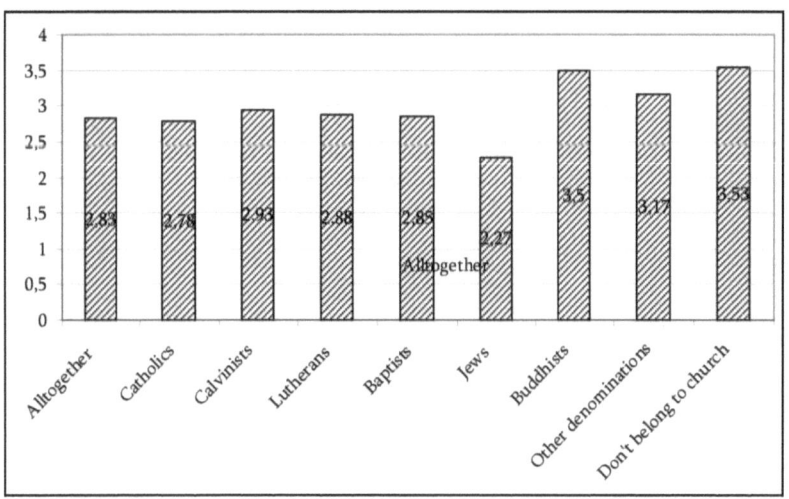

Chart 10: Responsibility churches in managing ecological problems, in different religious groups

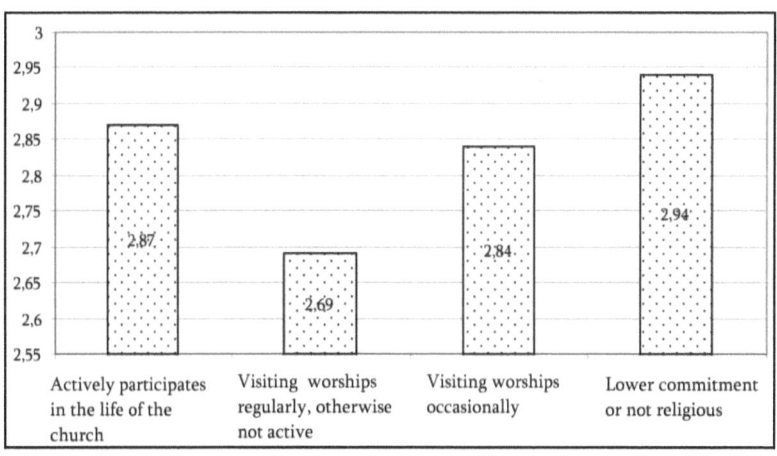

Chart 11: Responsibility churches in managing ecological problems, in relation to religious commitment, mean values on 1-5 scale

We couldn't find direct or linear relationship between strength of commitment to churches and the opinion about the environmental responsibility of churches. The weakly or non-committed respondents have the highest expectations, this value decreases with the augmentation of strength of commitment to churches, but reaches high level again in the most committed group. (Chart 11.) We got slightly controversial results when we asked respondents to specify, in their opinion who should act in managing environmental problems: government, NGOs, scientific life, public administration, churches, economic players, ourselves, and all of them or none of them (more than one answer was possible). Answers to this question showed that with the increase of religious commitment there is a parallel augmentation in the proportion of those who specified churches as necessary players in these efforts (13-13-18-20%). (Chart 12.)

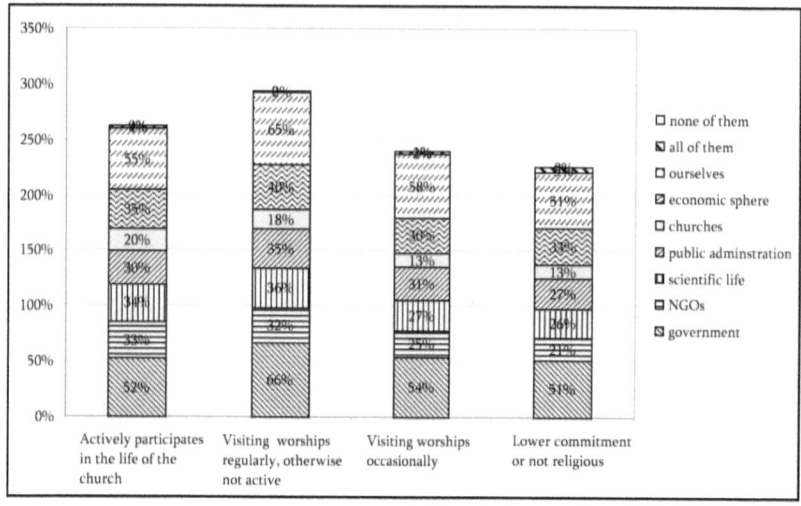

Chart 12: Who should act in managing ecological crisis? (more than one answer was accepted)

We also studied how churches' activity meets the believers' expectations. Generally we can state that believers are not satisfied with churches in this sense. Concerning churches in general, 47,1% of the respondents gave 1 or 2 on a 1-5 scale (1: not satisfied at all; 5: totally satisfied), and only 16% expressed his/her satisfaction with 4 or 5. When we posed the same question but churches in general was substituted wit Hungarian churches, the level of satisfaction decreased further on (4-5: 13,6%; 1-2: 50,5%). Respondents gave a bit better values to their own church than to other churches.

However we can say that believers are very poorly informed about initiatives and documents of churches concerning environmental issues. Only 16% of the respondents could mention any kind of church document, and 60% of the "Yes" answers was merely generality (e.g. "circular letters", "sermons, preaching", "papal messages", etc.), and only 40% (6,4% of the total sample) could name directly any kind of church document (our survey was carried out before the autumn of 2008, so before the release of the circular letter of the Hungarian Catholic Bishops' Conference or the publication of the World Council of Churches document in Hungarian).

Finally, we wanted to explore, what kind of activity is expected from the churches by their believers. For this we used an open question. Respondents could freely give suggestions what should churches do, without having answer possibilities. We merged given answers in eight categories:

1. Information, awareness raising
2. Religious teaching
3. Practical advice
4. Giving example, practical realization
5. Participation in and support of other initiatives
6. Other
7. Churches have nothing to do
8. No answer

Our results showed that respondents expect example-giving and practical realization (e.g. selective rubbish disposal, energy-saving solutions in church institutions, using and supporting alternative transport systems, etc.) This is followed by the claim to information, awareness raising and by religious teaching (in sermons, biblical education, religious schools, etc.) About a 9% of the respondents needs also practical advice from churches, and 8% participation in and support of other initiatives. 12% thinks that churches have no duties in this field. (Chart 13.) Giving example was least expected by Baptist believers, and most expected by Calvinists, while in the highest proportion (20%) members of the Jewish community wanted practical advices from their church. Giving information and awareness raising was supposed to be a duty of the church most widely in the Buddhist community, and Baptist and Jewish respondents agreed in the highest proportion that churches have no duties in environmental issues.

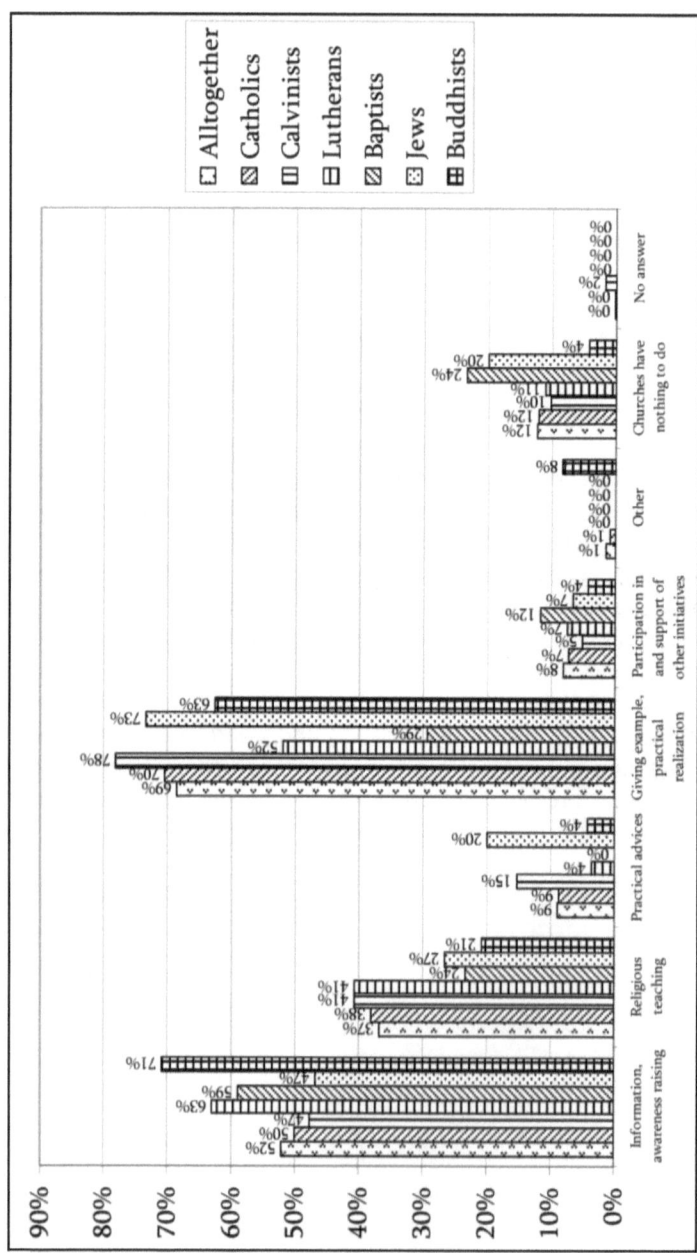

Chart 13: What the believers expect from the churches to do concerning environmental problems?

We also posed questions concerning cooperation of the churches with other players in combating environmental crisis. Three statements were given to respondents to value on a 1-5 scale their agreement with the statements (1: don't agree at all; 5: totally agree). These three statements were the following:

1. Churches should cooperate with each other in fighting (against) ecological problems;
2. Churches should cooperate with NGOs in fighting (against) ecological problems;
3. Churches should support every economic effort which leads to sustainable societies and ecosystems.

Answers showed that believers are most convinced of the necessity of cooperation among churches in environmental field, but also joint work with NGOs and the support of economic efforts are considered as important. (Chart 14.) Calvinist, Lutheran and Buddhist respondents required in the highest proportion this cooperation, but the difference is not outstanding compared to the mean. The Jewish and Baptist believers find the joint effort the least important, and they are far less aligned to cooperate with other churches (even the cooperation with NGOs is considered more important in this group). (Chart 15.)

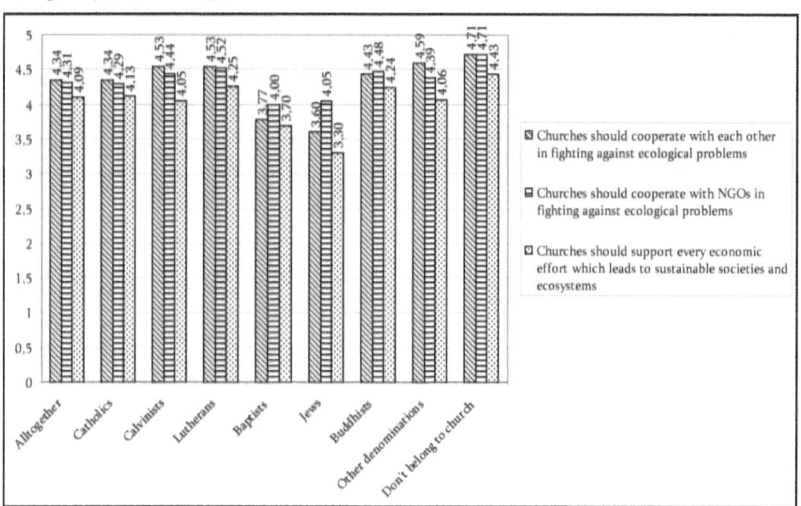

Chart 14: Who should churches cooperate with in your opinion ? (average agreement with the cooperation on 1-5 scale, mean values)

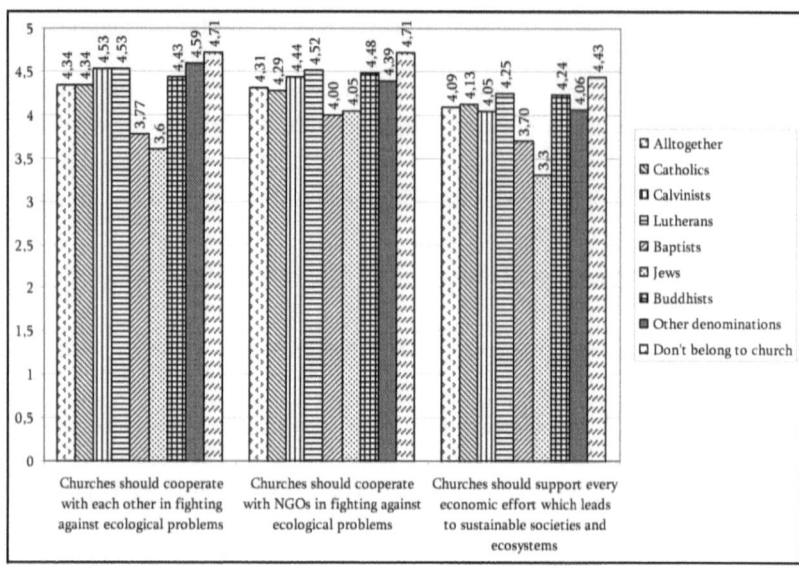

Chart 15: Opinions on the cooperation with different players (1-5 scale, mean values)

The comparison of different commitment groups showed that weaker commitment is tend to be in relation with a higher level of conviction about the importance of cooperation either with other churches or with the NGO and the economic sector. (Chart 16.)

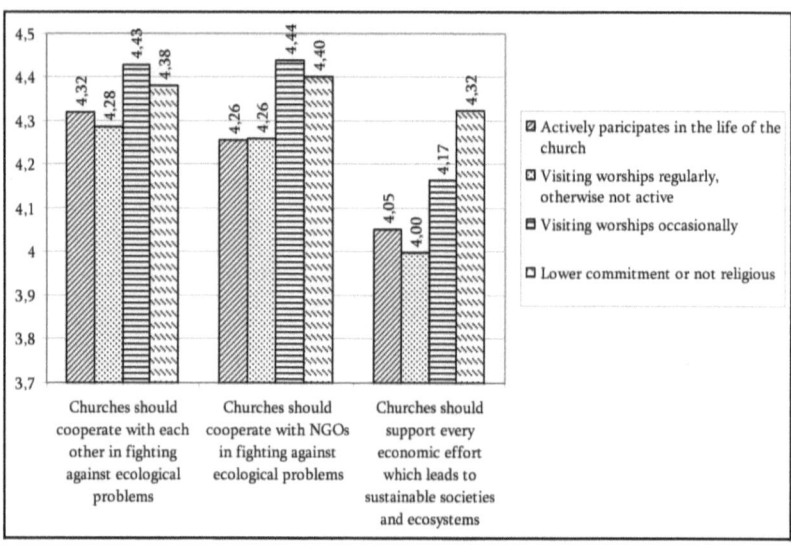

Chart 16: Mean values of the importance of cooperation in different commitment groups

Conclusion

In our study, which, according to our knowledge, is the first research in Hungary concerning environmental attitudes of religious communities, we reached the following conclusions. Answers of a sample of 800 persons showed that the strength of belonging to churches is in inverse proportion to the conviction of the seriousness of environmental problems. Those who are more active in the life of the churches consider ecological crisis less serious. Denominational commitment has a strong effect to this conviction. Buddhist believers see environmental crisis the most important danger (mean 4,48 on a 1-5 scale), but members of all churches, except Baptists (3,81) and Jews (3,9) gave values higher than 4 in this respect, this means that they regard environmental problems "very serious concern" or "the most important global problem".

These results support those theories which state that Christian tradition has a negative effect to environmental concern and attitude, and that this is not only a historical phenomenon but also presently can be detected. To study whether this experience is in relationship with White's hypothesis based on his "dominion thesis" or not, we surveyed the presence of the "dominion thesis" (which was defined by two statements) in religious communities. We experienced that among members of Jewish-Christian based churches there is a higher acceptance of the "dominion thesis" than among the Hungarian Buddhist community or than among those, who do not belong to any denomination or religious community. Regarding Jewish-Christian churches, in traditional protestant churches (Calvinists, Lutherans) we found a lower presence of this thesis, but the acceptance was over the mean in the Jewish community – but even here it didn't reach the medium level (average 2,68 on a 1-5 scale). There is an outstandingly high agreement with one of the statements defining "dominion thesis" in the Jewish and the Baptist community, however, the results here were a bit contradictory. In groups which were more strongly attached to churches we also found a higher level of acceptance of the "dominion thesis" than in weaker commitment groups. This acceptance reaches its maximum among those, who visit worships regularly, but otherwise they are not active in the life of the churches. Our final conclusion is that in Jewish-Christian churches we can identify a considerable group (20-30%) whose concept of human-nature relationship is based on the dominion thesis.

We also studied whether, besides of the adherents of the "dominion thesis", is it possible to identify another type of Jewish-Christian based approach to nature. We used the so called "good steward" approach, which is widely known in the international theoretical literature. Persons are regarded "good stewards" who accept responsibility for and moral imperatives to protect natural environment. We also defined the "good steward" approach with the level of agreement with two statements. We concluded, that in our sample there is a proportion of 30-40% respondents, who can be considered as "good steward". Highest ration of "good stewards" was detected among Buddhists (where more than 50% belonged to this group), in the lowest proportion among denominations we find them in the Jewish and the Baptist community. The far lowest proportion of "good stewards", however, was detected in the group of weakly or non-religious group. This backs our preconception that the "good steward" approach has its roots in religious tradition, what is in harmony with international results. (Kanagy-Nelsen 1995, Kanagy-Willits 1993) Generally "good stewards" consider environmental problems more serious, they attribute higher level of responsibility to churches, they are less satisfied with churches in dealing with environmental problems, they are (or could be) more active in this field and more informed of churches activity in this issue.

We also tried to assess how members of different religious communities in general see environmental activities and efforts of the churches. According to our results respondents attribute a medium level of responsibility to churches in managing environmental problems. Buddhists and the weakly or non-committed group consider this responsibility a bit stronger while Jews a bit weaker compared to the mean. The strength of belonging to churches decreases the level of the responsibility attributed to churches, which, however, reaches its minimum among those, who visit worships regularly, but otherwise are not active, and in the group of those who actively participate in the life of their church, reaches a relatively high level again. A 20% of this group reinforces at the concerning question that churches has no simply responsibility, but they also should practically act – proportion of those who answered so decreasing in parallel with the weakening of belonging to churches. A relative majority of believers is unsatisfied with activity of the churches in this field. In the first place among their expectations "giving example, practical realization" could be found (selective waste disposal, energy efficiency, etc.), followed by "information, awareness raising" and "religious teaching" (in sermons, preaching, biblical lessons, religious education). Other expectations (practical advice, participation in other initiatives) appeared only to a very small degree. Also few respondents thought that churches have no duties at all.

Our results showed that according to members of the religious communities churches should cooperate with other players. First of all the need for the cooperation among churches was expressed, but also the joint work with NGOs and support of economic efforts were considered important.

All in all we can say as a result of our study that environmental sensitiveness of religious communities is slightly lower compared to secularized society, but the problem is clearly present in their thinking. Besides of the traditional "dominion thesis" followers we can also identify the "good steward" group, a typically religious approach to nature, supporters of this concept can be found also in a great number in religious communities. Members of the churches consider dealing with environmental problems an important duty of the churches and they expect more activity on behalf of their church in this field.

References

Alternatív globalizáció a népekért és a Földért – Az Egyházak Világtanácsának dokumentuma és kísérő tanulmányok, Luther Kiadó – Védegylet, Budapest, 2008

Ann L. Owen – Julio Videras (2007): Culture and Public Goods: The Case of Religion and the Voluntary

Provision of Environmental Quality, *Journal of Environmental Economics and Management*, 54 September 2007, 162-180

Biel, Anders – Nilsson, Andreas (2005): Religious Values and Environmental Concern: Harmony and

Detachment, *Social Science Quarterly*, 86 (1), March 2005

Boyd, Heather Hartwig (1999): Christianity and the Environment int he American Public, *Journal for the Scientific Study of Religion*, 38 (1): 36-44

Eckberg, Douglas Lee; Blocker, T. Jean 1989 "Varieties of religious involvement and environmental concerns: testing the Lynn White thesis," *The Journal for the Scientific Study of Religion*, 28, 4, (Dec, 1989), pp. 509-517.

Felelősségünk a teremtett világért – a Magyar Katolikus Püspöki Konferencia körlevele a teremtett világ védelméről, MKPK, 2008. December 4.

Greely, Andrew (1993): Religion and Attitudes toward the Environment, *Journal for the Scientific Stufy of Religion*, 32 (1): 19-28

Guth, James L. – Green, John C. – Kellstedt, Lyman A. – Smidt, Corwin E. (1995): Faith and the Environment: Religious Beliefs and Attitudes on Environmental Policy, *American Journal of Political Science*, 39 (2) pp. 364-382

Hagevi, Magnus (2002): Religion and Environmental Opinion int he U.S. and Sweden, presentation at the *98th Annual Meeting and Exhibition of the American Political Science Association*, Boston, MA, August 29 –September 1., 2002

Hand, Carl M., Van Liere, Kent C. 1984 Religion, Mastery-Over-Nature, and Environmental Concern, *Social Forces*, 63(2):555-70

Kanagy, C. L. and F. K. Willits. 1993. A greening of religion? Some evidence from a Pennsylvania sample. *Social Science Quarterly* 74:674–83.

Kanagy, C.L. – Nelsen, H.M. (1995): Religion and Environmental Concern: Challenging the Dominant

Assumptions, *Review of Religious Research*, Vol. 37, No. 1 (September, 1995)

Religion and the 2008 Election:. A Pre-Election Analysis.; The Henry Institute National Survey on Religion and Public Life

Religion and the Environment: Polls Show Strong Backing for Environmental Protection Across Religious Groups; Pew Forum on Religion and Public Life Survey Reports (October 2004)

Shaiko, Ronald G. 1987. "Religion, politics, and environmental concern: A powerful mix of passions", *Social*

Science Quarterly 68: 244-262.

Sherkat, Darren E. – Ellison, Christopher G. (2007): Structuring the Religion-Environment Connection: Identifying Religious Influences aon Environmental Concern and Activism, *Journal for the Scientific Stufy of Religion*, 46 (1): 71-85

White, Lynn: *Historical roots of our ecological crisis*, Science, vol. 155. 1967.

Religious Research Perspectives

Religious Research in Europe

Viggo Mortensen

Religious Innovation and Pluralism in 21st century Europe (RIPE)

When the group that has formed the Network for the Study of Religious Innovation and Pluralism in contemporary Europe (RIPE) met for the first time in Aarhus, Denmark, 2006 it was reiterated that overall; there is a need to get a clearer picture of what is actually going on in the religious marketplace in Europe. Is what we are experiencing decline, revival, recycling or transformation of religion? Obviously conflicting tendencies can be observed, both privatization and de-privatization leading to an increased eclecticism on the background of a weakening of the traditional family structures of religious transmission. The ensuing fragmentation of the personal religious structure raises the question if it is at all possible in a modern European context to share common beliefs. A need was identified for studying what the "liberalization of the symbol market" entails for the individuals, for the institutions and for society as a whole. The weakening of the institutional governing systems of truths puts a heavy burden on the individuals. That can lead some people to move towards more structured religious communities, groups segregating and taking refuge into "bunker values" or "refuge identities". Thus individualization can paradoxically lead to the constitution or the invention of small closed community identities and strengthening traditionalist and fundamentalist trends within the religious traditions. This also constitutes a crucial political issue for society as a whole and a challenge for democracy. Moreover, pluralism can lead to relativisation. When more than one faith is recognized, all religions are being relativised, which again leads to secularisation and indifference. Others will focus on the supply side and stress that when pluralism increase the supply, then people is given a choice and "sale" is stimulated. Religion is then no longer a matter of necessity, but a question of choice to be considered in connection with choice of life style. Sometimes people make the choice blindly or they may even take over something by tradition. At other times people will – like in other consumer cases – make an informed choice, by which the function of religion in the modern society plays an important role. Scholars of sociology have brought forward the terms that religion may take care of the "collective memory", the "common discourse" or the "social capital". But one question remains: What provides the coherence of societies? Can consumerism and entertainment fulfil that role? Religion has in many societies played the role of giving coherence and identity to a given society. The Christian church used to and can in certain cases still administer part of this social capital in today's western society, but the share is declining, and declining rapidly because faith does not lead to commitment and taking responsibility.

The result of the workshop was the formation of a European network for Religious Innovation and Pluralism in 21st century Europe (RIPE) dedicated to study and analyze the cultural diversity and religious pluralism that comes with the changing cultural and religious landscape in Europe. The starting point is the fact that changes are happening. The next step was to explore the consequences for society, the individuals and the established religious institutions.

- The consequences for **society** can be explored in relation to such questions as
  1. the role of religion in the public domain, including civil religion and the legal framework concerning freedom of religion, and
  2. the governing of the relationship between church and state and the recognition of religious minorities.

- The consequences for the **individuals** can be explored in relation to the so called "return of religion". The reinvention of religion that is happening in contemporary Europe manifests itself in many forms, in the emergence of different forms of fundamentalisms and in a more loose turn to spirituality. Individuals are often caught in between and we see a development of hybrid identities and multiple belongings.

- The changes in the religious landscape have consequences for the **religious institutions**. The established religious institutions in Europe, i.e. the churches, are undergoing dramatic changes as they try to accommodate the new realities. A top priority is to study how they develop strategies for building interreligious relations by way of a dynamic theology of religions. New ecclesial models are tried out adapted to the changing religious and cultural landscape. The Christian and other religious diasporic communities contribute immensely to the new religious landscape in Europe which is so important to study in order to face the challenges of building interfaith harmony.

Cultural diversity and religious pluralism

Upon this background it was a natural choice for the next meeting of the RIPE network to propose the topic *Cultural Diversity and Religious Pluralism: the possible Dialogue in Europe*. This was the theme for the conference in Rome October 2007. Here the reigning diversity and religious pluralism in Europe was analyzed, and the following driving forces behind this development towards diversity and pluralism were identified:

- Globalisation followed by localisation
- Urban industrialisation and other macro structural tendencies that lead to a pluralisation of the religious spectrum
- Secularisation followed by de-secularisation or the return of religion
- Mediatisation & marketisation and other midrange structural tendencies
- Individualisation & hybridization and other micro social consequences that turns religion into a commodity that you choose in accordance with personal preference. Keywords: Transit & bricolage

Some will upon this background paint a very grim prospect at least for the majority religion. In a recent issue of the leading missiological journal *International Bulletin of Missionary Research (IBMR 31/3 July 2007)* the religious situation in Europe is in focus under the heading: *Europe: Christendom Graveyard or Christian Laboratory?* The main articles have titles such as *Godless Europe?* by Philip Jenkins and *Can Europe be saved?* by Lamin Sanneh. The notion of Eurabia is mentioned. Just to give you an impression here are a couple of citations:

> "Will the rapid pace of dechristianization push Europe to the fringes of the Muslim world as Eurabia? Will Spain revert to Islam? Will Britain become North Pakistan,France the Islamic Republic of New Algeria, Spain the Moorish Emirate of Iberia, Germany the new Turkey? Will Brussels and Belgium become Belgistan. Will Italy and Albania merge to become a new Albanian Islamic Federation? As Libya's president Qaddafi asserts: "There are signs that Allah will grant Islam victory in Europe without swords, without guns, without conquests. The fifty million Muslims of Europe will turn it into a Muslim continent within a few decades." (IBMR 31/3, p. 121)

A more thorough analysis and documentation is presented in Philip Jenkins book *God's Continent: Christianity, Islam, and Europe's Religious Crisis*. This is the third volume of his ambitious trilogy examining religion in global perspective. There was *The Next Christendom: The Coming of Global Christianity*, followed by *The New Faces of Christianity: Believing the Bible in* the Global South. In God's Continent, Jenkins seeks to counter what he views as the excessively dismal, even alarmist, analyses of the future of Europe.

As one has come to expect from Jenkins, God's Continent is full of information, and he develops a many faceted argument stressing that "both Christianity and Islam face real difficulties in surviving within Europe's secular cultural ambience in anything like their familiar historic forms." Both will have to adapt to what sociologist Peter Berger calls "Euro secularity," and, in fact, both are doing just that. Economically, Europe will continue to need large numbers of immigrants, particularly to support its welfare states with aging native populations. Immigrants will mainly be Muslim, and, while their birth rate is high, and much higher in their native countries, the rate among second- and third-generation immigrants in Europe is falling.

In general, Europe is not necessarily as secular as it appears to be. Jenkins draws on the work of Grace Davie and others to the effect that the European phenomenon is one of "believing without belonging." At the same time, Jenkins knows that not too much comfort is to be drawn from survey research suggesting that Europeans are still residually Christian. "Such evidence for 'latent faith' does not necessarily offer comfort for Christians in the longer term, as it is not clear how many decades cultural memories can survive. Residual Christianity may be in reasonable health a generation or so after institutional structures went into free fall, but the situation in thirty or forty years could be very different. We might presently be seeing only a transitional phase in religious decline, on the path from active affiliation to total indifference. Still, the picture of sudden Christian decline is more complex than it initially appears." At times, Jenkins directly challenges the prophets of the death of Europe; at other times, he simply claims that the situation is more complex than they suggest.

Jenkins offers a fine historical sketch of Christian-Muslim relations, countering the bizarre but widespread notion that Islam has typically been the victim of Christian assertiveness. The growth of Islam in Europe today has other causes than an on-going struggle against Christianity. It is "the empire that comes home". And then there is the desperate economic need for workers. The result is *that European nations in coming decades will have to take account of aspects of Muslim culture, or rather of the north African and Asian cultures brought by Muslim immigrants; but that is quite different from envisioning wholesale Islamization ... Yet matters are not so terrifying [as many contend]. While sections of European Islam in recent years have acquired a strongly militant and politicized character, we have to understand this as a response to temporary circumstances; moreover, hard-line [Islamic] approaches still command only minority support. In the longer term, the underlying pressures making for accommodation and tolerance will prove hard to resist."*

That is Jenkins' somewhat sanguine prognosis. He bases it on many factors. For instance, he says the religious fervour of most Muslims in Europe is greatly exaggerated. Secularization is taking the same toll among Muslims as among Christian young people. In dealing with Muslims, European states make the mistake of treating chiefly with the clergy, who are often in the pay of foreign powers such as Saudi Arabia and Morocco, and are not representative of most Muslims. In general, he says it is a mistake to treat Muslims *as Muslims* when, in fact, they are poor and marginalized immigrants who, in most cases, are only incidentally Muslims.

It is my contention that Jenkins seriously understates the religio-ideological challenge of Jihadism, the belief that every Muslim has an obligation to employ whatever means necessary to advance the world's submission to Islam. It is true, as he says, that such hard-liners are in a minority; hard-line fanatics are usually a minority. But, of a billion Muslims in the world and thirty million in Europe, a small minority can do a great deal of damage. For all the horror of the attacks to date, one can agree that it is noteworthy that there have been so few. Quite recently a Dutch report was published indicating that radical Islamism in Europe are deploying new tactics.

(https://www.aivd.nl/aspx/get.aspx?xdl=/views/aivd/xdl/page&SitIdt=25&VarIdt=13&ItmIdt=108805) Islamists are no longer in favour of using terror but has a more direct political message followed by an effort to create enclaves in society, where Islamic legislation reign. Democracy is denounced for putting humans above God. Tina Magaard, Danish researcher in Islamism states as she gives her evaluation of this new trend: "Islamism as political ideology attacks the software of society. Instead of ruining the computer as Al-Qaeda attempts, the new islamists will ruin or change the software, the basic values in the secular democracy." (Kristeligt Dagblad 11/10 2007) We should always remember that most of the Balkans was not conquered by Islam through force but they responded positively to the Islamic dahwa.

Jenkins rightly reminds us of the force of historical contingencies that can be neither anticipated nor controlled. But the conflicts we have had so far are intra-European struggles within an indisputably Christian narrative. Deists, atheists, and skeptics in that narrative are unmistakably Christian deists, atheists, and skeptics. Islam is, and understands itself to be, a militant counter narrative. It is, to use our academic jargon, the "other," and it is an "other" with no history of multicultural sympathy with the other to which it is "other."

Jenkins says European Christianity must accommodate itself to being a "creative minority." In relation to Islam, that sounds an awful lot like dhimmitude, in this case joined to secularism's toleration of Christians so long as they mind their manners; which means that Christians agree that their faith is a private religious preference without public consequence. A creative minority could have culture-transforming effects that we cannot now anticipate. But as a whole Jenkins presents us with a thought provoking overview that also should encourage reflections within religious institutions. In Denmark we have gone through a specific learning experience. I am talking about the so-called Mohammed or Cartoon crisis that I here will see as an expression of orientalism.

The cartoon crisis as expression of orientalism

An old adage within the ecumenical movement states that it is the world that is writing the agenda of the church. Today there can be no doubt that in Europe it is radical Islam, Islamism, which is writing the agenda of the world. Thus it should also be radical Islam that should be writing the agenda of the church. Due to several factors and among them a tendency to political correctness this has up till now not been the case, but there are indications that things are changing. I am thinking of the new emphasis within the Catholic church of reciprocity and the clearer voice coming out of the German churches. The reasons for these changes are the severity of the situation. As Lamin Sanneh writes: "The Muslim challenge implies that Europe can again be a continent only if it becomes God's continent. Yet whose God that is will determine what kind of continent Europe becomes" (s. 125). In Denmark we have had the incident of the Cartoon crisis and in Europe we have had the controversy around the Popes speech in Regensburg.

The Mohammed or the cartoon/caricature crisis 2005 was – seen from the vantage point of religious studies – a classic example of what we term orientalism. But it began with a murder and developed into a very severe crisis with around 150 killed and diplomatic relations severely hurt. To me this was a conflict that was ignited because of misunderstandings from both sides. The West displayed a blatant orientalism and was met by equally strong expressions of Occidentalism. If there is a lesson to be learned from this it can be summarized in four points:

- No room for double standards:
- What is said in the corner will be shouted out from the rooftops
- Islam is a strong religion

- The "Umma" is in place and functioning.

The changes in the European religious scene are obvious and our American observers give us the choice: Graveyard or laboratory. Although some of us can have a preference for the quietness and calm of well-preserved graveyards, to me there can be no doubt. I opt for the noisy and laborious laboratory. So this is what Europe is today: A laboratory where it is possible to experience and study what happens when a formerly mono-religious Christian continent turns multi-religious. The options are numerous and it is quite open in what direction it will go: religion can vanish; churches can disappear and be replaced by strong fundamentalist religions or by a weak religiosity that as a varnish is spread thinly like New Age religiosity already functions today.

Philip Jenkins observes that both Christianity and Islam face real difficulties in surviving within Europe's secular cultural ambience in anything like their familiar historic forms. Europe is a historical phenomenon, and Europe without its familiar historic forms is not Europe. To speak of the death of Europe is not to suggest that the continent called Europe will disappear. It is possible that "Eurosecularity" in sustained tension with an Islamo-Christian cultural ambience will flourish, at least economically, for generations to come. But, with the establishment of Eurabia or the Maghreb, Europe "in anything like its familiar historic forms" will be a memory. That is what is meant by the death of Europe.

The American author Richard John Neuhaus ends his thorough analysis of Jenkins Book as follows:

> "At a recent dinner party with European intellectuals, I put to an influential French archbishop Daniel Pipes' projection: Either assimilation or expulsion or Islamic takeover. That, he said, puts the possibilities much too starkly. "We hope for the first," he said, "while we work at reducing immigration and prepare ourselves for soft Islamization." Soft Islamization. It is a wan expression. Whether soft or hard, the prospect is that, in the not-so-distant future, someone will publish a book titled Allah's Continent. In fact, several Muslim authors have already published books with very similar titles, anticipating the future of the Europe that was. Needless to say, and historical contingencies being as contingent as they are, I very much hope that they turn out to be wrong."
>
> (The Much Exaggerated Death of Europe. First Things: A Journal of Religion, Culture and Public Life
> http://www.firstthings.com/article.php3?id_article=5488&var_recherche=%22the+much+exaggerated+death+of+europe%22)

The possible dialogue in Europe

But what is the alternative? The alternative to islamization and secularisation is dialogue, dialogical democratic communities. In Denmark like in other European countries we have had a very lively discussion on the role of religion in nation building and in the public square. The background is that Denmark like all European nations has gone through a process of secularisation and modernization. The result of this process was a naked public square. When religions come back in different forms, as it happens in Europe right now, there is a temptation to opt (again) for a sacred public square. From my viewpoint neither of these possibilities is good. We should develop a civic public square. On the basis of some core values and human rights, – including freedom of religion and the right to change belief without any repercussions whatsoever, and the rights of minorities, – the differences should be negotiated to ensure the maximum freedom for the individual. As it has rightly been pointed out: Religion can function both in a negative and in a positive way, but it is always a force to be reckoned with. When religions want to play a part in the nation building process and thus function as civil religion, they need to tone down their confessional identity and develop structures that allow for others to have full freedom of religion. Respecting minority views does not exclude that there can be a lead culture in a given society, as is the case with for instance pancasilla in Indonesia and folkchristianity in Denmark. Different metaphors have been employed to characterize the multicultural society that is the most likely result of the present globalization: Melting pot, salad bowl, symphony, and rainbow. I favour two other metaphors, artichoke and Lego. They underline both respect for diversity and the necessary drive towards unity. Diversity and plurality can indeed be celebrated but it can only come into full bloom if it is nourished by and contribute to the common good.

Here interreligious dialogue comes into play as a way to bridge the gap between different viewpoints. With Hans Küngs famous words: There is no peace between nations without peace between religions; and there is no peace between religions without interreligious dialogue. Dialogue we have in order to further understanding. In the encounter with "the other" one experiences both alienation and commonalities and the aim is to incorporate what is different into a common frame of reference or horizon, what the German philosopher Hans Georg Gadamer calls "Horizontverschemlzung". To understand is to change. I am different when I leave a dialogue compared to when it started. That is why dialogue is a risky business and truly difficult because you are requested both fully to encounter "the other" and keep your own horizon of understanding intact. Of the many forms of dialogue

(dialogue of life and action, the spiritual dialogue and the intellectual dialogue) those who focus on the more practical issues have the best possibilities to succeed. A good starting point is to act together in order to alleviate concrete suffering. If that proves successful a fruitful framework for a more extended dialogue is created. Interreligious dialogue is a good instrument to dismantle prejudices. The biggest threat to interfaith harmony is the lack of knowledge of "the other" and an inadequate understanding of one's own position.

My experience with interreligious dialogue has mainly been in the context of the Asian Europe Meetings (ASEM). Here I have learned that freedom of religion is the most important and also most contested issue within the dialogue. When everybody agrees on the fundamentality of this, the road can be cleared towards a tolerant society. It includes the following steps:

- What is to be tolerated is what is unacceptable
- In order to argue why one disagrees with the other one needs to argue on how to create a tolerant society.
- It must be clear what cannot be tolerated.
- The intolerant cannot be tolerated
- What can be tolerated is constantly debatable and must be solved in open discourse.
- Thus freedom of speech is indispensable.

Religious tolerance presupposes a discussion of what can be tolerated and what cannot be tolerated, and this is exactly what needs to be cleared through interreligious dialogue. Thus interreligious dialogue is a condition for the survival of religious plural societies.

As we have seen, the development is underlying certain megatrends that cause transformations that lead to new models. Protestantisation of religion will let secularisation prevail. Islamisation of Christianity will create a totally new agenda. How it will all develop remains to be seen. Recently the debate concerning state and religion has been reinvigorated under the catchword of the cohesion of society. Historically religions have in several cases played a pivotal role in providing for stability and coherence of society. That is why many people, concerned with the cohesion of a given society, are asking now how much diversity a society can include or just tolerate. It is clear how integration becomes key:

- If separation due to globalisation is impossible (the westphalian principle)
- If parallel development is unethical and unsustainable (apartheid), then integration is the only possibility.
- Integration presupposes tolerance towards the different and a clear position towards what is not tolerable.

If we do not want to restrict religious and cultural pluralism in our societies, then the different religions in pluralistic societies are confronted with a number of challenges and I will end with enumerating those:

- How can they develop the potential in their own religion for an attitude of respect and inclusiveness for adherents of other religions in order to promote peace and understanding between the different religious groups in society?
- How can the claims to universality and absoluteness in the religious traditions be handled, so that "the other" is not excluded from fully participating also in democratic processes of any given society?
- How can religions contribute positively to the common good of society? What can be brought to the common table as a gift from the various religious traditions?
- How can different religious communities relate to or contribute to the development of common values and norms in society so that they are not seen as threats to the stability of society but contributors to the cohesion of society?
- How can we do all this and at the same time respect the specific religious identities?

Our late modern period is characterized by the fact that nothing is absolutely certain. Absolute or universal truths are a little ridiculous. We live in a dialogical culture where it is uncommon to just automatically to adapt to transmitted established truths. In Europe Christianity is such a transmitted established truth with a very long history; and it is difficult to communicate its inherent truths claims in such a cultural environment. It goes especially for Protestantism. In a global culture so – through the media – fixated on the external and visibility, it is difficult to explain a form of religion that basically is about internal change. As the individual is justified by faith alone and not by works there is nothing to show! The message is only a rumour or a story, but if nobody listens the rumour will stop running. And this is exactly what has happened. We have in the last 50 years in Europe experienced a thorough loss of understanding and practicing of the Christian tradition. This loss of tradition makes itself felt now. The French sociologist Hervieu Leger has used the notion of ex-culturation of Christianity in Europe in order to name this development. The reason for this ex-culturation is that for the average European there is no physical need for religion. We are not hungry; we do not fear death; we do not mourn the loss of our eternal soul; we do not fear eternal damnation. In addition the basic family unit so important for transmission of inherited truths are undergoing as it seems irreversible changes. The lifelong holy matrimony built on a perceived natural order is changing into contractual partnerships and single parent relationships not conducive to formal transmission of religious heritage. Instead we see new types of religious socialization: The seeker, the pilgrim, the convert, the refugee.

The ruling class consisting of a secular elite seems to prefer an agnostic civilisation. The problem is if the people of Europe will accommodate to such a view, because there is still this hunger for alternative ways of looking at the world, a hunger for meaning, a hunger for God. The market does what it can to meet this hunger. The marketisation makes religion a commodity. From Feng Shui to holistic medicine, from aroma therapy candles to yoga weekends, spirituality is big business. It promises to soothe away the angst of modern living and to offer an antidote to shallow materialism. If you are not attracted to this offer at the vanity fair you can join the hardliners, because another trend is the growth of fundamentalism and neo confessionalism. Fundamentalism is growing in all major world religions, whether Islam, Hinduism, Judaism or Christianity. In addition we have seen a growth of aggressive atheism. I need not give examples here. Sales charts of books by Dawkins, Hitchens and others talking about the God delusion speak louder than words.

But there is still this hunger, and those possessed by that hunger will come together in communities where they will find their identity. They will come to know what they are by realizing what they are not. That is why, in such an engaged culture, dialogue will be of the utmost importance; dialogue of life and a dialogue of faiths. But we might expect that the climate for such interreligious dialogue is going to get a little harsher. The fundamental problem is of course that if a person is not firmly rooted in his or her own tradition the dialogue tend to be superficial and function as mere window dressing. This has in some corners given dialogue a bad name. In spite of that there is no alternative.

The Necessity of the Study and Research of Jewish-Christian Relations as a Coherent Field of Academic Inquiry

Judit Hermann

> Teach thy tongue to say
> *'I do not know,'*
> and thou shalt progress.
>
> (Maimonides)

Ever since 2005, when I received the invitation for the Sir Sigmund Sternberg Fellowship from the Cambridge based Center of Studies of Christian Jewish Relations/ CJCR /, I was dedicated to use every opportunity to build liaison and co-operation – both on personal and institutional level – between the Centre and the Hungarian institutions I was associated with. When I first entered the Library of the Centre this dedication became a devotion, almost a passion. I remembered the hardships we experienced because of the lack of literature and resources during more than a decade in our work within the Hungarian Christian Jewish Society, and here I found a special, expertly selected large library, a collection of materials connected to the different fields and aspects of Christian Jewish relations and dialogue culture in general. There were corners dedicated to the different theological aspects, separate spaces, even rooms filled with material about the ancient and medieval history, the political, sociological and ethical questions of the relations, a special Holocaust studies room of course, and a very interesting collection of studies in art, literature and film related to Christian Jewish relations. Only by browsing in the library one could have a sense that the research of this field is an interdisciplinary endeavor, by my opinion a paradigm of modern science in general. I have led the view for a long time, that the significance of the study and analysis of Christian Jewish relations lies in great degree in the fact that the nature of this relation, the problems and events emerging from it throughout its history provide a paradigmatic field for the deeper understanding of human society and the world in general. As the beloved late Pope John Paul II stated to Chief Rabbi Toaff: "Our encounter is a sign of hope for the world"[226]

The Library's material showed not just the interdisciplinary character of the field, but also suggested that the study of relations and dialogue culture constituted a coherent new branch of modern science.

---

[226] The Pope's Address to Professor Elio Toaff, Chief Rabbi of Rome, on the Occasion of the Tenth Anniversary of the Historic Visit to the Synagogue of Rome. 15, April, 1996.

I started my research work by collecting material about the great pioneers, the outstanding personalities who opened the door and helped the way for a new era in Christian Jewish encounter, especially during the last 50 years. A Pantheon opened in front of my eyes. Reading about Jules Isaac whose wife and daughter perished in Auschwitz, and who right after loosing them, in 1946 wrote *Jesus and Israel* and then immediately began organizing conferences between rabbis and priests sympathetic to his cause to change Christian teaching and the tradition of contempt towards Jews. Or I could mention the fascinating story of the meeting of Cardinal Bea and Rabbi Heschel paving the way for Nostra Aetate, or many stories of similar importance from which one could understand and follow the foundation of Judeo-Christian dialogue. The same way we can see the related focal issues of philosophy, from the works of Franz Rosenzweig to that of Levinas and many other contemporary thinkers paving the way for this new field of research, and we can follow the same process in theology in the thinking of many modern theologians, or read special resources for the study and understanding of the historical Jesus, mainly from works of great Jewish contributors starting from DavidFlusser to Geza Vermes. In the library and curriculum of CJCR we can find material about the core matters of the science of dialogue culture, one of the most important research fields in our contemporary world, from Martin Buber to David Bohm. I cannot emphasize enough to Hungarians how important it is to familiarize themselves with these scholars.

I started to prepare presentation materials on the members of this pantheon to create a kind of popular introduction, let's say a reading for the general public, for secondary school level, or as a lecture book used in universities. I also translated W. Simpson and Ruth Weyl's book *'The Story'*, a history of the International Council of Christians and Jews that presented using first hand testimony of participants the very process of this history of the dialogue and the establishment of many international Christian Jewish organization. I find this work necessary not only to provide material in Hungarian, which is very sparse, at least regarding the special results of the study of relations as an independent field. I am deeply devoted to this work because I consider it indispensable to inject down to root level and implant in the general public the knowledge about the results of these fifty years of development. I hold the view that when launching this process in 1947 the ICCJ's Seelisberg Conference was right in its initiative to recommend the education of clergy and the leaders of the society to render them knowledgeable in the basic points of the new aspects in the relations. The revelations about the importance of Christian Jewish relations could have altered the way of thinking of people who were in charge of education. This was very important. But a process that began 50 years ago stemmed from a wider and deeper need. The aspects of the relations touch many fields of our lives. I experience great interest when the topic arises among young and not so young people of every denomination and of different levels of education. I always encounter great interest and lack of information. The modern history of Christian Jewish relations has a concrete history and concrete development that has changed the world and altered world view in such a way that today we cannot talk about the role of religion and churches in society without proper knowledge of the 50 y ears history of Christian Jewish dialogue and relations. In a world that is ever more divided and faces so many cultural, social, economic and ethical challenges it would be so much harder to fall for different manipulations of opinion – nowadays frequently used as virtual weapons – if the knowledge about the results of this research field were elaborate and widely available to the public.

Let me recall a recent example from my personal experience. During the first days of the outbreak of the recent Gaza conflict, here in Hungary my fellow members in the Equestrian Order of the Holy Sepulcher of Jerusalem – highly educated and devoted Catholics – initiated a prayer session for peace. While discussing on the internet the reasons and purposes of the prayer session – a discussion that by my opinion raised a lot of theological and political questions worthy of clarification – two of the knights, my fellow members in the Order, had a debate and disagreement about what it was John Paul II had eventually said about praying for the Jews, and if he had talked about the subject, what had he meant by it. I thought this discussion was a good example of how much harder it would be to hold false ideas or propagate wrong directions if basic resources were readily available in public. While reading this discussion I could glance at the book in my desk: "*Spiritual Pilgrimage. Texts on Jews and Judaism by John Paul II*" published by Eugene Fisher and Leon Klenicki[227]. Professor Fisher who is adviser of the National Conference of Catholic Bishops of the USA was Sternberg Fellow in CJCR just before I arrived there. He understood the importance of preparing materials in Hungarian, and kindly gave me the right of translation of this book. I am working on it now hoping that back home I'll find a medium for understanding its significance. The book is part of the many contributions that are presently emerging as a special field in research and studies about the work and contribution of Pope John Paul II. In the present situation, when the recent developments, among them the Vatican's movements, seemingly altered the path of reconciliation and put obstacles in front of Christian Jewish relations to such an extent that for a while it looked like I

---

[227] Crossroad Herder Book New York 1995.

should change almost every statement of my lecture; it is extremely important to be able to see the situation as a whole. We must do everything to help to develop this holistic approach in the wide society. Concerning the history of Christian Jewish relations I can say that in the last 50 years we have achieved great results. These achievements could help to recognize moments of a complicated and hard conflicts as momentums of a hard struggle and evolution of thoughts. The results of our research can help us to see these events as part of a painful process of the emerging deep changes in our world view, recognize attacks on this process and distinguish manipulations. For this it is indispensable to implant basic facts and information in the wider public about the achievements of the relations and dialogue.

I am happy to say that the Centre of Study in Christian Jewish Relations understands this need. The Cambridge based institute that celebrated the 10th anniversary of its foundation in the autumn term of the 2008/09 academic year, can state that by the end of 2011 nearly 200 of its students will have a postgraduate degree in Christian Jewish relations as a special field of academic inquiry. During this decade more than 2000 students have visited the Centre and have been associated with it in the different fields of the academic work. Let me quote from the anniversary commemorations: "Theologians, political scientists, historians, classicists, policemen, engineers, art historians, literary studies specialists and many others have and continue to pass through the Centre to study Christian Jewish relations." I have to add here: to study it at a top academic level. Let me proudly say: on a "Cambridge level", as the Centre worthy of the great Cambridge tradition has become a leading academy in the field in Europe and in the world in general. Since 1998 the MA and other postgraduate degrees given by the Centre have been approved by the distinguished Cambridge based Anglia Ruskin University where Christian Jewish Relations became one of the University's largest MA programs. This paved the way by 2006 for CJCR to open the course of *Master of Studies in Christian Jewish Relations*, a degree approved by the University of Cambridge. The Master of Studies degree offered by the Centre is in conjunction with the Faculty of Divinity and the Institute of Continuing Education of the University of Cambridge. The Faculty of Divinity which is one of the oldest Faculties of the University of Cambridge accepts that the MSt includes sufficient training towards the minimum requirements for a Cambridge PhD level.

This Faculty of the University has always been at the forefront in theological studies that had a great impact on the processes in the development of world view and whole social systems.

CJCR, which has been an Associate Member of the Cambridge Theological Federation since 1999 – understands and follows the very nature of this interdisciplinary field, and brings together many scholars and professionals apart from theology too who share an interest in advancing education about Jewish Christian relations.

The aim of implanting knowledge in wide circles was assisted by the 1999 launching of the Distance Learning program that CJCR students could join via correspondence or the Internet. Now the MSt course in conjunction with the Institute of Continuing Education of the University of Cambridge promotes lifelong studies. It just shows what a modernizing effect the study of Christian Jewish relations can have in general, that CJCR's MSt program is the first occasion when the Cambridge University allows the participants undertake a substantial part of their learning on the Internet and accepts the study by E-learning.

I frequently encounter great surprise and astonishment among young Hungarians, even among university students, when I say that one can acquire a Cambridge University approved MSt degree in Christian Jewish relations. It would be the subject of another study and lecture how this statement would sound today in the wider public in Hungary.

It also would require a special lecture to present the latest achievement of the Centre of great importance. In 2006 CJCR broke new ground and paved the way for the study of Muslim-Jewish relations. The Centre of Studies in Muslim Jewish relation, the CMJR, in conjunction with the Institute of Continuing Education of the University of Cambridge offers a certificate in Islam/Jewish relations. CJCR and its sister Centre CMJR today comprise the Woolf Institute of Abrahamic Faith.

Recommending just a few important publications of the Institute, allow me to mention first of all the handbook, titled *Valuing Diversity* that has been prepared by the Institute to provide material for teachers to meet the goals in the compulsory British national curriculum to promote national cohesion. I also have to recommend to you the outstanding publications of CJCR's many distinguished authors. The full list is available on the Centre's Website (www.woolfinstitute.cam.ac.uk/cjcr). Let me mention here two titles relevant to the subject of our conference: Lucia Faltin, & Melanie Wright: *The Religious Roots of Contemporary European Identity*[228], and Edward Kessler & James Aitken: *Challenges in Jewish-Christian Relations*.[229]

---

[228] London & New York: Continuum. 2007.
[229] New York: Paulist Press 2006.

But first of all I have to draw to your attention a pioneering work, the first comprehensive guide: Edward Kessler and Neil Wenborn: A *Dictionary of Jewish Christian Relations*[230], that comprises more than 700 entries defining the many factors connected with the study of the historic and ongoing Jewish Christian relations. Edward Kellser, founding and executive director of CJCR under the auspices of the Centre, and Neil Wenborn with the cooperation of Cambridge University Press created a Dictionary that is an excellent reference book in the academic studies of the field, but in the meantime is also a really enjoyable read and introduction to the subject that is worthy of wide public interest. I do hope that it will be available soon in Hungarian.

I am very grateful that the Conference provided me with the opportunity to present this subject and CJCR. The Centre's work plays an important role in contemporary Europe. I take it as a sign that the presentation takes place within the programs of the preparation of cultural capitalship of Pécs for 2010 and in the meantime the 800th anniversary of the foundation of Cambridge University. I do hope these years will give opportunity to establish and strengthen liaisons between the University of Pécs and the Woolf Institute in Cambridge, and Pécs follows the example of Szeged, the twin city of Cambridge and combines forces to build an important cooperation, a building block of a modern and united Europe.

Thank you for your attention.

The program combines religious, philosophical, biblical and cultural studies, with history, political sciences and international relations to explore the role of Christian Jewish relations in a wider society.

---

[230] Cambridge University Press 2005, First Paper Back 2008.

What is Emerging in Western Europe / USA? The Emerging Church in the Post-Christendom Culture – Strengths, Weaknesses, Opportunities and Threats

Norbert Izsák

This piece of writing is an attempt to present the new, so called emerging church movement. As we will see, it is not easy to define what it is, or to be more accurate, what it is emerging to be. Some of the data and opinions presented in this study come from the particular, sometimes peculiar emerging church perspective. I have done everything in my power to refrain from over-generalization, and where I had seen it fit, I tried to balance emerging church theoreticians' opinions with other data or opinions. However, I still have to admit that the author has been somewhat influenced by the honest enthusiasm and transparent attitude of many emerging church people. I must confess that their (so far) conscious avoidance of power and institutional authority – I could not help it – has been more than appealing to me, who comes from a country, where organised religion traditionally relies on power and institutional authority. Since I come from an evangelical background, some of the starting points and references may be different from a researcher coming from the Catholic Church for instance. I do apologize for that.

In evangelical churches of the western hemisphere, and also, in some mainline churches, such as the Church of England, the word 'emerging' has become a divisive word. It seems to evoke emotions. If one promotes an activity or a church programme as 'emerging', he or she will most likely have immediately excited or angered a lot of people.

So what *is* the emerging church? It is by no means easy to define the emerging[231] church. Most of the discussion about it is controversial to say the least and even its leaders are sometimes confused, when they are to give a definition. The researchers Eddie Gibbs and Ryan K. Bolger work with this statement: 'the emerging church is a goal or a process, and it has not yet completely arrived. If anything, it is in its infant stage.'[232] It is true, emerging church leaders have a hard time identifying themselves. Many times they only know what they are emerging from (the traditional church), but they do

---

[231] In this paper, we will use 'emergent' and 'emerging' interchangeably, although more and more thinkers make a distinction between them.
[232] Eddie Gibbs & Ryan K. Bolger, *Emerging Churches: Creating Christian Community in Postmodern Cultures* (London: SPCK, 2006) p. 43.

not know what they are emerging into.[233] In fact, the Californian Spencer Burke (he himself being labelled emerging) states that emerging churches are non-existent today.[234]

So, why should then we bother to spend our time defining something that does not exist yet? Well, in fact, there are hundreds, if not thousands of so called emerging churches. However, there is a strong ideal, which these churches are shooting for, but they are also very aware of the fact that they have not reached the goal they are trying to reach. It is also worth noting that the language of these emerging church leaders is different from that of traditional evangelical leaders. The latter refer a lot to 'objective truth' and often speak in strong statements regarding theology, doctrines and church life, whilst the former like to ask questions and – some think it is the consequence of post-modern thinking – usually are afraid of using black and white statements. Therefore, many an emerging church mover and shaker will only refer to their movement as an emerging conversation, some would argue, a 'fragile, embryonic and diverse conversation'.[235] Emerging churches are so disparate that there are exceptions to any generalisations. Most are too new and too fluid to clarify, let alone assess their significance. There is no consensus yet about what language to use: 'new ways of being church'; 'emerging church'; 'fresh expressions of church'; 'future church'; 'church next'; or 'the coming church'. The terminology used here contrasts 'inherited' and 'emerging' churches.[236] The picture is further blurred, when we take into consideration the fact that this emerging church or conversation for the outsiders seem to give a fragmented picture. The somewhat loose relationship they are in is maintained in chat rooms, through blogs, websites and more recently conferences.[237] As a result, almost every relevant information on the emerging church can be found on the internet.

Since the movement basically lives its life on websites, it may be relevant to quote Wikipedia on it. In December of 2010, according to Wikipedia, the emerging church is 'a Christian movement of the late 20th and early 21st century that crosses a number of theological boundaries: participants can be described as evangelical, protestant, roman catholic, post-evangelical, Anabaptist, Adventist, liberal, post-liberal, reformed, charismatic,

---

[233] Gibbs & Bolger, *Emerging*, p. 28
[234] Gibbs & Bolger, *Emerging*, p. 42
[235] Peter Rollins, *How not to Speak of God* (London: SPCK, 2006) p. 5.
[236] Stuart Murray, *Church After Christendom* (London: Paternoster Press, 2004) p. 73.
[237] Gibbs & Bolger, *Emerging*, p. 29.

neocharismatic, conservative, and post-conservative.'²³⁸ Well, this is not extremely helpful. The definition goes on to say that 'participants seek to live their faith in what they believe to be a »postmodern« society. What those involved in the conversation mostly agree on is their disillusionment with the organized and institutional church and their support for the deconstruction of modern Christian worship, modern evangelism, and the nature of modern Christian community.'

From an insider's perspective, the yearning of the emerging church can be summarized by Mark Scandrette's rather brave, but vague definition: 'the emerging church is a quest for a more integrated and whole life of faith. There is a bit of theological questioning going on, focusing more on kingdom theology, the inner life, friendship/community, justice, earth keeping, inclusivity, and inspirational leadership. In addition, the arts are in a renaissance, as are the classical spiritual disciplines. Overall, it is a quest for a holistic spirituality.'²³⁹

This holistic spirituality, however, is different from today's general 'holistic teachings'. It is based on traditional Christian values. Many emerging church leaders would claim that they do not teach anything new: they only rediscover something that has been lost in the modernist age. With a lot of self-reflection, one of them said: 'if we do sound somewhat revolutionary, we would like to think we are promoting the self-same revolution that was precipitated through the world-shattering life and ministry of Jesus Christ and the early Christian movement.'²⁴⁰ The emerging church claims to be totally biblical and 'unmoving on the core Christian doctrines', just perhaps 'unconventional'.²⁴¹

Being unconventional also means that the emerging church rejects the Christendom mentality. In the first 1500 years of Christianity, Christian thinkers and leaders did not primarily think in nations. The main focus was the realisation of the Kingdom of God in Europe even at the price of such abuses as the Crusades or the Inquisition. Larger Christian churches believe now that politically enforcing Christianity on the people, the violent realisation of Christendom is not acceptable any longer and it is foreign to Jesus' teachings.²⁴² Nevertheless, it takes time for the Church to move from

---

[238] http://en.wikipedia.org/wiki/Emerging_church; accessed on December 1, 2010.
[239] Gibbs & Bolger, *Emerging*, p. 42.
[240] Michael Frost & Alan Hirsch, *The Shaping of Things to Come: Innovation and Mission for the 21ˢᵗ-Century Church* (Peabody: Hendrickson, 2003) p. ix.
[241] Frost & Hirsch, *The Shaping*, p. ix.
[242] Kaufmann, Franz-Xaver, Christentum und Christenheit, In: Gordan, Paulus, *Evangelium und Inkulturation (1492-1992)*, (Graz: Styria, 1993) pp. 101-128.

a situation where it occupied an eminence from which it addressed the nation as acknowledged spiritual and moral guardian, to one where there is no single spiritual or moral reference point, and where the Church is one voice among a number of voluntary pressure groups.

Emerging thinkers often emphasise the fact that the Bible was not written in modernity, but in premodernity.[243] Still, many practices and paradigms of today's mainline churches are rooted in the modernist worldview. This latter started briefly before the Renaissance and ended in the 20th Century. The main assertions of modernity were the following: the pursuit of order, the loss of tradition, the separation of the different spheres of reality.[244] The evangelical church in the age of modernity embraced all of the above, but the emerging church seeks to transition to postmodernity. That latter is just as different from modernity as the premodern time of the early church. In fact, emerging church gurus teach that the majority of current church practices are cultural accommodations to a society that no longer exists.[245] Which means, that many of the previous, modernist accommodations must be broken down and new, culturally relevant approaches have to be found. Though in modernity the church lost much of its previous influence, many contemporary evangelical and mainline denominations still think that their worldview should be central in the culture and the best way to achieve that is to tell society how they have to get their acts together. In other words, although the world de facto lives in a post-Christendom era, where the church is considered to be one of a million recreational and non-profit organizations, often, the church still functions in the Christendom mode: it thinks and acts like it has a central and powerful place in society.

The emerging church rejects the Christendom-type modus operandi. Just like the early church, it does not seek to be legitimised by politicians, does not want benefits from the power (yet) and does not assume that everyone should listen when it speaks. The emerging church does not wish to fight the culture with preaching; instead it is offering an alternative lifestyle.

This, however, does not mean that the emerging church is apolitical. Steve Chalke, the founder of Oasis and Faithworks and generally considered an emerging church leader, thinks that Christians are awakening 'to the political dimension of their faith', because the gospel has 'a direct application to

---

[243] Leonard Sweet (ed.), *The Church in Emerging Culture: Five Perspectives* (Grand Rapids: Zondervan, 2003), p. 16.
[244] Gibbs & Bolger, *Emerging*, p. 17-18.
[245] Gibbs & Bolger, *Emerging*, p. 19.

politics'.²⁴⁶ Moreover, at a conference, organized by emergentvillage.com in September 15-17 of 2008, the participants discussed the question: 'should the emerging church support the creation of the Religious Left against the Religious Right?'²⁴⁷ In Chalke's interpretation this is a radical return to the early church. He argues that the word 'ekklesia' the New Testament church used to describe itself was not a religious term, but 'a secular, political term used to describe a gathering of people called for a political purpose'. Based on this, Chalke concludes that the early church recognized that it had a political as well as a spiritual mission.²⁴⁸

But when it comes to politics, the emerging church recognizes that non-Christian authorities and people can be friendly towards the Gospel. Brian D. McLaren argues that the apologetics of the modernist era are too defensive and often mistake potential friends for enemies. The combativeness of today's (evangelical) apologetics considers the audience as enemies instead of students or clients, and treats them accordingly. By doing so, apologists are burning, rather than building bridges.²⁴⁹

Emerging church proponents like to think that 'the Christian church is dying in the West.'²⁵⁰ They would probably legitimately claim that the Church is facing several serious problems in our age. A few years ago, every week fifty-three thousand attendees were leaving the institutional church in Europe and in North America. At that rate – scholars claimed a few years ago – by 2030, mainstream Christianity, at least in Britain, will have largely disappeared.²⁵¹ This decline is fairly universal: throughout the Western world, Christianity has fallen on hard times. No matter how they are reported and interpreted, the statistics of church attendance and membership all paint the same picture, right across all denominations and all theological persuasions.²⁵² Evangelical mega church pastors often like to use modern management lingo. Well, any business losing clients at this rate

---

[246] Jonathan Bartley, *The Subversive Manifesto: Lifting the Lid on God's Political Agenda* (Oxford: The Bible Reading Fellowship, 2003) p. 8 (Steve Chalke's forward)
[247] http://www.emergentvillage.com/events/2008-emergent-theological-conversation, accessed on 6 Dec 2007.
[248] Bartley, *The Subversive*, p. 8 (Steve Chalke's forward).
[249] McLaren, Brian D., *The Church on the Other Side: Doing Ministry in the Postmodern Matrix* (Grand Rapids: Zondervan, 2000) p. 73-79.
[250] Riddell, Michael, *Threshold of the Future: Reforming the Church in the Post-Christian West* (London: SPCK, 1998) p. 1.
[251] Lynch, Gordon, *After Religion: 'Generation X' and the Search for Meaning* (London: Darton, Longman and Todd, 2002) p. 3.
[252] Drane, John, *The McDonaldization of the Church: Spirituality, Creativity, and the Future of the Church* (London: Darton, Longman and Todd, 2000) p. 2.

would be doing some serious reconsidering of its methods and objectives. Nowadays, there is more and more talking about it, however, very little visible change is happening. Evangelical pastors and theologians seem to have a hard time adjusting to the challenges of a new world, not few of them expect the world to adjust to their church life and way of doing ministry. A lot of them are simply unwilling to realize that Christendom, as an overarching cohesive body of belief and morals held to by the great majority of people in the 'West', is evaporating.[253]

The Enlightenment worldview has promised that more knowledge and more research would solve every problem and cure every illness. The heart of the rational worldview rests on logic, reason, and predictability. However, rationalism prevents people from recognizing the mysteries present in their lives. Operating from this worldview, persons interpret every unexplained event as something about which we do not yet have the answers; with more knowledge and more time, understanding will come and the mystery will disappear.[254] In a way, western rationalism and western ways of doing church have cut people off from their spiritual roots.[255]

This may be one reason why some of the people most concerned about pursuing a relationship with God have left organized religion. Many of them have sensed that protestant and evangelical churches, despite all their language, have no real spiritual depth.[256] As a result, today's seekers do not normally include the church on their 'shopping list' of places to investigate because they regard the church as being devoid of true spirituality.[257] A lot of people think that the church is utterly unspiritual. It is not that they think the church is wrong, they think the church is boring and completely irrelevant.[258] In fact, many people see the structures of institutional religion as impediments to their spiritual pilgrimage.[259] Meanwhile, the Western church is in danger of becoming spiritually bankrupt, spiritual disciplines are more

---

[253] Finney, John, *Recovering the Past: Celtic and Roman Mission* (London: Darton, Longman & Todd, 1996) p. 1.

[254] Rice, Howard, *The Pastor as Spiritual Guide* (Nashville: Upper Room, 1998) pp. 40-41

[255] Ellis, Roger & Seaton, Chris, *New Celts: Following Jesus into Millenium 3* (Eastbourne: Kingsway, 1998) p. 159.

[256] Rice, *The Pastor*, p. 40.

[257] Johnson, Philip & Clifford, Ross, *Jesus and the Gods of the New Age: Communicating Christ in Today's Spiritual Supermarket* (Oxford: Lion, 2001) p. 12.

[258] Booker, Mike & Ireland, Mark, *Evangelism – Which Way Now: An Evaluation of Alpha, Emmaus, Cell Church and Other Contemporary Strategies for Evangelism* (London: Church House Publishing, 2003) p. 171.

[259] Rice, *The Pastor*, p. 40.

talked about than practised.[260] It is no exaggeration to say that there is a crisis of spirituality within Western Christianity.[261] A whole generation, and what is worse, the new culture seem to be lost for the church. The new generation does not fit in the old models of church.

Whilst the Church is facing serious problems, a lot of non-churchgoing people are opening up to spiritual experiences. The emerging generations are very spiritually minded and open.[262] Many people, even successful people are not satisfied with the material rewards of Western culture, they feel empty inside, and they have a sense of incompleteness.[263] According to Finney, 90 per cent of people describe themselves as spiritual beings and over 60 per cent of them pray.[264] As the modernist matrix disintegrates, people are turning to deeper and supra-rational sources to provide meaning for their lives. The most enthusiastic participants in this quest envisage the current period of history as a flowering of spiritual evolution.[265] It is believed by many that the hunger that draws people to cults, New Age experimentation, or the occult is the hunger for God that is primary in our age.[266] Magazines are full of spiritual advice; new spiritualities continue to rise in the Western world.[267]

However, most people's spirituality is in the 'quest mode', they feel they are on a journey, but the destination is fairly unclear.[268] Their spiritual life is a process, a pilgrimage.[269] For many people today the journey is more important than the destination. Searching for the truth seems to be more attractive than finding a set of truth or doctrine and subscribing to them intellectually.[270] One of the beneficial side effects of the importation of Eastern forms of spirituality has been the rediscovery of the rich tradition of mysticism within Christianity.[271] Emerging church thinker Rob Bell states that 'Jesus is more compelling than ever. More inviting, more true, more

---

[260] Riddell, *Threshold*, p. 11.
[261] Ellis & Seaton, *New Celts*, p. 129.
[262] Kimball, Dan, *They Like Jesus, but Not the Church: Insights from Emerging Generations* (Grand Rapids: Zondervan, 2007) p. 11.
[263] Rice, *The Pastor*, p. 39.
[264] Finney, *Recovering the Past*, p. 43.
[265] Riddell, *Threshold*, p. 11.
[266] Rice, *The Pastor*, p. 38.
[267] Finney, John, *Emerging Evangelism* (London: Darton, Longman and Todd, 2004) p. 13
[268] Mellor, Howard & Yates, Timothy (eds.), *Mission and Spirituality: Creative Ways of Being Church* (Sheffield: Cliff College, 2002), pp. 15-16.
[269] Miller, Gordon L., *The Way of the English Mystics: An Anthology and Guide for Pilgrims* (Tunbridge Wells: Burns & Oates, 1996) p. 12.
[270] Drane, *The McDonaldization*, p. 175.
[271] Miller, *The Way*, p. 11.

mysterious than ever. The problem isn't Jesus: the problem is what comes with Jesus.'[272] They think 'Christianity has been smothered by churchianity', and they want to leave that baggage behind.[273] Many people are critical of the Church; they view churchgoers as being hypocrites, bigots and out of touch with reality.[274] No wonder that one of the goals of the emerging church is authenticity. Even emerging church critic D. A. Carson recognizes that the movement's desire and quest for genuineness is valid: 'to expose such inauthenticity is a good thing, to hunger for authenticity in all our existence, not least our walk with God and with other Christians, is also a good thing.[275]

Traditionally, spiritual life flowed out of and was a consequence of doctrine. People believed certain things about God and as a result experienced the spiritual. Today, a lot of non-church goer, non-dogma believing people experience something during their lifetime (about 63 per cent of British people), and then based on the experiences, they will form some sort of theology. Experience leads to doctrine.[276] This is unacceptable for most evangelical church leaders. So, the problem really is twofold: on the one hand people open to spirituality do not seek the church for answers while on the other hand, the church is unable to use the existing energy and move it towards faith. Either it demonizes the spiritual initiatives of the world or gives them the cold shoulder, but generally speaking fails to acknowledge the true spiritual thirst behind it.

On the other hand, the emerging church embrace spirituality as in their view, 'mystery (...) is not a fancy or spiritual word for ignorance that we can conquer by more knowledge; nor does it designate a secrecy that we can penetrate by painstaking search.'[277] It seems to be a paradox, but one serious reconsideration the emerging church has done, has to do with the idea of holy places. In order to keep its missional focus, the emerging church seems to reject the idea of holy places. They seek to tear down the sacred-secular divide. 'Sacralization in emerging churches is about one thing: the destruction of the sacred/secular split of modernity.'[278] As a result they do

---

[272] Bell, Rob, *Velvet Elvis: Repainting the Christian Faith* (Grand Rapids: Zondervan, 2005) p. 12.
[273] Riddell, *Threshold*, p. 58.
[274] Mellor & Yates, *Mission and Spirituality*, p. 19.
[275] D. A. Carson, *Becoming Conversant with the Emerging Church: Understanding a Movement and its Implications* (Grand Rapids: Zondervan, 2005) p. 49-50.
[276] Finney, *Recovering the Past*, p. 42.
[277] Dawn, Marva & Peterson, Eugene, *The Unnecessary Pastor: Rediscovering the Call* (Grand Rapids: Eerdmans, 2000) p. 67.
[278] Gibbs & Bolger, *Emerging*, p. 66.

not wait for people to come in to a church building, but they take their type of spirituality to common places, where people are. Emerging church thinker Dan Kimball would go as far as to say that today's usage of the word church is corrupted. Many people would 'go to church', like they go to a store. They would 'attend a church', like they attend a school and they 'belong to a church', like they belong to a club with its programmes.[279] Kimball states that 'we can't go to church because we are the church.'[280] One of the aims of the emerging church is to change this perspective that reduces 'church members' to passive membership. The emerging church wants to teach people that they are the church,[281] and being in a community is at least as important as adhering to a set of doctrines.

For elevating something else on the same platform as perfect theological conviction (may it be orthopraxis vs. orthodoxy), the emerging church receives its fair share of criticism from traditional evangelical leaders. For example, John MacArthur clearly bashes emerging church leader Brian D. McLaren and accuses him of preaching a 'social gospel'.[282] Roger Oakland from Understand the Times Ministries (this organization has seven evangelical Calvary Chapel pastors on the board)[283] has published a book, Faith Undone.[284] In it, Oakland resembles the emerging church to New Age and labels it very destructive. He also teaches widely in Calvary Chapels in the United States about the supposed heresies and dangers of the movement.[285] Evangelical churches have a hard time admitting that protecting true doctrine often means protecting their own influence in society, in other words, the Christendom paradigm. As Leonard Sweet, an emerging church proponent puts it, 'all our doctrines are at best castles in the air. Fifth-century church historian Socrates Scholasticus thought that »all theological disputes were to be treated as a mere fig leaf for contentions about power and authority«.'[286] There is a general feeling in emerging churches that all power corrupts, and therefore one of the main concerns of

---

[279] Dan Kimball, *The Emerging Church: Vintage Christianity for New Generations* (Grand Rapids: Zondervan, 2003) p. 93.
[280] Kimball, *The Emerging*, p. 91.
[281] Kimball, *The Emerging*, p. 94.
[282] http://www.youtube.com/watch?v=OH1yOmij7Q4, accessed on 1 Dec 2007.
[283] I find it amusing that Calvary Chapel seems to take a very antagonistic stand against the emerging church, knowing that 30 years ago a lot of people had similar sentiments with regards to Calvary Chapel.
[284] http://www.understandthetimes.org/faithundone.shtml, accessed on 1 Dec 2007.
[285] http://www.youtube.com/watch?v=MV9yBowu6s8, accessed on 1 Dec 2007.
[286] Sweet, *The Church*, p. 37.

church leaders should be the conscious, on-going fight against the lures of power and authority.

This may be one reason why many emerging churches do not care about numbers. In fact, the emerging conversation rebels against the cult of numbers. The evangelical church growth movement assumes that the main purpose of the church is to multiply itself. Therefore, matters such as peace, justice, development and the fight against poverty are encouraged as long as they bring in more people into the church. Quantitative expansion is the top priority. [287] The emerging generations rebel against this technocratic attitude.

In many evangelical churches, members still put a great emphasis on immediate conversion. Almost everyone is expected to say on what exact date he or she became "saved". One of the past abuses the emerging church reacts against is the inability to allow people space and time to process beliefs.[288] According to McKnight, conversion is a process, and it should be recognized that what one person might think of as less-than-a-full-conversion may be an early dimension in the process of conversion.[289] Emerging churches would mostly acknowledge that at its core, conversion is a process of identity formation in which a person comes to see himself or herself in accordance with the gospel of Jesus Christ.[290] In these new forms of church people are given a chance to belong before believing.[291] And that is rather helpful, since 69 percent of adults in England come gradually to faith.[292]

It is no secret that the emerging church rebels against the existing, traditional church structure and by the same token against traditional forms of leadership. Would this mean that the emerging church does not need leaders? For hundreds of years, people have tried to find the perfect biblical structure for the church and its leadership. However, the truth is that the Jewish, historical synagogue type was transformed by the needs of the

---

[287] Verkuyl, Johannes, *Contemporary Missiology: An Introduction* (Grand Rapids: Eerdmans, 1978) p. 189.
[288] Webber, Robert, *Listening to the Beliefs of Emerging Churches: Five Perspectives* (Grand Rapids: Zondervan, 2007) p. 36.
[289] McKnight, Scott, *Turning to Jesus: The Sociology of Conversion in the Gospels* (Louisville, KY: Westminster John Knox Press, 2002) p. 3.
[290] McKnight, *Turning to Jesus*, p. 4.
[291] Ellis, Roger & Seaton, Chris, *New Celts: Following Jesus into Millenium 3* (Eastbourne: Kingsway, 1998), p. 74.
[292] Finney, *Recovering the Past*, p. 41.

Gentile world, where the early church was functioning.[293] Some contemporary authors suggest that 'we should be foolish to look for a precise blueprint for the ministry in the pages of the New Testament (...) most of the advances derive from the needs of the situation rather than from any preconceived normative plan.'[294] The emerging church claims that the New Testament leadership was continually situational and contextual.[295]

Some emerging leaders totally reject the forms of leadership that were commonly in use in recent years. Many are creating new church environments without any form of leadership and want to stay in an unstructured or even anti-structured form of church life. This is clearly a reaction against understanding leadership as controlling, top-down and professional.[296] Some emerging leaders think that it is virtually impossible to be an honest, God-honouring leader in the present culture. The pastoral role 'in a century of buy-it consumerism and fix-it psychologism, has become so powerful that it defeats all individual efforts to work within it.' It is so secularized and politicized that it is not a venue for genuine Christian ministry. Only lay leadership can overcome the barriers of the culture.[297] The emerging church is trying to introduce a different, perhaps more eastern model of leadership. Lord Montgomery thought that 'leadership is the capacity and will to rally men and women to a common purpose, and the character which inspires confidence'.[298] A more conservative approach to leadership is John R. Mott's definition: 'a leader is a man who knows the road, who can keep ahead, and who can pull others after him'.[299] President Truman said: 'a leader is a person who has the ability to get others to do what they don't want to do, and like it.'[300] The assumption here is that the leader always knows what is best for the group and will get the lazy, ignorant followers to open up their eyes and see: the leader was right in telling them to move ahead and without realizing, the couch potato followers learned to like the right thing. Some eastern philosophers totally disagree with this definition. Lao-Tse, the Chinese thinker thought a 'leader is best, when

---

[293] Finney, John, *Church on the Move, Leadership for Mission* (London, Daybreak, 1992) p. 110.
[294] Michael Green, quoted in King, Philip, *Leadership Explosion, Maximising Leadership Potential in the Church* (London, Hodder and Stoughton, 1987), p. 41.
[295] Roxburgh, Alan J., *The Sky is Falling: Leaders Lost in Transition* (Eagle, ID: ACI, 2005), p. 149.
[296] Roxburgh, *The Sky is Falling*, p. 146.
[297] Dawn & Peterson, *The Unnecessary*, p. 5-6.
[298] Sandler, J. Oswald, *Spiritual Leadership* (London: Lakeland, 1967), p. 19.
[299] Sandler, *Spiritual Leadership*, p. 19.
[300] Sandler, *Spiritual Leadership*, p. 19.

people barely know he exists'.[301] The Catholic theologian, Henri Nouwen was convinced, that 'the Christian leader of the future is called to be completely irrelevant and to stand in this world with nothing to offer but his or her own vulnerable self. That is the way Jesus came to reveal God's love.'[302] In this respect, leaders of the emerging church are more like spiritual guides, rather than authoritarian bishops or mega church pastors.

Many emerging church leader would agree with Gabriel Marcel, who taught that life is not so much a problem to be solved, but a mystery to be explored.[303] 'Life is not something we manage to hammer together and keep in repair by our wits; it is an unfathomable gift.'[304] Such a mystery does need spiritual guides to explore and to penetrate. Part of the task of any spiritual guide is to recognize human uniqueness and thus to respect and value each person's particular pilgrimage. The disturbing nature of cults and some hardcore evangelical churches resides in their frightening uniformity. People strain themselves to pretend that they are something they are not. Everyone is trying hard to be like everyone else; everyone is trying hard to be like the leader.'[305] However, a spiritual guide does not have to be perfect; he or she can afford to be honest, transparent and broken. A guide does not have much to lose. In an emerging church leaders are not supposed to be problem solvers, but guides, who are open handed and do not force themselves upon a group of people. Their security and confidence do not come from the position they have, but from their own spiritual journey and experiences. This maybe one of the reasons, why the emerging church seems to listen to those groups of people who are on the margins of the society: broken homosexuals, downcast divorced people and the like. Those, who would not easily fit in to a white middle class, somewhat typical evangelical church.

From their perspective, just as the apostle Paul gave up Judaism with all its laws to affirm God for the Gentiles, the emerging church is on its way to give up traditional Christianity in order to affirm Jesus to a post-Christian world. Is it going to work or is it going to turn into an extreme, mainline church criticizing cult? Or is the emerging church just a new movement that is not institutionalized yet? Is it just a simple attempt to apply contextual theology

---

[301] LePeau, Andrew T., *Paths of Leadership: Guiding Others toward Growth in Christ through serving, following, teaching, modelling, envisioning* (London: Scripture Union, 1984), p. 10.
[302] Nouwen, Henri J. M., *In the name of Jesus: Reflections on Christian Leadership* (New York: Crossroad Publishing Company, 1989) p. 17
[303] Peterson, Eugene H., *The Contemplative Pastor: Returning to the Art of Spiritual Director* (Grand Rapids: Eerdmans, 1989) p. 72.
[304] Peterson, *The Contemplative Pastor*, p. 72.
[305] Rice, *The Pastor*, p. 42.

in the postmodern world? Is it a brave attempt to live an uncultured life in a post-Christian, postmodern society? Is it only appealing to secular people, because it has no structure? Will it become institutionalized within 5-10 years even though one of the main purposes of the movement is to avoid institutionalization? Can a movement survive without some form of institution? One author suggests that 'cultural creations need managers – lest they die in the same ivory tower where they were conceived.'[306] Well, we are not able to give the final word on this movement or conversation until a little bit later, when the emerging church will have emerged a little more.

---

[306] Bauman, Zygmunt, *Liquid Life* (Cambridge: Polity, 2005) p. 59.

Bibliography

Bartley, Jonathan, *The Subversive Manifesto: Lifting the Lid on God's Political Agenda* (Oxford: The Bible Reading Fellowship, 2003)

Bauman, Zygmunt, *Liquid Life* (Cambridge: Polity, 2005)

Bell, Rob, *Velvet Elvis: Repainting the Christian Faith* (Grand Rapids: Zondervan, 2005)

Booker, Mike & Ireland, Mark, *Evangelism – Which Way Now: An Evaluation of Alpha, Emmaus, Cell Church and Other Contemporary Strategies for Evangelism* (London: Church House Publishing, 2003)

Carson, D. A., *Becoming Conversant with the Emerging Church: Understanding a Movement and its Implications* (Grand Rapids: Zondervan, 2005)

Dawn, Marva & Peterson, Eugene, *The Unnecessary Pastor: Rediscovering the Call* (Grand Rapids: Eerdmans, 2000)

Drane, John, *The McDonaldization of the Church: Spirituality, Creativity, and the Future of the Church* (London: Darton, Longman and Todd, 2000)

Ellis, Roger & Seaton, Chris, *New Celts: Following Jesus into Millenium 3* (Eastbourne: Kingsway, 1998)

Finney, John, *Emerging Evangelism* (London: Darton, Longman and Todd, 2004)

Finney, John, *Recovering the Past: Celtic and Roman Mission* (London: Darton, Longman & Todd, 1996)

Frost, Michael & Hirsch, Alan, *The Shaping of Things to Come: Innovation and Mission for the 21st-Century Church* (Peabody: Hendrickson, 2003)

Gibbs, Eddie & Bolger, Ryan K., *Emerging Churches: Creating Christian Community in Postmodern Cultures* (London: SPCK, 2006)

Johnson, Philip & Clifford, Ross, *Jesus and the Gods of the New Age: Communicating Christ in Today's Spiritual Supermarket* (Oxford: Lion, 2001)

Kaufmann, Franz-Xaver, Christentum und Christenheit, In: Gordan, Paulus, *Evangelium und Inkulturation (1492-1992)*, (Graz: Styria, 1993)

Kimball, Dan, *The Emerging Church: Vintage Christianity for New Generations* (Grand Rapids: Zondervan, 2003)

Kimball, Dan, *They Like Jesus, but Not the Church: Insights from Emerging Generations* (Grand Rapids: Zondervan, 2007)

King, Philip, *Leadership Explosion, Maximising Leadership Potential in the Church* (London, Hodder and Stoughton, 1987)

McKnight, Scott, *Turning to Jesus: The Sociology of Conversion in the Gospels* (Louisville, KY: Westminster John Knox Press, 2002)

McLaren, Brian D., *The Church on the Other Side: Doing Ministry in the Postmodern Matrix* (Grand Rapids: Zondervan, 2000)

LePeau, Andrew T., *Paths of Leadership: Guiding Others toward Growth in Christ through serving, following, teaching, modelling, envisioning* (London: Scripture Union, 1984)

Lynch, Gordon, *After Religion: 'Generation X' and the Search for Meaning* (London: Darton, Longman and Todd, 2002)

Mellor, Howard & Yates, Timothy (eds.), *Mission and Spirituality: Creative Ways of Being Church* (Sheffield: Cliff College, 2002)

Miller, Gordon L., *The Way of the English Mystics: An Anthology and Guide for Pilgrims* (Tunbridge Wells: Burns & Oates, 1996)

Murray, Stuart, *Post-Christendom: Church and Mission in a Strange New World* (Carlisle: Paternoster, 2004)

Nouwen, Henri J. M., *In the name of Jesus: Reflections on Christian Leadership* (New York: Crossroad Publishing Company, 1989)

Peterson, Eugene H., *The Contemplative Pastor: Returning to the Art of Spiritual Director* (Grand Rapids: Eerdmans, 1989)

Rice, Howard, *The Pastor as Spiritual Guide* (Nashville: Upper Room, 1998)

Riddell, Michael, *Threshold of the Future: Reforming the Church in the Post-Christian West* (London: SPCK, 1998)

Rollins, Peter, *How not to Speak of God* (London: SPCK, 2006)

Roxburgh, Alan J., *The Sky is Falling: Leaders Lost in Transition* (Eagle, ID: ACI, 2005)

Sandler, J. Oswald, *Spiritual Leadership* (London: Lakeland, 1967)

Sweet, Leonard (ed.), *The Church in Emerging Culture: Five Perspectives* (Grand Rapids: Zondervan, 2003)

Verkuyl, Johannes, *Contemporary Missiology: An Introduction* (Grand Rapids: Eerdmans, 1978)

Webber, R., *Listening to the Beliefs of Emerging Churches: Five Perspectives* (Grand Rapids: Zondervan, 2007)

http://www.emergentvillage.com/events/2008-emergent-theological-conversation, accessed on 6 Dec 2007.

http://www.youtube.com/watch?v=OH1yOmij7Q4, accessed on 1 Dec 2007

http://www.youtube.com/watch?v=MV9yBowu6s8, accessed on 1 Dec 2007.

http://www.understandthetimes.org/faithundone.shtml, accessed on 1 Dec 2007.

Authors

Botos, Katalin

Economist, university professor in Pázmány Péter Catholic University – PPCU, Heller Farkas Institute of Economic, Department of Environmental Law, Budapest and University of Szeged (Hungary). Former state secretary, minister, head of Banking Supervision. Main field of research: public finances, demography, economic consequences of ageing, economic history, economic policy, international economics, ethics and economics. Guest professor of several European universities, member of European Business History Association. Among the publications: "State and Future of the Hungarian Banking System. Compendium of Studies on Central European Financial Systems" (London, 1998). "What Can Be Espected after Joining EU? Lisbon Targets and Hungary" (Budapest, 2004).

Faltin, Lucia

She has been involved in the study and practical involvement in interfaith relations for nearly two decades. Her main area of interest is European integration and the relationship between religious and secular sphere in this process. She has spent 12 years in Cambridge at the Woolf Institute dedicated to the study of relations between Jews, Christians and Muslims. She co-edited a volume The Religious Roots of Contemporary European Identity (with Melanie Wright, publ. Continuum London and New York, 2007 and 2010). She recently returned to her native Slovakia to work in the field of philanthropy and is also doctoral researcher at the University of Cambridge (UK).

Hermann Priesler, Judit

Economist, Member of the Executive Board of the Hungarian Christian Jewish Society. Visiting Scholar at St.Edmund's College University of Cambridge (2005). Sternberg fellow of Centre for the Study of Jewish-Christian Relations - CJCR Cambridge, University of Cambridge. (2005). Dame of the Vatican's Order of the Holy Sepulchre of Jerusalem. Some professional experiences: the Bishop's Office in the Diocese of Pecs: Press Officer and Event organizer (1994-1999); Project "Understanding Open Society": project manager (1999-2002). Among the publications: "The international Structure of Interfaith Relations, Hungarian CCJ Year Book (2002); Omega Brochures Translation and Preface to Henri Boulad SJ's lectures on modern Christian theology, Korda (1998-2004). Translations and editing: educational material and articles for Christian Jewish Society.

Izsák, Norbert

Norbert Izsák is assistant professor at the Pentecostal Theological College of Budapest (Hungary). He has an MA in practical theology from the University of Manchester, an MA in history and is currently working on his PhD in history at the University of Pécs. His area of research is new religious movements, faith and politics in the USA, but he is also interested in church leadership models and paradigms.

Jávor, Benedek

Ecologist, environmental activist, scientific advisor of Pázmány Péter Catholic University, Department of Environmental Law (Hungary). His research areas include environmental ethics, religions and ecology, ecological politics. Founder and till 2008 spokesperson of the environmental NGO Védegylet - Protect the Future. Since 2010 member of the Hungarian National Assembly (**Green Party "Politics** can be different").

Knoll, Reinhold

Professor, Institute of Sociology, University of Vienna (Austria). Docent at the Karoli Gaspar University, Budapest (1998). Docent at the Goedoelloe University for Culture Sciences (1998, 1999). Studies and research on: history and theories of sociology; Humanism and Enlightenment, an history of Austrian philosophy since 1450. Member of the Vienna Catholic Academy. Among the publications: "Faith between the domination of an order and the salvation's expectation" (Vienna 1996); "Beyond society: cultural-sociological contributions in memory of Robert Reichardt" (Klausen-Leopolsdorf, 2000). "Thoughts on Television" (Gödöllő, 2000).

Korpics, Márta

Born in 1966, Zalaegerszeg. Senior lecturer at the Institute of Literature and Linguistics, Illyés Gyula Faculty of University of Pécs. She has a PhD in linguistics (2009). Her main research interests are sacral communication, religion and communication, and the pilgrimage in modernity. Among the publications: "Sacral Communication", Ed. with Dóra P. Szilczl together (Budapest, 2007); "Religions and Churches in a Common Europe. Hungary", Co-authored with János Wildmann (Budapest, 2010).

Mortensen, Viggo

Professor of Systematic Theology and director of the Center for Multireligious Studies at the Theology School of the Aarhus University (Denmark). Teaching areas: Ethics and Philosophy of Religions. Former director of Lutheran World Federation, based at the Department of Theological Studies at the University of Geneva, Suisse. Director of the project "Danish Pluralism." In his most recent scientific publications he has addressed the issues of the relationship between globalization, global ethics and interreligious dialogue in a multireligious framework, the dialogue between science and religion, the dialogue among peoples of different faith, the future of "Global Christianity ". Founder of the European research network R.I.P.E. - Religious Innovation and Pluralism in 21st century Europe, Aarhus, DK, 2006 (www.ripe-project.eu)

Nagy, Endre J.

Professor of Sociology. Graduated in Law, Ph.D. in Juridical and Political Sciences, habilitation in History, doctor of Hungarian Academy of Sciences in Sociology. Active in Institute of Mental Health at Semmelweis University, Budapest (Hungary). Main fields of research: History of Sociology and Social Political Ideas in Hungarian, Traditions of Liberal Philosophy in Central Europe. Among the publications: "Scientific Trends in the Research on Public Administration", Co-authored with L. Lőrincz and L. Szamel (Budapest, 1976); "Idea and Reality. Essays on the History of Hungrian Sociology" (Budapest, 1993); "Adventures in Sociology. Selected Essays in Sociology (Szombathely, 2003).

Pickel, Gert

Professor in Church and Religion Sociology, Faculty of Theology, University of Leipzig (Germany). Previous experiences at the Research Centre for Social Science, University of Bamberg (1992-1996); collaborator at the Europa University Viandrina, Frankfurt (Oder) for comparative Culture Sociology. Main specific issues of the research activity: quantitative and empirical Religion Sociology; comparative research on democracy and democratic processes; comparative methodology in Political Sciences and Social Sciences. Studies and analysis on the religious situation in East Europe; the role of the religious values for societies and churches; the complex effects of the secularization processes. Chairmanship member, Section Religion Sociology, German Society of Sociology. Member of spokesman of the working group "Politics and Religion", German Union for Political Sciences. Member of Scientific Committee, research project on church belonging, German Evangelical Church. Among the publications: "Religion and Religiousness in the Unified Germany: Twenty Years after the Revolution" (Wiesbaden, 2011); "Religion Sociology: an Introduction to the Central Thematic Areas" (Wiesbaden, 2011).

Rasmusson, Arne

Professor in systematic theology, Department of literature, history of ideas, and religion, Gothenburg University (Sweden). Teaching areas: theology, ethics. Visiting Research Scholar, The Divinity School, Duke University, N.C.,USA (1997-98); Resident Member, Center for Theological Inquiry, Princeton, N.J., USA (2002); Visiting professor, the Faculty of Theology, Stellenbosch University, South Africa (2005, 2007, 2010). Main projects: "Church, Theology, and the Liberal Nation-state"; "Theological Ethics and Neuroscience: On Morality and the Embodied Mind". Among many publications: the book "The Church as Polis: From Political theology to Theological Politics as Exemplified by Jürgen Moltmann and Stanley Hauerwas", University of Notre Dame Press, (1995); the articles: "Church and War in the Theology of Karl Barth" (2011), "the curious fact that ... the Lord always puts us on the just side': Reinhold Niebuhr, America, and Christian Realism" (2012); "Science as salvation: George Lakoff and Steven Pinker as secular political theologians" (2012).

Ricceri, Marco

Expert in social and labour policies, is acting as secretary general of the EURISPES, a primary Italian research institute in the economic and social sectors (see web site www.eurispes.it). Ricceri is also: professor at the Link Campus University in Rome (Italy) – Faculty of Political Sciences for the following course: " European Institutions"; coordinator of the Ethic Committee of the A.E.I. – European Agency of Investments, Geie, Bruxelles; enrolled in the list of "Pool of Reviewers" of the ESF-European Science Foundation, Strasbourg, for: "European Social Policy", "Industrial Relations". Specific research areas: European integration process. Previous working experiences: researcher, the National Study Office of CISL (Free Italian Trade Union); Chief Officer for the Economic Policies at the Parliamentary Groups of the Italian Chamber of Deputies. Ricceri was substitute member of the E.E.S.C.–European Economic and Social Committee, advisor of the Italian Ministry for Scientific Research.

Rixer, Ádám

Associate professor, Károli Gáspár University of the Reformed Church, Faculty of Law, Department of Public Administration in Budapest (Hungary). Special studies and publications on the issues: "Religion and Law", "Religion and Politics", "Civil Society". Expert of the Soros Foundation program about Rom minority. Advisor of Family Service Support Chance (Budapest, VII District), and of the Foundation for Nonprofit Enterprise. Docent at the Corvinus University (2005-2007). Special Prize XXI. OTDK, Section Political Sciences 1993); Prize "Pro Juventute Facultatis Award" (1998, ELTE Law

Faculty). Member of the Religious Society (Hungary), and the Hungarian Political Science Association. Among many articles and essays: "The Relationship between State and Religious Communities in Hungary" (Studia Iuridica Caroliensa, 2010); "The Church as a Non-governmental Association" (Collega, 2005).

Torres Gutierrez, Alejandro

Chair of Law at the Public Law Department, of the Public University of Navarre, (Spain). Extraordinary Prize of PhD, of the Law School of the Complutense University of Madrid, year 2000. Visiting Scholar at the University of Berkeley, (USA), Visiting Professor at the Universities of Salzburg, (Austria), Catholic University of Portugal, and Coimbra, (Portugal), and Bologna, (Italy). His main books and papers are focused on religious freedom in Spain, Austria and Portugal, and the legal status of minorities and multiculturalism.

Wildmann, János

Economist and theologian (Degree in Luzern/Switzerland). PhD in Catholic Theology at the University of Vienna (1991), habilitation at the Evangelical Theological University of Budapest (2007). He was the leader of the Centre of Religion and of the Sociology of Religion Research Group at the Department of Sociology, Faculty of Humanities at the University Pécs (2003-2009). Since 2011 he is professor at the John Wesley Theological College in Budapest (Hungary). Main fields of research: practical theology and sociology of religion. Among the publications: "Catholic Mirror. The Hungarian Church and European Integration" (Budapest, 2005); "The message of Reformcouncil" (Budapest, 2006); "Religions and Churches in a Common Europe. Hungary", Co-authored with Márta Korpics (Budapest, 2010).